NAVIES IN HISTORY

NAVIES IN HISTORY

Clark G. Reynolds

NAVAL INSTITUTE PRESS
Annapolis, Maryland

Library of Congress Cataloging-in-Publication Data

Reynolds, Clark G.
Navies in history / Clark G. Reynolds.
p.   cm.
Includes bibliographical references and index.
ISBN 1-55750-716-3 (hardcover : alk. paper). —
ISBN 1-55750-715-5 (pbk. : alk. paper)
1. Naval history. I. Title.
D27.R46   1998
359'.009—dc21   98-6112

Printed in the United States of America on acid-free paper ∞

Contents

◆

Essays

◆

Illustrations

Figures

Diagrams
by BartArt

Maps
by Richard D. Kelly Jr.

◆

A Historical Reconnaissance

"PRIMER" is defined as an introductory book on a subject. "Reconnaissance" is the preliminary survey or scouting of an area. This book is both: a basic account of navies throughout history upon all the oceans of the world.

Students of naval history include undergraduates and their professors, government officials and armed forces personnel, scholars, journalists, and interested lay people. After reading a chapter of particular interest—in effect, reconnoitering the period—the student may elect to study aspects of it in greater depth by reading specialized books, articles, and documents. The target objective might be a college research paper, broadened historical knowledge, or simply intellectual satisfaction. The section on Further Reading is a list of selected sources on specific subjects.

Signposts of historical importance—key naval terms, persons, weapons, and battles—are rendered in **boldface** or *italics*. Common literary practice dictates that all names of ships be italicized (or underlined), which the student must do in a term paper. The maps and the appendixes—Functions of Navies in History, Modern Naval Ranks, The Ship, and Warship Profiles—are intended as ready references for the student while reading the book. Because a sense of geography is absolutely essential for understanding naval operations, the reader is encouraged to utilize the maps at the end of the book as he/she goes along.

NAVIES IN HISTORY

1

Navies

"SEAMANSHIP," declared the Athenian Pericles, "is an art. It is not something that can be picked up and studied in one's spare time; indeed, it allows one no spare time for anything else." Although the great Greek statesman made this observation more than 4 centuries before Christ, it has held true throughout history.

Any ship is a carefully designed and crafted floating machine which operates at the mercy of winds and seas. Its very survival and effectiveness depend largely upon the skills and experience of its officers and crew in shiphandling. When a vessel is also a weapons platform—a ship of war—it requires even more technical sophistication of its personnel.

Seafarers are therefore consummate professionals; amateurs have no place at sea. Their physical world is circumscribed by the confines of their ship, their universe by the endless waters and skies round about them. As practical individuals, sailors throughout history have not generally had the time or the inclination to deal with the theoretical aspects of their work. They are ship drivers, not philosophers.

By the same token, students and devotees of navies—and aspiring career officers—are usually attracted to naval history by its "business end"—the high adventure and fascination of naval wars, battles, and leaders. The reader of this book may therefore prefer to skip this first chapter and move directly into the "action." The careful student, however, will profit by first becoming familiar with naval terms and certain historical characteristics of different types of navies.

Navies in History

Power

For better or worse, the urge to attain power is a basic trait of human nature. One common feature of all peoples in all times has been the use of power in order to survive, prosper, and achieve dominion—over nature and over enemies. Human institutions have not evolved at an even pace for all peoples, leading to disparities and thus conflict. The most basic human grouping has been **tribal**—nomadic hunter-warriors, herders, and simple farmers. A dynamic tribal chief with dominion over other tribes became warlord of a **feudal** society, defended by an army of loyal soldiers. Certain villages, towns, and feudal estates developed into **city-states, nations,** and/or **empires.** These **great powers** extended their dominion at the expense of less-advanced and less-powerful tribal and feudal peoples—and competed against one another. Only then did true naval power develop.

All states in history started out small. Several which achieved great power status exerted **hegemony** (from the Greek word for "leadership") over other peoples. Such political and economic supremacy eventually came to mean general domination of the European continent with a powerful army or rule over oceanic areas and distant lands with a large navy. Small nations which never achieved great power status existed at the sufferance of the larger powers, usually as allied, client, or subject states.

The great powers of history may be generally categorized in 1 of 2 geographic contexts—predominantly continental or maritime. This categorization helps in understanding how great powers developed their national strategies and the naval component.

Strategy is defined as the plan or method for attaining broad political, economic, and military goals in peacetime and in war. The major strategic tool of a great **continental power,** with its long land borders to defend, has been the **army.** The key strategic force of a great **maritime power,** which lacks land borders but is dependent on overseas trade, has been the **navy.**

Naval Philosophy

The systematic study of how nations have utilized their navies in the past did not begin until relatively late in history—the late 1800s. Before that time, ever since antiquity, the proper **roles and missions** of navies were determined by the experience of their political and naval leaders and forebears. Such knowledge was based on tradition, habit, need, and sometimes the imitation of other navies.

One of the themes developed by naval and historical analysts since the 1890s has been the strategic differences between continental and maritime great powers, especially how these powers had utilized their navies in the past. Although history is never repeated exactly, general patterns of national behavior help explain the strategic and naval actions of both types of great powers. One common limitation, however, has been the finite amount of available national resources: money, manpower, and raw materials. Indeed, no warring nation in history ever enjoyed unlimited resources to develop overwhelming strength equally on land and at sea.

Put another way, in major conflicts between a great power on the land and one on the sea, neither was ever able to create a superior army *and* a superior navy (much less also a supreme air force in recent times). When a nation was superior at sea, it required an ally or coalition of allies to provide the necessary manpower and main army to defeat the enemy on land. Similarly, a great power supreme on land required naval allies in order to achieve victory at sea. Neither antagonist was able to "go it alone."

Purely land wars were another matter altogether, while purely naval wars—between 2 great maritime powers—were exceedingly rare. The classic examples of the latter type of conflict were the 3 Anglo-Dutch wars of the late 1600s, which focused on simple slugging matches between the opposing fleets.

The basic determining strategic factor of the great power throughout history has been geography. The continental state, even if it had one or more coastlines, was shaped by long land borders regarded as military frontiers. It required a large standing (permanent) army and fixed fortifications to defend the country against possible overland attack. The maritime state was insular, either a real island, a peninsula, or virtually isolated because of natural physical barriers and/or the absence of a genuine overland threat. Unlike the continental state whose economic wealth was based on agriculture, the maritime state achieved prosperity through overseas trade and required a large standing (permanent) navy to protect the **merchant marine,** its commercial vessels.

Because geographic conditions, and a possible favorable political situation, rarely existed for the emergence of genuine maritime great powers, only 5 of them existed in history: ancient Athens in the 5th century B.C.; Renaissance Venice during the 14th and 15th centuries; the 17th-century Netherlands; 17th- to 20th-century England/Great Britain; and the 20th-century United States. All the other great powers of history, whether or not they built formidable navies, were basically continental.

Functions of Navies in History

The ways that continental and maritime great powers utilized their navies (outlined in Appendix 1) were the result of the general national and strategic characteristics which defined the state: geographic, political, economic, sociocultural, and military. These characteristics and naval functions pertained continuously over time, not only during wars.

The **continental power** was comprised of a large land mass vulnerable to overland invasion, making military security its most fundamental national requirement.

Politically, therefore, the continental government was highly centralized, authoritarian, and reactionary—a monarchy or totalitarian dictatorship. It maintained internal security by wielding absolute control over the people and by violently suppressing dissenters. The army and the official state church were major political agencies for controlling the masses; the king, queen, or dictator was often an army general and/or virtual religious godhead. A state secret police protected his/her person.

Economically, the continental state was based largely on state-run agriculture in order to feed the large population and army. This entailed a 2-class socioeconomic system: a small landed aristocracy and a massive peasantry and workforce, a carryover from feudalism. The titled landowners (or party functionaries in more recent times) controlled the wealth of the countryside and assured the power of the king/queen/dictator, who originated from the aristocratic class. Peasants and workers were kept in real or virtual servitude by the aristocracy, and they fulfilled the huge manpower needs of the army. Whatever middle class (merchants, bankers) existed was minuscule and rigidly manipulated by the state, which controlled and managed the entire economy. Even if the continental nation had seaports, a merchant marine, and a navy, the nautical element of the economy was subordinated to agriculture.

Culturally, the continental state's society was closed and conservative, resistant to any change which might undermine the authority of the state. Obedience and conformity left no room for individual freedoms—to create, to criticize, or to practice other religions than the state's. High art, toleration, imported ideas, and general literacy were discouraged, unless they happened to serve the needs of the state. Innovation and invention might occur, as in the development of a navy and weapons, but none of these proved decisive because of authoritarian controls and the overpowering requirements of national security.

Militarily, the army was the senior military service of the continental state. Its manpower, economic, and technological requirements consumed the bulk of the defense budget. (In the 20th century, land-based air forces were linked closely to the army, given the continental nature of their missions.) The field (and air) marshals and generals, being key leaders in the state, dominated strategic policy, including the uses of the navy. Admirals enjoyed little political power or influence on strategy.

The **missions of the continental state's navy** were therefore subordinated to those of the army. Ideally, in time of war, the navy required one or more allied navies in order to attain sufficient strength to fight a maritime enemy. Such alliances, however, usually proved unsatisfactory due to differences over shared command and control of operations. The navy of the continental state had 6 major missions:

1. Assumed a fundamentally **defensive strategic posture.** In order to ensure the army's ability to take the offensive on the continent, the navy supported the army whenever necessary. Because of the expense and time required for building warships, the navy sought to minimize its losses and was therefore reluctant to take unnecessary risks in battle. The navy's needs could never be allowed to impinge significantly on those of the army.

2. Maintained a **sufficiently strong fighting fleet** in home waters to restrict or deter the superior fleet of the maritime enemy from blockading or invading the coast. A continental navy constructed a sizeable fleet of large battle-capable warships which it concentrated in one or more major ports ready to sally forth against an enemy naval force. Ship for ship, these were often technologically superior to their enemy counterparts and thus posed a deadly challenge. When vastly outnumbered, however, the continental fleet was neutralized from taking the initiative.

3. **Defended against invasion.** The navy augmented the army's coastal fortifications to help repel amphibious invasions of the homeland along the coast, lakes, and/or rivers and to assist the army in protecting overseas colonies.

4. **Attacked enemy commerce** (*guerre de course*). Using single warships or small squadrons of them, the navy raided the enemy's merchant marine. If enough of these raiders were successful, they would be imposing a **commercial blockade** of the enemy's coast. The objective was to weaken the enemy's economy sufficiently to force it to terminate the war. Such commerce raiders could also be diverted to protect their own overseas merchant shipping by escorting **convoys.**

5. **Engaged in coastal and combined operations** with the army. This entailed sealifting troops along short stretches of coastal waters, lakes, and rivers as part of land campaigns. The navy could be used to transport a large army over water for an **offensive** amphibious invasion of another country. This was only possible, however, when no formidable enemy fleet opposed it. When that occurred, however, the result was usually disastrous for the continental navy, tied as it was to protecting the army's transport ships for such an invasion.

6. Maintained a **strategic bombardment capability.** This **offensive** naval mission to attack the enemy homeland developed with the advent of long-range aircraft and missiles in the 20th century. It was used by continental navies only as a deterrent, never in actual fighting.

The **maritime power** was isolated from overland attack because it was an actual or virtual island nation. Its geographic insularity had to be combined, however, with a favorable location adjacent to major sea routes of international trade. Lacking that, the maritime state would have been economically isolated from the overseas commerce upon which its growth and prosperity depended.

Politically, being free of the military imperative of maintaining continental defenses, the maritime state was able to focus on the development of civil institutions more liberal than those of continental states. That is, the individual predominated over the state. Democracy was born in ancient Athens and resurfaced in varying degrees in the 4 maritime powers noted above. Humanism (individual values) and humanitarianism (promotion of human welfare) went hand in hand as these few representative governments evolved out of their original feudal or authoritarian roots. Civil law protected individual rights and freedoms.

Economically, the maritime state depended on commercial trade and therefore embraced free enterprise by private merchants, what eventually became *bourgeois* (middle-class) **capitalism.** The middle class generally predominated over the smaller propertied agricultural (and later industrial) upper class and over the lower working class, thereby defining the socioeconomic character of the maritime state. Individual merchants and investors formed shipping companies in order to make profits which they reinvested in lucrative international trade. Such companies also engaged in overseas exploration and colonization and often armed their merchant vessels for self-defense, thereby augmenting the navy. The merchant class required peaceful order on the high seas and accordingly promoted the development of **international law** to guarantee its legal right to trade and thereby assure the nation's prosperity. This required the suppression of international outlaws which restricted or attacked trade—**pirates** and certain foreign powers.

Culturally, the comparatively liberal institutions of the maritime state fostered freedom of speech and religion; promoted high art, creativity, and invention; advanced science, industry, and education; and remained open to ideas, immigrants, and goods from all over the world. Self-interest, of course, often gave rise to the excesses and greed common to human nature, but the emphasis was always on individual rights rather than subservience to the state.

Militarily, the navy was the senior service of the maritime state. In order to ensure the safety of the merchant marine on the high seas, primary funding for national defense went into a superior navy capable of ruling the sea. Admirals predominated in strategic policy, while generals were charged with administering the relatively small army for home and colonial defenses and for overseas expeditions.

The **missions of maritime state's navy** served as the basis of national strategy. In time of war, however, the maritime power depended absolutely on one or more allied armies to defeat the enemy army on the continent. When the maritime nation's own army participated, the navy sealifted it to the continent. There the army generally cooperated successfully with the coalition forces and sometimes even provided overall command of them. The navy of the maritime state had 7 strategic missions:

1. Assumed an **offensive strategic posture.** In order to ensure uninterrupted trade on the high seas—against enemy fleets and commerce raiders—the navy asserted control over shipping lanes. In peacetime, this meant enforcing the international laws propounded by the state. In wartime, the goal was to achieve **command of the sea** by denying its use to the enemy. Because this navy's operating arena was primarily oceanic rather than coastal, it came to be regarded as a "blue-water navy."

2. Maintained **the strongest battle fleet in the world** in order to control the seas. In so doing, the navy, by its permanent existence and readiness, was able to deter rival powers from going to war. Or, if they did, the battle fleet actively sought out enemy fleets to engage and destroy them in battle.

3. **Defended against invasion.** If temporarily unable to eliminate the enemy fleet and/or an enemy invasion armada, the navy used its warships in aggressive maneuvers (raids and diversions) to keep the enemy navy preoccupied until the fleet could concentrate for a major battle. This stratagem of naval activity came to be known as the **fleet in being.**

4. **Protected merchant shipping.** In peacetime, the navy deployed smaller warships to patrol sea lanes and to capture or destroy the vessels of maritime outlaws—pirates and smugglers. In wartime, squadrons or single warships hunted down enemy raiders, attacked enemy merchantmen (*guerre de course*), and/or **escorted convoys** of merchant ships through disputed waters.

5. **Blockaded enemy coasts.** Squadrons patrolled enemy coastal waters to deter enemy vessels from leaving port or to destroy them if they did. The blockade was either **close** and **direct** (continuous patrols within sight of land) or **open** and **indirect** (only 1 vessel keeping watch, ready to alert a larger force at its anchorage some distance away). The blockade was primarily a **naval** one as long as the enemy fleet lay at anchor. Otherwise, it was a **commercial** blockade to immobilize enemy merchant shipping. It could simultaneously be both naval and commercial.

6. Engaged in **combined or amphibious operations.** The navy sealifted and supported the army and/or specialized marine infantry forces in offensive invasions or temporary hit-and-run raids of the enemy homeland and colonial possessions. The fleet's support of landings entailed shore bombardment, logistical (supply) backup, and the ability to withdraw the landing force. Overseas **advanced bases** were usually required before such offensive amphibious operations could be undertaken.

7. Engaged in **strategic bombardment.** Naval vessels of 20th-century blue-water navies were used as platforms for long-range naval aircraft and guided missiles to attack the enemy homeland, including naval installations. Along with land-based air forces, these naval weapons systems also acted as deterrents to war.

The **missions of small states' navies** were to defend and police local waters and attack warships of nearby enemies during regional conflicts at sea. When drawn into conflicts between great powers, the small states depended largely on their alliance with one of the major powers. Some engaged in effective commerce warfare (*guerre de course*) although never decisively.

The history of the United States provides a typical example of a nation which began as a small state with a commensurately small navy but which eventually grew into a maritime great power:

1775–1900   Small power, small navy (except for the Civil War)
1900–1945   Great power, major navy (but coequal with Great Britain)
1946–   Hegemonic great power, the strongest navy in the world

Naval Terms

The study of navies requires a general familiarity with a few basic terms, herein simplified.

Naval strategy. The actual plans, in peacetime or wartime, for the use of the navy as part of the **national grand strategy** in concert with diplomacy, economic measures, and the army (and air forces more recently). In the broad sense, naval strategy has been a component of **military strategy,** unless the latter term is specifically applied to the use of armies.

In contrast to armies, which in wartime remain in constant close contact with enemy armies during long campaigns and numerous battles, **naval power** has been applied subtly over months and even years in blockades, commerce warfare, and the like. Formal fleet-versus-fleet engagements were few and not always decisive. This was the case both in **total wars** waged for complete victory and in **limited wars** over trade rights, colonial territories, piracy, and so on.

Maritime great powers, notably Britain and the United States, often adopted a **strategy of concentration** when involved in conflicts with continental powers, usually during total wars but sometimes in limited wars as well. This was essentially a **maritime strategy of hit and hold.**

To **hit or concentrate** on defeating the main enemy fighting force (the continental nation's army), the maritime state provided funds, arms, general supplies, and eventually its own smaller army to sustain the vast manpower of its allied continental army.

Simultaneously, the maritime state used its navy to **hold or isolate** the enemy nation from outside supply or reinforcement. This entailed the destruction or neutralization of the enemy fleet and merchant marine by battle and blockade, the capture of the enemy's overseas possessions, and landings on the enemy coast—hit-and-run raids and the eventual invasion assault by its own army to augment the coalition army.

Naval policy. The programs of the navy to carry out the **roles and missions** assigned it by the government. This included determining optimum **force levels** of the numbers and types of warships and weapons and developing the **doctrines** of how they were to be utilized (in fleet battles, amphibious operations, convoy escort, etc.).

Naval administration. The organization and management of the navy by its high command ashore, including ship construction and repair, weapons development, personnel training and affairs, fleet and base maintenance, medicine, and coordination of the sealifted **naval infantry** or **marine corps.**

Naval tactics. Techniques of battle against enemy fleets, in commerce warfare, and in amphibious operations. Simply put, tactics are how to fight a battle, strategy how to fight a war.

Naval supply or logistics. Provisioning the navy with fuel, ammunition, tools, spare parts, and dry stores (the necessities for sustaining life at sea). A force of supply ships was called **fleet train** (Britain) and **service squadron** (United States).

Naval communications. This term has 2 meanings. Technologically, it is the system of **signaling** or talking between ships (and with the shore and aircraft), often in code. Referring to shipping, it is the system of sea lanes or routes along which commercial and naval vessels travel (recent U.S., SLOC, sea lines of communications).

Naval ranks. The exact titles of naval officers and enlisted crewmen have evolved and differed between navies over the years, but by the late 20th century they generally followed those of Britain and the United States, with ranks equivalent to those of armies (see Appendix 2).

Officers receive formal commissions from the government. An **admiral** (by descending seniority—fleet, full, vice, or rear admiral) or **commodore** usually commands a force of 2 or more warships: a **squadron, flotilla,** or **division; a task force** of several of these units; or an entire **fleet.** As such, the admiral or commodore flies a special identifying "flag" in his command ship, that is, the **flagship.** Hence, an admiral or commodore is a **flag officer.**

The **captain** commands 1 ship as its "skipper," although his/her formal rank may be lesser than that of actual captain. The second-in-command is known as the **executive officer.** The lesser ranks are, by descending seniority, **commander, lieutenant commander, lieutenant, lieutenant (j.g. [junior grade]),** and **ensign.**

Among enlisted personnel, the **warrant officer** holds a special position of seniority among noncommissioned officers. The next level is comprised of several grades of **petty officer,** from **chief** through 3 lesser classes. Finally, the ordinary **seaman** is rated through successive grades.

Naval fraternity. The closely knit camaraderie engendered by the teamwork required of **ship's company**—the crew, of which each sailor is known as a **deckhand,** collectively as **all hands.** They are **shipmates** who live, work, and fight within the close confines of onboard living **quarters,** working **spaces,** and battle **stations.** Loyalty to an individual ship has been especially pronounced when certain members of the crew have served a lengthy **tour of duty** aboard the vessel, especially in battle.

Naval personnel, officer and enlisted alike, have traditionally been bound by a common love of life at sea and a consequent distaste for life ashore—whose inhabitants sailors derisively label "landlubbers." Sailors share a specialized language derived largely from the components of and practices on board a ship. Their uniforms have been distinctive from those of armies—often of "navy blue" or white. Sailors' behavior during brief and infrequent "liberty" periods ashore is not surprisingly raucous. Punishments for misdeeds afloat and ashore are meted out during "captain's mast" (trial) and confinement in the "brig" (ship's jail). The ship remains the special tie that binds.

Admirals have tended to behave apolitically once ashore, outside their watery element. They have consequently tended to be less adept in competing for funds with generals, statesmen, and the private sector. With ships so expensive, admirals have been conservative when threatened with having to replace their vessels with untried ship types or new weapons and especially when faced with downsizing the fleet at all—simply because many years are required to rebuild it up to fighting strength. And intense rivalries have existed between officers who specialize in various environmental modes of naval warfare—during the 20th century these were surface gunships, naval aviation, and submarines.

Warships. (Basic terms in Appendix 3.) **A ship is not a boat!** In the age of sail, a square-rigged **ship** was so designated by having at least 3 main masts; vessels with fewer main masts had specialized designations such as **frigate, sloop,** and **bark.** Since then, a ship has been any vessel that can carry a boat on board. The major exception to this rule is the submarine, an underwater boat (U-boat). Gender-wise, warships have been traditionally designated both as masculine—a **man-of-war**—and feminine—she, her, several alike being "sister ships."

A **privateer** during the age of sail was a privately owned armed merchant ship authorized with a **letter of marque and reprisal** by its government to attack enemy shipping during wartime. Without the letter such a vessel was regarded as a **pirate,** operating outside international law, its crew as criminals subject to the death penalty.

A **capital ship** was an early-20th-century designation for the largest and most powerful type of naval combatant—first the **battleship,** later the **aircraft carrier** and **submarine.** Warships which have escorted or supported these, or operated independently, have been **cruisers, frigates,** and **destroyers.** Smaller warships have included **gunboats, minesweepers, landing craft,** and a plethora of auxiliary vessels for transport, supply, repair (**tenders**), hospitalization, and so on.

Making warships function effectively and efficiently has been the eternal task of sailors. Seamanship is all-consuming work, as Pericles knew very well in the earliest days of navies.

2

Antiquity

(2000 B.C.–A.D. 400)

Navies first appeared in the eastern Mediterranean and Aegean seas during the 2nd millennium B.C. Over preceding centuries, boats and barges had transported trade goods and soldiers upon the Tigris and Euphrates Rivers of Mesopotamia, Egypt's Nile, between the Aegean islands, and along the coastal waters of the Levant (modern Syria, Lebanon, Israel). Oars, along with paddles and poles, had provided the principal means of propulsion, although some Nile River craft had made use of a square sail sometime before 3000 B.C.

The adoption of the sail to Aegean rowed craft around 2000 B.C. provided auxiliary power in the tricky currents and winds of the open sea. This innovation not only stimulated longer-distance commerce but enhanced opportunities for seaborne plundering by rival states and freelance pirates. The offensive and defensive uses of navies therefore figured prominently in the ancient world as continental kingdoms and the first maritime states competed via Mediterranean sea routes.

The Maritime Minoans. The first maritime-oriented civilization was that of the Bronze Age Minoans, centered on the island of **Crete.** From about 2000 B.C. their oar/sail-powered merchant ships established trading settlements or colonies among the Aegean islands, on mainland Greece, and in Egypt and the Levant. By 1700 B.C. their extensive trade required active naval countermeasures against seaborne raiders. The Minoans apparently employed the **armed merchantman,** whose crew utilized lances, swords, slings, and bows and arrows to defend the vessel, attack pirate settlements, and perhaps capture rival islands. Insular Crete required no fortifications, but the volcanic destruction of the island trading entrepot of Thera, 60 miles to the north, in about 1628 B.C. probably weakened Minoan naval defenses.

Continental Egypt and the Mycenaeans. Egyptian civilization, long isolated from overland invasion by the Sinai Desert, lost the Nile Delta to the army of the Hyksos about 1650 B.C. Like earlier Egyptians, the conquerors depended heavily upon Levantine port city kingdoms such as Ugarit and Byblos for maritime trade and naval operations. Native Egyptians expelled the Hyksos to establish the 18th Dynasty in the late 1500s and create a continental empire with its military frontier at the Euphrates River in Mesopotamia. Levantine ships supplied and supported the army in pacification operations against the Mitanni in Palestine until the mid-1400s B.C.

Simultaneously, the warrior Mycenaeans of mainland Greece moved their war chariots and troops by sea to conquer Minoan Crete and overseas settlements. By 1400 B.C. the continental Mycenaeans had forged an empire out of the southern Greek mainland and the Aegean islands and established a trade network. To police their coast, islands, and shipping, they created a navy and may well have developed the first rudimentary warship—the **war galley**—for attacking enemy ships and coasts. In spite of such maritime activities, however, Mycenae remained essentially a warrior state (or confederacy of states).

For 2 centuries Mycenaean armies and warships subdued and enslaved mainland, coastal, and island peoples of the Aegean and guarded their own land and sea frontiers. Their most celebrated overseas achievement occurred in the **Trojan War** about the 1230s B.C. A Mycenaean expeditionary army, sealifted aboard hundreds of vessels, besieged and defeated the city of **Troy,** located at the Dardanelles (Hellespont), the strait through which all Black Sea shipping passed. This victory, however, secured their northern frontier only briefly.

"The Sea Peoples." Beginning about 1250 B.C. massive migrations of Indo-European tribal peoples pushed by land and sea into the Aegean and Levant, forcing the inhabitants to flee. Collectively labeled "Peoples of the Sea" by the Egyptians, they destroyed the Mycenaean cities and empire in the 1220s B.C. and sailed directly to Libya, with which they allied for attacks on the Egyptians in the Nile Delta. Egypt created a defensive maritime police force which helped its army repel these forays. The major land-and-sea advance of the Sea Peoples, however, pushed into the Levant, crushed the Hittites, and destroyed Ugarit.

About 1176 B.C. Pharaoh Rameses III assembled a great army, much of it on board ships, and destroyed the Sea People's fleet of warrior-laden vessels off the Syrian coast in the first major naval engagement of record. It was basically a land battle at sea—shipboard soldiers in hand-to-hand combat—which was apparently decided by superior Egyptian archery. Rameses parried another western attack on the Delta, but Egypt withdrew behind the Sinai Desert and abandoned its continental empire.

Canaanite survivors and Sea Peoples occupied the Levant. The most dynamic of the latter were the Philistines, who founded 5 thriving port cities along the southern coast named for them, Palestine. There, however, they soon came into conflict with a truculent tribal hill people, the Hebrews.

Phoenicians and Greeks. The Canaanites restored and enlarged older northern Levantine port towns, notably **Tyre** and **Sidon,** as centers of a new Iron Age culture, the Phoenicians. Skilled in seafaring, the Phoenicians focused on commercial activities. Exposed on the land side, their cities had little choice but to accept client status under the militaristic Assyrian continental empire soon after 1100 B.C. The Phoenicians cooperated with the Hebrew kingdom of Israel in destroying Philistine power in the 900s B.C. In the next century they began establishing distant overseas colonies throughout the western Mediterranean, in particular **Carthage** in North Africa.

The Phoenician (or **Punic**) maritime colonies became increasingly important when, in the 700s B.C., the Assyrian army marched into all the mother cities—except for Tyre. Situated on an offshore island protected by its navy, Tyre successfully withstood several sieges because the Assyrians lacked ships. When the new continental empire of Babylon crushed the Assyrians in the 600s B.C., the Phoenicians provided a fleet for an unsuccessful Egyptian attempt to stop the Babylonian onslaught. Again, in the early 500s B.C., only Tyre could counter these attacks by the nonmaritime Babylonians.

The Sea Peoples' onslaught around 1200 B.C. left the Aegean in a long cultural dark age typified by tribal and feudal warfare. Rampant piracy led successive island rulers to exert what later Greek historians termed **thalassocracy,** naval control over certain waters. Gradually, by the 800s B.C., independent Greek city-states emerged on mainland **Corinth, Athens, Sparta** and elsewhere and on several Aegean islands. Some of these states established overseas colonies in Ionia (western Turkey) and the western Mediterranean, notably **Syracuse** in Sicily. Greek merchant ships all required naval protection, especially those which brought vital wheat from the Black Sea.

Greeks and Phoenicians became maritime rivals who attacked and captured each other's merchantmen. This rivalry extended to the western Mediterranean, where Greek colonists competed with their Phoenician (Punic) counterparts centered at Carthage. These Greeks also had to contend with the Etruscan state of northwestern Italy. Greeks, Carthaginians, and Etruscans built warships which fought pirates and each other beginning in the late 700s B.C.

The Galley. The most maneuverable vessel for fighting at sea during antiquity was the galley, a ship powered by oars but equipped with an auxiliary mast and square sail, lowered during battle. The common merchant galley was vulnerable to boarding by an attacking galley and to seaborne raiders when pulled up on the beach, the common practice for overnight respites, long-term stays, and winter storage.

Probably in the late 700s B.C. the Phoenicians added a sturdy bronze-sheathed underwater ram at the bow for piercing enemy hulls and a second bank of oars to some of their galleys. These ram-equipped galleys—**penteconters**—varied in size to accommodate up to 40 rowers. The earliest known naval battle between fleets of galleys occurred in the mid-600s B.C., when Corinth defeated its rebelling colony of Corcyra in the Adriatic Sea. Greek colonists from Ionian Phocaea, who settled in southern France and Corsica, devised ramming tactics for their 60 penteconters which defeated 100 Punic and Etruscan galleys off Corsican Alalia about 540 B.C. This battle seems to have acted as the catalyst for the development of a more powerful galley—the trireme.

The **trireme** (*trieres*) was the first specially built true warship. Probably initiated by the Phoenicians and/or the Corinthians, it was adopted by most navies between about 540 and 525 B.C. These sturdy 120-feet-long war galleys were propelled by 170 rowers in 3 superimposed banks of oars; each carried up to 30 officers and marines. Rival fleets of triremes developed naval tactics which required constant training of crews to maneuver in battle for ramming speeds up to $9\frac{1}{2}$ knots and/or for boarding. Many Greek navies excelled in ramming, but Corinth, the Phoenicians, and most later navies preferred grappling for an infantry battle at sea.

During the same century, the Greeks pioneered the all-sail, round-hull merchant ship for transporting the vast amounts of Black Sea grain. To overtake these lumbering merchantmen, which averaged about 6 knots, pirates continued to depend on the smaller fast galley.

Persian Invasions of Greece. In the mid-500s B.C., the warrior Persians overran the Near East and drew upon Phoenician ships for their invasion of Egypt. When the Persians convinced 2 Greek city-states in Ionia to supply warships for the conquest of the eastern Aegean in 530 B.C., the tyrant of Ionian Samos, Polykrates, used his powerful triremes to crush the fleets of the 2 wayward cities. But when Polykrates then courted the Persians, his crews mutinied and caused his destruction. The Persian army completed its conquest of Ionia and cut the Greek grain route to the Black Sea. Under King Darius, Persia consolidated its continental empire and relied upon subject Phoenicia, Egypt, and Cyprus to provide a huge fleet to help put down a revolt by the Ionians in 499 B.C.

When the Persians besieged coastal Miletus the Ionians assembled over 350 triremes and penteconters at the island of Lade. The brilliant Ionian commander **Dionysius** of Phocaea devised ramming tactics against the superior imperial fleet, but in the naval battle of **Lade** in 494 B.C. many of his galleys withdrew prematurely, signaling defeat. Miletus fell, and with it Ionian resistance. Darius, to secure his Aegean frontier, issued an ultimatum to the mainland Greeks to submit to his authority.

The city-states of Greece rallied together to resist the Persian threat. The Greeks entrusted naval leadership to maritime, democratic **Athens** with the largest fleet, although oligarchic **Sparta** with its excellent army had overall command. The Persian army, supported by hundreds of subject galleys under Phoenician leadership, crossed the Dardanelles in 492 B.C. and moved down the coast of Greece. A violent storm, however, destroyed some 300 ships and their 20,000 men, forcing King Darius to withdraw.

He tried again 2 years later by "island-hopping" directly across the Aegean, his army on board 400 transports and 200 triremes. The troops landed at the beach of Marathon on the Attican peninsula, only to be driven into the sea by Greek infantry, forcing Persia to make another ignominious retreat.

For the next confrontation the opposing navies adopted separate tactical doctrines which typified opposing continental and maritime powers throughout subsequent history—the proverbial "elephant" (Persia) and "whale" (the Greeks).

The Persian/Phoenician solution was **quantitative:** outbuild the enemy. Darius raised a fleet of 650 triremes, plus hundreds of transports, for massive frontal ramming attacks to overwhelm the enemy. Each trireme carried 30 soldiers for missilery (arrows, spears) and boarding for hand-to-hand combat. Then the 200,000 troops would be landed to defeat the much smaller Spartan-led Greek army and destroy Athens.

The Greek/Athenian tactical doctrine was **qualitative:** develop maneuvers by which to neutralize the enemy's superior numbers. These tactics were designed to prevent boarding, with only 18 troops on board each trireme for missile fire. Although under the nominal command of a Spartan admiral, the brilliant Athenian naval leader **Themistocles** strengthened his city's fleet to 250 triremes, reinforced by 124 from the allied Panhellenic League, and drilled their crews in tactical maneuvers.

The key offensive tactic of the Greeks was the *diekplous* ("sail through"), perhaps invented by the Phoenicians and perfected by the Phocaeans. Columns of triremes charged forward between the approaching enemy ships, using their rams to sheer off the enemy's oars. Each Greek trireme turned sharply around the stern of its crippled victim and drove its ram into the hull. It then backed off so its ram did not get stuck in the enemy hull and be exposed to boarding. Stricken triremes did not generally sink. They only became immobilized, unable to board enemy ships or escape, thereby miring the fleet in utter confusion as the Greeks continued their individual attacks.

Persian and Greek triremes clash in the Bay of Salamis, 20 September 480 B.C. Using tactics of maneuver, each Greek galley sheers off the oars of an opponent before plunging its bronze waterline ram into the side of the enemy hull near the stern. As the defeated triremes of the Persian subject navies crowd together in confusion, the one led by Queen Artemisia of Halicarnassus rams one of her own ships to cover her escape. She is seen in white, standing and facing the stern and its 2 steering oars (the rudder was not invented until the 1300s). Ancient vessels did not have the crow's nest atop the mast as imagined by 19th-century artist Kostas Volanakis. (Hellenic Navy)

In 480 B.C. the new Persian emperor Xerxes followed Darius's original route across the Hellespont and down the coast. His 1,200 triremes and many smaller galleys and transports covered the seaward flank of the army. In July, Themistocles took 271 galleys up the coast to a sheltered shore at the narrow strait of Artemisium. No sooner had Xerxes's fleet appeared in mid-August than a 3-day storm dashed some 400 of its triremes against the rocky coast. The Greeks then audaciously attacked several advancing Persian triremes, capturing 30 of them.

Xerxes tried to entrap the Greek fleet by sending 200 triremes around it, only to have these battered by another storm. The Greeks, reinforced to 300 triremes, met some 450 attacking Persian galleys in the naval battle of **Artemisium** on 20 August. Both fleets suffered heavy losses, and the Greeks had to retire south-

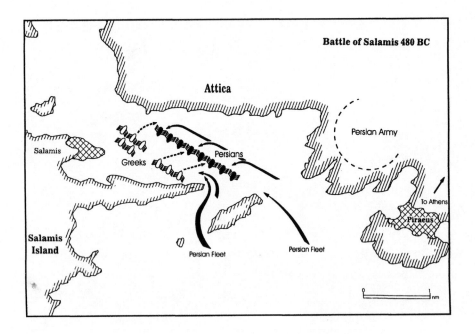

ward when the Persian army overran the Spartan army contingent at Thermopylae, where it had been blocking Xerxes's overland descent on Athens.

Disheartened, the Greeks abandoned Athens and fell back to a defensive wall south of the narrow isthmus of Corinth, where the Spartan-led army hoped to stop the Persians. Themistocles, however, had such confidence in his crews and tactics that he refused to obey the withdrawal order. Also, it would have meant pitting his 310 triremes in the open sea off the isthmus against the enemy, now reinforced to perhaps 1,000 galleys. He had to evacuate the people of Athens, which the Persians then captured and burned. But Themistocles kept the fleet offshore. On 20 September, he brought his ships into the sheltered strait between **Salamis** Island and the Athenian coast. There the Greeks brilliantly crushed the Persians, forcing them to abandon their invasion (see essay).

Athenian Empire. Greek arms, land and sea, counterattacked to neutralize Persian and Phoenician sea power. The Greek fleet burned the beached Persian fleet at Ionian Mycale in 479 B.C., liberating Ionia and then Cyprus. In 478 B.C. a Greek fleet captured Byzantium at the Bosphorus entrance to the Black Sea, thereby reopening the grain route, and supreme naval command passed to Athens. In the west, Greek Syracuse destroyed the beached Carthaginian fleet at Himera, Sicily, in 480 B.C. and 6 years later defeated the Etruscan navy at Cumae,

Battle of Salamis

In order to conquer Greece in 480 B.C., Persian emperor Xerxes had to destroy the Panhellenic fleet, the existence of which threatened the maritime supply routes of his army as it invaded Greece. The 4 squadrons of his imperial fleet, which outnumbered the Greeks by perhaps 1,200 to 310 galleys, spent the night of 19–20 September sealing off the escape routes from the Bay of Salamis. Themistocles, the de facto Greek commander, planned to exploit the confines of the narrow strait to nullify Persian superiority. He also had his crews get a night's sleep while the Persian rowers toiled at the oars establishing their blockade.

At dawn, the Persian imperial fleet of subject peoples entered the 1000-feet-wide strait in line-abreast: Phoenician triremes on the right, Ionian Greeks on the left, Cilicians and Cypriots in the center. The refreshed Greek crews sallied forth in line-abreast in perfect discipline, mostly free citizens fighting the Persian aggressor ("galley slaves" date from the A.D. 1400s) and singing their battle hymn. When the Persians attacked, the Greeks formed into 3 columns and moved forward, Spartans and Corinthians on the right, Athenians in the center and left.

The 50 triremes of Corinth moved ahead while the rest of the Greeks backed water in apparent retreat. It was a ruse, however: the Persians charged forward, creating a gap in their left flank. As they emerged from the confined strait, Themistocles seized the moment to execute his deadly *diekplous* maneuver. His Athenians rowed forward at battle speed to plunge their rams into the exposed sides of the Phoenician triremes. Simultaneously, the galleys of Aegina fell upon the flank of the Ionians. Calamity spread to the flanks and rear as the Greeks rammed enemy hulls and rained missiles upon their crews.

The battered lead Persian ships succumbed to the Greek attacks one by one, instigating a chaotic Persian retreat. The perfectly disciplined Greeks prevented Xerxes from bringing forward his rearmost ships. Xerxes, in spite of his defeat, was most impressed by Artemisia, queen of Halicarnassus who had succeeded her late husband in command of 5 Persian ships. She escaped capture by aggressively sinking another vessel (unknown to Xerxes, one of his own!). The Persians lost at least 200 triremes, whose crews drowned, not knowing how to swim. The Greeks lost about 40 vessels, whose survivors swam ashore. Xerxes, fearing his escape route would be cut by the Greek navy, elected to abandon the campaign, thereby ensuring the independence of all Greece.

southern Italy. In 478 B.C., Athens formalized the anti-Persian alliance by establishing the Delian League, which most Ionian and Aegean city-states voluntarily joined.

Athens became the first maritime-oriented great power in history. Geographically situated on the Attican peninsula, it became a virtual island when Themistocles had a defensive wall erected across the neck, minimizing the need for an army. Politically, Athens was the world's first democracy, governed by a wealthy class of merchants whose vast overseas commerce made Athens the trading hub of the Mediterranean world. These merchants used their excess profits to finance, maintain, and command Athenian warships themselves, raising and provisioning the crews as well. Democracy and naval power went hand-in-hand as Athens sowed the seeds of Western civilization.

Athenian foreign policy aimed at maintaining peace and stability in the Aegean—a Pax Atheniana—in order to preserve Athens's democracy and prosperity. The chief agency was the standing Delian League fleet of some 200 triremes, mostly Athenian, kept at peak strength for annual training maneuvers and overseas operations. As the expense of maintaining warships became too great for some junior league members, they substituted cash, used to finance additional Athenian triremes. When the admiral **Pericles** succeeded to the leadership of Athens after 460 B.C., he increased the fleet to 300 galleys, plus 100 in reserve, and even wrote the requirement for maintaining naval supremacy into the Constitution of 432 B.C.

Throughout the course of the century, Athens transformed the Delian League into its own **maritime** empire, formally in 448 B.C. Its strategy was twofold: to deter or eliminate major continental enemies, and to police the empire for internal stability. The navy accomplished both.

The Athenian fleet destroyed Persia's navy at the Eurymedon River, western Asia Minor (modern Turkey), in 466 B.C. and supported an Egyptian revolt against Persia in the 450s B.C. Simultaneously, however, a wary and jealous Sparta, which had refused to join the Delian League, emerged as the new continental rival to challenge Athenian hegemony. Athens kept Sparta isolated in the Peloponnesian mainland by allying with Argos and Megara, whose armies stood against Sparta south of the isthmus of Corinth.

Internal imperial policing meant pacifying Greek city-states which courted Sparta in order to drop out of the league and stop paying fleet taxes to Athens. When such cities revolted, Athens used warships and sealifted troops to crush them. Corinth and Aegina were the first to suffer such a naval defeat off the latter island in 458 B.C. Growing Athenian power drove Sparta, Corinth, and other jealous states to form a rival Peloponnesian League. In 431 B.C., when Athens dispatched warships to Corcyra, then fighting Corinth in the Adriatic Sea, Sparta declared war on Athens.

Peloponnesian War (431–404 B.C.). Between 431 and 421 B.C., maritime Athens and continental Sparta failed to break each other's supremacy at sea and on land respectively, even with the help of allied city-states. Sparta built a small fleet of triremes to control the Gulf of Corinth, only to suffer 2 naval defeats by the superior tactics of the Athenian admiral Phormio in 429 B.C. Four years later **Demosthenes** landed an Athenian amphibious force which besieged and captured Peloponnesian Pylos, while a Spartan army overran the Greek mainland north of Athens, hoping to cut the Black Sea grain routes. A formal peace came out of the stalemate in 421 B.C., followed by an undeclared "cold war."

Athens made the fateful decision to enlarge its empire westward by dispatching a large fleet and expeditionary force to subdue Syracuse in Sicily in 414 B.C. Sparta and Corinth promptly declared war. Using a new Corinthian reinforced ramming prow, these allied navies trapped and destroyed the 200 Athenian triremes and expeditionary force inside the harbor of **Syracuse** the next year. Between 411 and 407 B.C., however, the brilliant Athenian political and naval leader **Alcibiades** quelled a revolt of the Ionians, restored control over the Aegean, and defeated inexperienced Spartan naval commanders at the battles of Cynossema, Abydos, and Cyzicus, where he annihilated the main Spartan fleet.

The major Athenian casualty in this long war, however, was its democratic institutions. The heavy military requirements resulted in a despotic government which removed Alcibiades in 407 B.C. and even executed 6 admirals for spurious reasons after their crushing victory over a new Spartan fleet at Arginusae, Ionia in 406 B.C. Sparta turned to a new admiral, **Lysander,** whose fleet the next year surprised and destroyed the anchored and beached 180-trireme Athenian fleet at **Aegospotami** near the Dardanelles. This cut Athens's vital sea route to the Black Sea, whereupon Sparta instituted a land-sea blockade of Athens which starved it into submission in 404 B.C.

A resurgent Persia played Athens and Sparta off against each other over the ensuing half-century, as Athens rebounded from its defeat to eliminate Sparta at sea and embroil the Aegean in a series of revolts and wars. The net result was the fatal weakening of all the Greek city-states and the Persian Empire, leaving them vulnerable to newly emerging continental powers weaned on Hellenic Greek culture. These were Hellenistic Macedon and Rome.

Alexander the Great. After King Philip of Macedon conquered most of Greece by land in 338 B.C., his son Alexander did the same to the Persian Empire. In 334 B.C. he liberated the subject peoples of Ionia, Cyprus, Phoenicia, and Egypt who had provided the 400 warships of the Persian navy. Most of these joined Alexander in besieging and defeating insular Tyre in 332 B.C. He then freed Egypt, where he founded the great seaport bearing his name, Alexandria, as the hub of a 400-ship naval defensive network. After his death in 323 B.C., his generals founded dynasties in separate parts of his empire which fought over the next 125 years. Their largest galleys carried powerful shipboard catapults useful for attacking cities, but their main strength lay in their armies.

Carthage, Syracuse, and Rome. In the western Mediterranean, Punic Carthage and Greek Syracuse fought on land and sea for a century (409–306 B.C.) for control of Sicily. Both were innovators in naval architecture. Around 400 B.C., Carthage developed the *quadrireme* and Syracuse the *quinquereme,* enlarged versions of the trireme but with varying arrangements, respectively, of 4 and 5 banks of oars and/or men to the oar, plus shipboard catapults. Although larger galleys were later built, the quinquereme proved the most efficient and was eventually imitated by the Romans. All warships retained the ram, but the infantry battle at sea remained the preferred naval tactic. The only innovation was to expedite grappling—the Syracusan *corvus* (crow) or boarding bridge. Adopted by the Romans, c. 260 B.C., the corvus worked but made the ship top-heavy, liable to capsizing, and was soon abandoned.

Continental Rome recognized Carthaginian maritime supremacy in the western Mediterranean and only built galleys in the late 300s B.C. to fight local pirates. It was dragged into the larger naval wars when Carthage, in control of most of Sicily, threatened southern Italy in 264, leading to declarations of war against the Punic state by Rome and Syracuse.

Punic Wars (264–201 B.C.). Waged for control of Sicily, the **First Punic War** (264–41 B.C.) remained basically stalemated because of Rome's superiority on land and Carthage's at sea. Rome built and usually kept a 200-galley fleet in service for boarding actions and invasions of Sicily and North Africa, where the Roman legions attacked Carthaginian ports by land. Rome's fleet even won stunning naval battles off Sicilian **Mylae** (260 B.C.) and **Ecnomus** (256 B.C.) and North Africa's Cap Bon (255 B.C.). But Roman nautical inexperience led to a naval defeat off **Drepanum,** Sicily (249 B.C.) and the loss of several transport fleets in disastrous storms. Carthage consequently kept its besieged Sicilian ports supplied by sea.

Rome doggedly kept outbuilding Carthage in ships until a favorable opportunity presented itself for naval victory. Rome broke the stalemate in 242 B.C. by constructing 200 improved quinqueremes manned by experienced crews to blockade Drepanum. A quiescent Carthage rushed 170 quinqueremes into service, but with green crews they were crushed by the Roman fleet off the

Aegates Islands in 241 B.C. Its garrisons in Sicily cut off, Carthage sued for peace and surrendered all Sicily to Rome (except for independent Syracuse).

Rome extended its hegemony over the western Mediterranean until challenged by Carthage in Spain, bringing on the **Second Punic War** (219–201 B.C.). Now the strategic tables were reversed: the Roman navy dominated the seas, while the Carthaginian army under Hannibal marched overland from Spain to invade Italy via the Alps. He crushed the Roman legions, forcing the Romans into their walled coastal city in 217 B.C. Based in the roadstead of Ostia, the Roman navy operated from the **interior position,** shifting fleet units to threatened points and keeping Hannibal from being reinforced by sea. It isolated Carthaginian Spain and transported an expeditionary force there which eventually conquered the region in 206 B.C.

Rome's fleet won control over the Adriatic Sea by defeating the Macedonian ally of Carthage and eliminating piracy there (216–207 B.C.). When Syracuse declared war on Rome, and Carthage raised a new fleet to challenge Rome in Sicily, the Roman navy landed an army which besieged and conquered Syracuse (212 B.C.), frightened away the Punic fleet, raided North Africa (214–210 B.C.), and won 2 naval battles near Carthage (208, 207 B.C.). By 204 B.C. Rome was ready to sealift the 30,000-man army of Scipio Africanus to the enemy city. The 400 transports were escorted by 285 galleys from Sicily to North Africa. Hannibal had transports built to return to Carthage, only to be crushed by Scipio at the Battle of Zama in 202 B.C. Victorious Rome stripped Carthage of its overseas possessions, burned its warships, and turned it into a vassal state.

Roman Imperial Expansion. In spite of a republican constitution, Rome had become a continental empire during the Punic wars, dominated by army leaders. The success of its navy, however, enabled it to accept the appeal of the Greek maritime city-state of **Rhodes** for help in 201 B.C. Rhodian Sea-Law (*Nomos Nautikos*) had codified international rules for shipping, but the navy of Rhodes was not big enough to enforce them against pirates and Alexander's warring successor states. The result was Rome being drawn into the region's power struggles for the next 2 centuries.

To feed and administer its growing dominions, Rome depended on merchant ships, protected by the navy. When the eastern kingdoms—Macedonia, Greece, Syria—resisted these intrusions, Rome conquered them by land and sea between 200 and 133 B.C.

Unwisely, however, Rome then allowed its victorious navy to deteriorate in the face of endemic piracy throughout the Mediterranean. The most concerted threats were the fleets of 1,000 Cilician pirate galleys in Asia Minor and Crete and the new 400-galley navy raised by King Mithradates of Black Sea Pontus. Allied against Rome in 89 B.C., they overran much of the Aegean, attacked the coasts of Italy, and even destroyed a Roman fleet in its home harbor of Ostia. A Roman expeditionary force finally managed to conquer Crete in 72 B.C., and **Pompey the Great** was given extraordinary authority to destroy all Mediterranean piracy. In 67 B.C., he launched a systematic campaign using over 500 Roman and allied warships and 120,000 troops from Gibraltar to the Black Sea; they utterly destroyed the Cilician pirates. Two years later Rome defeated Mithradates.

Roman Civil Wars. Internal power rivalries ensued between Roman military leaders. From 49 to 48 B.C. Pompey used his naval strength to trap the army of rival Julius Caesar in Greece, but Caesar drew Pompey away from the coast to defeat his army. Caesar was briefly dictator of Rome before being assassinated. The new tenuous Roman government gave command of the navy to Pompey's son **Sextus Pompeius,** who however used it for piracy and personal conquests throughout the Mediterranean. **Octavian,** one of a triumvirate of government leaders, organized a fleet under **Agrippa** to fight Sextus in 38 B.C. In spite of 2 defeats, Agrippa streamlined his 370-ship fleet with reinforced waterline beams, propelled grappling hooks (the *harpago*), larger catapults, and fire arrows to seek a decisive battle. It occurred off **Naulochus,** Sicily, in 36 B.C., where Agrippa destroyed or captured most of Sextus's 300 warships.

A new rivalry followed between Octavian and Mark Antony, who had divided up the Mediterranean between them. Antony consolidated his rule over the eastern half by allying with Queen Cleopatra of Egypt and there building a Roman-Egyptian fleet of nearly 500 large galleys. Antony and Cleopatra moved their fleet to **Actium** at the western end of the Gulf of Corinth in Greece in 32 B.C. There Octavian and Agrippa attacked and defeated it with 400 galleys the next year. Antony and Cleopatra escaped to Egypt, where they committed suicide. Rome then annexed Egypt.

Pax Romana. In 27 B.C. the Roman Empire officially replaced the republic, Octavian became emperor as **Caesar Augustus,** and stability prevailed throughout the entire Mediterranean world under Roman administration. Augustus restructured the navy to operate in the littoral areas: 50 triremes based at Misenum near Naples, and provincial squadrons of light, swift, 2-banked galleys (*liburnians*) based at Ravenna on the Adriatic coast, at Egyptian Alexandria, and on the coast of Syria. These kept down piracy from the Black Sea to the Red Sea to the English Channel. By the time of his death in A.D. 14, Augustus had brought genuine peace to the Mediterranean world: the Pax Romana, international stability enforced by Roman arms.

For the next 2 centuries, however, Rome's major defenses depended upon the army legions on the frontiers. The system began to unravel due to internal stresses and tribal invaders which steadily entered the Mediterranean by land and sea. Civil wars of great armies and fleets culminated about A.D. 300, when the victorious emperor Constantine built a second capital city at the more easily defended Constantinople situated at the entrance to the Black Sea. The city of Rome fell to barbarians in A.D. 410, while Constantinople battled a truculent Persian Empire.

With the demise of western Rome and its navy, the ancient world of Europe entered a cultural dark age. Navies had figured prominently in the rise of Western civilization, protecting trade and ensuring the international order essential to urban cultures. When that order finally disintegrated, political chaos ensued.

3

Middle Ages and Early Renaissance

(c. 400–c. 1500)

MEDIEVAL EUROPE AND ASIA were fragmented by migrating tribal peoples, feudal kingdoms, and sprawling empires which did most of their fighting on land. The Mediterranean basin, however, remained an arena of major maritime and naval rivalries—between European Christians and the Europeans against the Muslim empires of the Middle East.

Byzantine Empire. Situated near the site of ancient Byzantium, Constantinople occupied a peninsula on the European side of the Bosphorus. With fortified walls blocking the landward approach and the seaward sides, the city was a virtual island. The Byzantine navy protected overseas trade and colonies and repelled attacks from the Aegean via the Sea of Marmara and the Dardanelles on the south and west and from the Black Sea on the north and east.

Because the Byzantine Empire depended on its army to protect its European and Persian frontiers, the navy economized on manpower by developing the 2-banked *dromon,* powered by 2 sails and 100 oarsmen. During the 7th century, a napalmlike inflammable concoction known as **Greek fire** was introduced. Projected from a sheathed tube, it clung to sails and clothes and could not be extinguished by water. It was a closely guarded secret until eventually imitated by the Arabs. Emperor Justinian undertook the reconquest of the western Mediterranean from the barbarians in the 6th century. His brilliant commander Belisarius used the army and navy to defeat the Vandals at sea and capture their capital at Carthage in 533, take Sicily in 535, and regain Italy from the Goths, Ostrogoths, and Franks by 562.

Byzantine-Arab Wars. A century later, the Arab Muslim conquest of Persia, Egypt, and eastern North Africa included the capture of the Byzantine naval bases of Tyre in 638 and Alexandria in 641. Absorbing the ships and crews of the conquered ports into their fleets, the Arabs mounted raids as far afield as Sicily and, via the Persian Gulf, the Indian Ocean. The Byzantines responded with massive naval construction, including a 3-masted dromon for boarding actions and 2 smaller galley types for ramming.

The new Arab fleet defeated a much larger Byzantine force in the **Battle of the Masts** west of Cyprus in 655 and mounted a 5-year land-sea blockade of Constantinople before being driven away in 678 by the deadly Greek fire in its first major employment. The Byzantines, plagued by barbarian raids and revolts of its naval district (*theme*) fleets, failed to prevent the Muslims from capturing Carthage in 698. Allied to a Bulgar army, however, Byzantine forces frustrated an Arab siege of Constantinople in 718. Flame-throwing dromons drove away the enemy fleet, the remnant of which was destroyed in 2 storms. After the Byzantines won a naval battle off Cyprus in 747 the Arabs turned east to suppress pirates in the Persian Gulf and initiate a trade offensive into the Indian Ocean.

Sea warfare was endemic for the next 3 centuries. The Byzantine navy repulsed 3 Kievan Russian seaborne attacks in the Black Sea. The navy of Italian Venice won control of the Adriatic Sea. The galleys of Charlemagne, king of the Franks, defeated Spanish Muslim ships in the Balearic Islands, which later fell to the Muslims. Arab fleets twice defeated Byzantine fleets in the waters of Sicily to conquer the island. Arab forces also took Byzantine Crete in 827, only to lose it again in 961. Muslim control of western Mediterranean waters was, however, finally challenged by the fleets of emerging Venice, Genoa, and Pisa.

The Northmen. As Charlemagne attempted to unify western European Christendom in the late 700s, the barbarian tribes of northwestern Europe formed the kingdoms of Denmark, Sweden, and Norway. These hardy warrior states fought each other for control of Scandinavian waters—the North Sea and Baltic Sea—and attacked the coasts of Charlemagne's empire and the British Isles. Their enemies knew them as Northmen, Norsemen, Normans, Varangians, and **Vikings.** Their standard warship—designed for boarding actions and coastal raids—was the 24-oar, single-decked, single-sail galley which evolved into the 60-oar oceangoing dragon-headed longship (*drekkar*).

During the 800s dragon ships by the hundreds transported attacking Viking armies into Europe by sea and by river. From the Gulf of Finland in the Baltic, they moved up the rivers of Russia to establish an empire at Novgorod and Kiev, pressing on to the Black Sea to become mercenaries in the Byzantine navy. From the North Sea, they overran the Netherlands and Normandy, established a base at the Isle of Wight in the English Channel, and moved up the Seine River to besiege Paris.

Viking attacks on England, Scotland, and Ireland prompted the creation of an English navy, the only one to oppose them. Anglo-Saxon King **Alfred** of

Wessex, one of several English kingdoms, initiated the construction of 60-oared warships in 875. He and his successors repulsed the Vikings and created 3 permanent naval squadrons to protect English merchant shipping in the North Sea, English Channel, and "Western Approaches" to the Channel.

Although the navy of Viking Norway dominated the Baltic and North Seas by 911, in fierce naval battles and campaigns between the 960s and 1030s Denmark conquered England and Norway for control of northern waters. Norwegian **Harald Hardraade** then returned from Byzantine service against the Arabs to restore Norway's independence, defeat Denmark in several naval battles, and invade England. The latter goal was also adopted by Duke William of Normandy.

By the time the Anglo-Saxon Harold became king of England early in 1066, the English had allowed their navy to deteriorate. Harald Hardraade easily landed in northern England in September, but Harold's army defeated and killed him in battle days later. William immediately crossed the Channel and occupied the port of Hastings, where Harold attacked him in October, only to be killed there. This victory of William "the Conqueror" not only sealed the fate of England but also ended the Viking wars.

Italy and the Crusades. The Normans responded to an appeal for help from the Pope in Rome by dispatching an army and 150-galley fleet to the Mediterranean in the 1060s. They conquered Arab Sicily, the island of Malta, and southern Italy and invaded Byzantine Albania in the Adriatic. But the defeat of the Byzantine army in 1071 by the emerging Muslim Turks caused all Christendom to initiate the Crusades to liberate the Holy Land in 1095.

The merchant ships of the Italian city-states of Venice, Genoa, and Pisa and the new Norman Kingdom of the Two Sicilies transported most of the Crusading armies to the Holy Land and supplied their feudal kingdoms there for 2 centuries. During the few naval battles, Christian rams, archers, and boarders usually prevailed over Muslim naval arms, which included Greek fire. These ships became adept at amphibious attacks on North African Muslim ports, using missile fire provided by crossbowmen high aloft in the ships' rigging and crow's nests.

Venice diverted the Fourth Crusade to help it attack and capture Constantinople by amphibious assault in 1203–4, the fleet being commanded by the ruling doge (duke) of Venice, **Enrico Dandolo.** The Venetians established their own imperial rule over Byzantine lands until rival Genoa and its navy helped the Byzantines recover Constantinople in 1261. Meanwhile, tribal Mongols swept out of Asia into the Middle East, forcing the last Crusaders to quit the Levant (except for Rhodes) in 1291.

Imperial Venice. The republic of Venice was essentially maritime and commercial in nature, ruled by a patrician class of rich but responsible merchant families. The city was located upon a group of islets in a lagoon of barrier marshes and mud flats at the north end of the Adriatic Sea, ideally positioned to trade with eastern and western Christendom and the Muslim world. Venice also reaped the ideas and knowledge that made it a cultural leader in the Italian Renaissance, underway by 1300.

The formidable Venetian navy of 2-banked, 3-masted "great galleys" and their citizen crews escorted merchant convoys, battled pirates, and protected overseas colonies from maritime rivals. Venice's bald aggression against the Byzantine Empire in 1204 prompted incessant conflict with Genoa, situated on the north-western coast of Italy. Genoa also had to contend in the western Mediterranean with Pisa, Spanish Aragon, France, and the Two Sicilies. These 5 western rivals fought a series of interrelated naval wars between 1282 and 1302, mostly over Sicily. The scale of these struggles was typified by the largest fleet of great galleys ever deployed—165 by Genoa in 1295 and manned by 35,000 sailors and soldiers. The end result was the destruction of Pisan naval power, Aragon's annexation of Sicily, and a naval balance in the western Mediterranean between Genoa and Aragon.

In the eastern Mediterranean, Adriatic, and Aegean Seas, Venice and Genoa fought 4 naval wars for maritime supremacy (1253–84, 1293–99, 1350–55, 1378–81). Venice quickly regained many of its Aegean–Black Sea trading privileges and was joined by the Byzantines and Aragon in the third war against Genoa. The climax of many naval battles occurred in 1380, when Venice destroyed the main Genoese fleet. Genoa conceded naval supremacy over the entire Mediterranean to Venice, enforced by its standing fleet of 80 war galleys.

Venice thereafter extended its colonial possessions along both coasts of the Adriatic, stationed a fleet at Corfu to command the entrance to the Adriatic, and used its navy to dominate the Gulf of Corinth, Athens, and much of the Greek Morea (Peloponnese). Venice also expanded its holdings overland into Italy, partly to counter Florence, the inland authoritarian republic which conquered coastal Pisa in 1406. Florence then created a navy and briefly allied itself with Venice, but in the 1450s they fought each other.

Ottoman Empire. The Ottoman Turks became Venice's new major enemy. Like the Mameluke Turks who overran Egypt and Syria, the Ottomans converted to Islam while conquering Anatolia (modern Turkey) and invading the Balkans during the 1300s and early 1400s. Because the Venetian navy and Constantinople stood in their way, they built galley warships and a naval base at Gallipoli at the entrance to the Dardanelles, only to be defeated there by a Venetian fleet in 1416.

Sultan Mehmet the Conqueror expanded his fleet to eliminate these obstacles in his plan to conquer Christian Europe. In 1453 a combined Ottoman land-sea assault captured **Constantinople,** bringing an end to the Byzantine Empire. Turkish armies and warships then absorbed most of Venetian Morea, Genoa's last Aegean islands, and the Black Sea coast. Venice and Turkey fought from 1463 to 1489, the former unable to confront the latter's army, the Turkish fleet unwilling to face Venice's. Venice successfully defended Crete and Cyprus, while Crusader Knights held on to Rhodes. But the Ottomans fashioned a powerful fleet built around Anatolian pirates to crush the Venetian navy in 3 battles in Greek waters in 1499.

Venetian political and naval hegemony did not recover, largely because Venice was overextended on the Italian mainland and in the western Mediterranean. Maritime Aragon had conquered Norman Naples in 1455, and in 1462 continental Castile captured Gibraltar, the vital strait to the Atlantic, from the Muslims. In 1469 Aragon and Castile united as the kingdom of Spain, Europe's first modern nation-state. Spain relied on Genoa to administer its economy and on Genoese seafarers such as Christopher Columbus to expand its overseas trade. Venice encouraged an emerging France to counter the Spanish influence in Italy, whereupon France conquered Florence in 1494.

Its military resources divided between land and sea, Venice ceased to be a major European power after 1500. Henceforth, Ottoman Turkey and Venice traded commercial goods and fought as naval rivals but only as part of the larger Christian-Muslim religious struggle.

England and France. Medieval feudalism gradually yielded to growing commercial towns in northern Europe, and dynastic wars plagued the developing kingdoms of England and France. The English crown employed private armed merchantmen and royal galleys to protect its sea communications to its possessions in France. Piracy and occasional but indecisive cross-Channel expeditions, blockades, and naval battles with galleys and sailing ships pitted the English against France throughout the 13th century. In the end the English navy was supreme.

The 2 rivals fought the **Hundred Years' War** (1338–1453) over western French lands. French sailing ships employed the first (ineffective) cannon in a typical boarding action off **Sluys** in 1340, but they were defeated by the 300-ship English fleet. Raised to 738 vessels, the latter blockaded and captured French Calais and landed an army in Normandy which defeated the French in 1346–47. Three years later the English navy captured a convoy from French-allied Castile at the battle of **Winchelsea.**

England's subsequent neglect of its navy led France and Castile to strengthen theirs. In 1372 an English fleet tried to relieve its besieged garrison at the port of La Rochelle, but the allied fleet nearly annihilated it using flaming arrows. The navies thereafter transported troops and made amphibious raids in this fundamentally land war. It finally ended in 1453, when France succeeded in driving England from the continent, except for Calais.

The Hanse. Baltic and North Sea waters were contested by Denmark, Sweden, and independent German coastal and river towns which created the Hanseatic League in the late 1200s. This informal economic confederation, centered at Visby and dominated by **Lübeck,** pooled its warships to fight pirates and grew in naval strength. In the 1340s Denmark initiated a strategy of weakening the Hanse and Sweden. It culminated with the Danes' capture of Visby in 1361 and the imposition of commercial tolls for passage through the Danish Sound, the vital straits linking the 2 northern seas.

The Hanseatic fleet counterattacked by capturing the capital of Denmark, Copenhagen, only to be defeated by the Danish fleet at the battle of Helsingborg in 1362. The dictated peace was broken in 1368 when the Hanse retook Copenhagen and forced Denmark to exempt Hanseatic merchantmen from the Sound tolls. Although Denmark soon absorbed Sweden and Norway, the Hanse won more trading concessions in another Danish war in the early 1400s and from England after Hanseatic warships ravaged that country's eastern coast in 1474.

Although the Hanseatic fleet played a key role in liberating Sweden from Danish rule in the 1520s, the following decade an allied Danish-Swedish fleet crushed the Hanse navy. When Lübeck independently sided with Denmark against Sweden in the 1560s, the league disintegrated, and Lübeck's navy was destroyed by its enemy.

International Law. Because no great civilization existed to articulate and enforce maritime laws, the Middle Ages were characterized by disorder and piracy upon the seas. When the early Byzantine emperor Justinian attempted to restore the Pax Romana in the 500s, he resurrected the ancient Rhodian Sea-Law to codify rules of commerce; it included the death penalty for giving barbarians knowledge of shipbuilding.

No such codes for adjudicating maritime claims existed thereafter until the Norman conquest of England in 1066. The English and French then revived Justinian's laws for an admiralty court located on the English island of Oléron off the French coast. The Normans took these **Judgments of Oléron** with them to the Mediterranean in the 1070s, where they were adopted by the Italian maritime republics, the Crusaders, and the Byzantine Empire. One of the Italian republics, Amalfi, after being conquered by the Normans in the 1130s, improved upon the judgments. These **Amalfitan Tables** were recognized throughout the Mediterranean until 1570.

As the Renaissance heralded early modern European civilization, maritime towns and emerging nation-states embraced these legal precedents. In the 1200s, the Judgments of Oléron provided the basis for the Sea Laws of Visby, which guided the Hanseatic League. In 1403, England officially adopted the judgments for its trade relationships with other countries. And later in the century Spanish Aragon applied its own maritime law, the *Llibre del Consolat,* in its struggle with Muslim states in the western Mediterranean.

The adjudication of international maritime law between disputants was a European legal convention. It dealt with such matters as the uses of the sea to fish and trade, the right to levy tolls, the right of neutrals to trade with warring rivals, and defining piracy. Its effectiveness depended upon all involved parties accepting it and/or upon the ability of the dominant navy to enforce it. As an institution of Western civilization, however, international law was alien to—and therefore ignored by—the tribal, feudal, and non-Western peoples on whom it was imposed, especially after 1500.

Asian Navies. The lands of East, South, and Southeast Asia were divided into dynastic kingdoms and feudal states which engaged in trade, piracy, and some naval operations on rivers, lakes, and coastal waters. Combinations of sails and oars characterized Asian vessels, including multimasted junks and sampans and a Chinese treadmill-propelled paddle-wheeled boat which carried archers.

Indian Ocean. The Muslim offensive down the Persian Gulf in the 600s brought Middle Eastern traders to several seaport towns of India, Indonesia, and China. One Indonesian kingdom which welcomed them was Srivijaya, which controlled both sides of the critical **Malacca Straits,** through which all seaborne traffic passed between India and China. The Arabs monopolized this trade, shifting to Indonesia after the Chinese closed the port of Canton to them in 878. Maritime Srivijaya policed these waters for centuries against endemic pirate peoples such as the Chola state of India in the 1000s.

Indochina. The piratic Champa kingdom of Vietnam in the 1170s built a riverine force of single-banked galleys armed with rams of ivory and copper-sheathed wood to invade the Khmer kingdom of Cambodia. Moving up to Mekong River into the lake of Tonle Sap, its warriors looted the Cambodian capital. The Khmer quickly fashioned a similar fleet of river galleys to defeat the Chams on the lake, drive them back down the Mekong, and conquer Vietnam.

China. Centuries of overwater forays to Korea schooled the Chinese in naval architecture and fighting by the time the Wu dynasty initiated overseas trade to Indochina and Malaya in the 300s. When a Japanese fleet invaded Korea in the 660s, a combined Chinese-Korean force repelled it at the naval battle of Haku-son-ko, bringing Korea under Chinese control. The Chinese government also provided warships to protect its merchantmen against Vietnamese pirates in the South China Sea.

Unable to stop the Mongol invasion of China north of the Yangtze River in the 1120s, the **Sung dynasty** moved the capital from Peking to a city south of the river, transformed its overland economy into a maritime one, and created an admiralty and navy of 11 squadrons along the Yangtze. From the large naval base at Hangchow, the Sung pacified Vietnamese waters, enabling new large merchant ships to penetrate the Indian Ocean and undermine the Arab trade monopoly. When Mongol ships attacked on the Yangtze and near the Shantung peninsula in 1161, a Sung fleet of over 300 warships and armed merchantmen drove them back using rams, flaming arrows, and—new to naval warfare—rockets and catapulted gunpowder-filled fragmentation bombs.

A fresh Mongol attack in 1235 caused the Sung to expand its Yangtze naval defenses to 20 squadrons, but they suffered steady losses over ensuing decades. In 1270 **Kublai Khan** commandeered captured Sung ships and crews to force the entire Korean merchant marine into his fleet. Four years later it ferried an army across the Korean Straits to southern Japan until a storm destroyed half its 900 ships. In 1279 the great Khan destroyed the Sung fleet at Yai-shan off Canton and established the Yuan dynasty over all China.

Amassing an armada of over 3,500 vessels for another invasion of Japan in 1281, Kublai Khan was able to overcome fanatical Japanese boat crews only to have his fleet virtually annihilated by a typhoon—what the Japanese termed a "divine wind" (*kamikaze*). His successors then suffered attacks by Japanese pirate fleets along the Chinese and Korean coasts and by South China Sea raiders during the next century. The southern province of Fukien revolted and between 1348 and 1368 destroyed the Yuan navy and dynasty.

Under Emperor Yung Lo, the new Ming dynasty set about creating a virtual maritime empire. Developing Nanking in the south as his capital and main naval base, Yung Lo built a fleet of 400 warships and 2,500 light vessels to protect his huge merchant marine against pirates from Japan to the Malacca Straits, including his conquest of northern Vietnam in 1407. Between 1405 and 1433, Admiral **Cheng Ho**, a Muslim in Ming employ, carried out 7 overseas expeditions in 62 large junks armed with cannons, other guns, rockets, and bombs to expand Chinese trade. Pacifying much of Indonesia, Cheng Ho based at Malacca to suppress Indian Ocean pirates and Ceylon (modern Sri Lanka) and to garner trade with India, Arab East Africa, and the Turks in the Persian Gulf and Red Sea.

Fundamentally a continental empire, however, China soon came to regard its maritime activities as an anomaly. Overland advances by Tamerlane and the Mongols against the northern frontier forced Yung Lo to shift the capital back to Peking and reinforce the army. Upon his death in 1425, his successors dismantled the navy, leaving Chinese merchantmen at the mercy of pirates everywhere, including Vietnam which successfully revolted in 1427. Overseas trade was gradually terminated and the construction of large seagoing vessels forbidden.

Japan. Aside from pirate vessels and the use of water craft in internal conflicts and a few forays to Korea, the feudalistic warrior clans of Minamoto and Taira kept Japan fairly isolated. Their long feud climaxed in the naval battle of Dannoura in the Inland Sea in 1185, when missiles and boarders from some 100 Minamoto rowed junks destroyed 500 Tairan boats. The victors allowed their navy to decline and were spared the 2 Mongol invasions of the late 1200s only by the fortuitous storms discussed above. Japanese naval expertise was maintained by Japan's subsequent piratic operations against the Chinese, which included a siege of Nanking in 1555.

In the 1580s, the new Japanese dictator Toyotomi Hideyoshi outlawed piracy and ordered the construction of 2,000 ships for the invasion of Korea and ultimate conquest of China. Employing 700 of them as transports, he landed his army at Pusan in southern Korea in 1592. It advanced overland to Seoul, there to await reinforcements by sea and river. When the enfeebled Ming dynasty did nothing, the Koreans built and trained a formidable fleet for tactical maneuvers.

Admiral **Yi Sunsin** developed the "tortoise ship"—a galley with reinforced ram, broadside guns, and a covered armored turtle-back deck from which spikes projected to deter boarders. Supported by wooden ships, Yi used 2 of these vessels to sweep the Yellow Sea during the summer of 1592, raining flaming arrows and ramming in line-ahead tactics to sink hundreds of Japanese transports and warships in several naval engagements. The Chinese army drove the Japanese back to Pusan, where Yi's ships pummeled their fleet until it evacuated the army.

In 1597, Hideyoshi launched a second invasion of Korea, now seriously weakened at sea due largely to Admiral Yi's removal by political opponents. The Japanese navy defeated the Koreans in 2 battles, but the Chinese army held its ground in Korea. Yi, recalled to duty, used his navy to win at sea even without his tortoise ships (apparently shipwrecked), causing the Japanese army again to fall back on Pusan. The Ming dynasty had meanwhile restored its navy, which now reinforced Yi, who was determined to prevent the Japanese evacuation after Hideyoshi's death in 1598. In the battle of Chinhae Bay, Yi defeated the superior 400-ship Japanese fleet but was killed in the process. Heavy ship losses on both sides caused the antagonists to make peace.

Except for endemic piracy, the experience of the several Asian states in maritime and naval affairs had been sporadic and ancillary to their basically continental concerns. No longer would Asian nations operate warships without taking into account the navies of Europe, which penetrated Eastern waters with increasing aggressiveness throughout the 1500s.

4

Iberian Global Empires

(c. 1500–c. 1600)

In 1494 the kingdoms of Spain and Portugal signed the Treaty of Tordesillas dividing up the unexplored regions of the world between them. From the Iberian peninsula of southwestern Europe, which they shared, their seafarers utilized advances in shipbuilding and navigation to create overseas colonial empires. Both nation-states required formidable navies to fight their opponents: Muslims of the Mediterranean Sea and Indian Ocean, Protestants of northern Europe, and pirates in American and Asian waters.

Warships. Spain was fundamentally a continental state whose superb army fought France for hegemony in western Europe. The navy in a subordinate role carried troops for the customary infantry battles at sea. Spain continued to rely on the great galleys of Italian Genoa, including the new galleass—single-banked with 25 oars to a side (5 men per oar)—for ramming and boarding, augmented by cannon and the lighter firearms in raised fore- and after-castles. It was easily maneuvered in **line-abreast tactics** for boarding actions in confined waters.

Both Spain and Portugal utilized the armed, round-hulled sailing ship of North Atlantic design for long-distance global voyages of exploration—Spain westward to America and China, Portugal south via western Africa and eastward to India by the 1490s. To engage enemy fleets on the high seas, the Portuguese developed the all-sail **galleon**—a sturdy though sluggish multimasted floating fortress which mounted up to 80 cannon in the castles and on broadside gun decks for salvo firing. The galleons of both Iberian navies carried up to 800 troops for boarding. England and the Netherlands developed sleeker and swifter galleons with fewer soldiers in order to fire broadsides and retire before boarding could occur. When such galleons began to maneuver in **line-ahead tactics,** they came to be known as **ships-of-the-line.**

Mediterranean Stalemate. Spain landed an army in Italy in the 1490s, forcing the French to withdraw, and helped Venice withstand an Ottoman attack during the war of 1499–1503. Jealous of Venetian power, however, Spain allied with France and Austria in a ground war against Venice, 1508–16. This contest ended Venice's imperial pretensions on land but left the republic as the Christian naval buffer against the Turks in the Adriatic Sea. Meanwhile, 1492 to 1518, the Spanish drove the last Muslim Moors from Iberia and, with the Portuguese, employed privateers to wage war against Muslim pirate strongholds in North Africa.

Portugal simultaneously penetrated the Indian Ocean and successfully attacked the shipping of the Mameluke Turks. When the Christians threatened the Muslim holy cities of Mecca and Medina in 1516, the Ottoman Turks dispatched a fleet down the Red Sea which conquered the Mamelukes and checked the Portuguese. The Ottoman sultan, Selim the Grim, unified the Muslim world and in 1519 accepted the offer of the veteran Tunisian pirate **Barbarossa** (Khair ed-Din) to turn North African Algeria into the western Muslim frontier against the Christians.

The next sultan, Suleiman the Magnificent, elected to invade Europe by land, using defensive fleets to hold the Black Sea, Red Sea, and Algeria. His navy did capture Rhodes in 1523–24 to secure the army's communications to the Balkans. But Charles V, the Austro-Spanish Holy Roman Emperor, attacked the Ottoman Empire in 1530, beginning with Genoese admiral **Andrea Doria**'s capture of several North African coastal towns. Suleiman appointed Barbarossa high admiral of his navy to build a new fleet for a counterattack.

Allowed to winter his fleet at French Toulon, Barbarossa in 1534 carried out devastating raids on the western coast of Italy. Admiral Doria responded with an allied fleet of 500 galleys from Spain, Italy, and Malta (to which the Crusader Knights of Rhodes had relocated) that captured North African Tunis in 1535. Barbarossa's fleet parried by destroying Port Mahon on Minorca in the Spanish Balearic Islands. From 1537 to 1540 Suleiman conquered all Venetian strongholds in the Aegean and Adriatic except Crete and Cyprus. Muslims and Christians kept fighting but in a general stalemate throughout the 1550s.

Spanish Imperial Expansion. In one generation, 1502–27, Italian and Portuguese explorers in Spanish service (notably Columbus and Ferdinand Magellan) conquered the tribal natives of the Caribbean Sea and the feudalistic Aztec, Maya, and Inca kingdoms of the Americas and crossed the Pacific to claim the Philippine Islands. To capture the Aztec capital Tenochtitlan (modern Mexico City), located on an island in Lake Texcoco, Hernando Cortez had his shipwrights construct 13 2-masted, 30-oared brigantines. In 1521 he used these and 16,000 canoes carrying over 25,000 allied Indian warriors to supplement the firepower of his troops in overwhelming the Aztecs and their 50 large war canoes.

American gold and silver plate enabled Spain to sustain its armies and navy in achieving hegemony in Europe and defending the empire. Lacking a middle class, Spain now depended upon the merchants of the subject Netherlands, in place of Genoa, to direct its trade with northern European manufacturers. This created a dangerous internal problem when many of the seafaring Dutch embraced the Protestant Reformation of 1517 opposing the Catholicism upheld by the Spanish crown.

Realizing that its *conquistadors* (conquerors) of the Americas could not defend themselves against rival Europeans, Spain closed American colonial waters to foreign merchantmen in the 1530s. This legal edict for economic monopoly proved hollow because it could not be adequately enforced against attacks on Spanish shipping across the Atlantic by pirate corsairs from England, the Netherlands, and France.

Philip II, the new King of Spain, therefore instituted annual escorted convoys in the 1550s to protect the plate-laden ships transporting American treasure across the Atlantic. The system was formalized in 1568 as the *Armada Real* — 2 to 12 galleons accompanying 2 yearly convoys each way between the Caribbean "Spanish Main" and Iberia, augmented by Spanish and Portuguese galleons between their coasts and the Azores Islands. But Spain's enemies also formed squadrons of up to 12 ships each to attack convoy stragglers and coastal towns on both sides of the Atlantic. The convoy system was nevertheless successful in deterring direct corsair attacks on the escorted plate fleets for more than 2 centuries.

Portuguese Imperial Expansion. Portugal, lacking the manpower and resources to engage in overland ventures anywhere, concentrated on maritime and naval enterprises. Expeditions of powerful Portuguese galleons crushed all local opposition at sea, landed troops to establish coastal enclaves, and from these bases regulated native sea trades in West Africa, Brazil, and the Indian Ocean. They then attempted to exclude all European competitors from sharing their monopoly. This all occurred during the reign of King Manuel I, 1495–1521.

The main Portuguese attack was in the Indian Ocean. The galleons first bombarded the port of Calicut on the Malabar western coast of India and drove off attacks by Arab sailing dhows in 1500 and 1502. Then **Alfonso de Albuquerque** instituted a brilliant naval strategy to ensure Portugal's permanent control over the trade of South Asian waters. He discerned that 3 key waterways linked the Indian Ocean with other vital sea lanes. These **terminal points** therefore had to be commanded by his warships: the Strait of **Bab el-Mandeb** to the Red Sea (and eastern Mediterranean beyond); the Strait of **Ormuz** to the Persian Gulf; and the Straits of **Malacca** to the South China Sea (and the Pacific).

Albuquerque and **Francisco de Almeida** implemented this tightly coordinated strategy against the widely separated and decentralized peoples of the region between 1507 and 1515. Operating from the **interior position**—fortified bases along the Malabar coast and Ceylon—their warships and troops viciously attacked, defeated, and intimidated the poorly armed defenders of each strait. They seized coastal positions at the mouth of Bab el-Mandeb. They conquered and fortified the entrance to Ormuz, thereby deterring a Muslim fleet in the Persian Gulf. And they besieged and occupied Malacca, posting a permanent naval squadron there to patrol the straits.

In order to shift their warships between the 3 straits as needed, the Portuguese strengthened their **strategic center,** Malabar India. From there the main permanent squadron rushed north to Diu to counter a combined Mameluke-Gujarat Indian fleet but was defeated in 1508. Reinforced, Almeida returned the next year to destroy the enemy fleet, followed in 1510 by Albuquerque's seaborne conquest and conversion of Goa into the Portuguese capital in India.

From Goa, Portuguese warships blockaded the western ports of India, forcing all Arab and Indonesian merchant ships to trade through Goa. India's rulers submitted to the Portuguese commercial monopoly and allowed them to fortify other key ports. Albuquerque then halted all trade to the Red Sea, crippling the Mamelukes and discouraging their successor Ottomans from counterattacking. The Portuguese also extended their control southward from Bab el-Mandeb to the Arab East African port towns of Mombasa and Kilwa.

Portuguese galleons and galleys maintained an aggressive posture in Asian waters. The occupation of Bahrain inside the Persian Gulf in 1521 provided a base for ravaging Muslim seaborne trade and repelling Indian-Ottoman attacks on Ormuz in 1546 and 1552. Portuguese warships repulsed 4 separate Indonesian descents on Malacca (1518, 1538, 1572, 1575), conquered the spice-rich Molucca Islands of Indonesia, established trade relations with Japan, and forced their way into Chinese markets. Driven off by a Chinese Ming coastal fleet in 1522, the Portuguese turned to smuggling until they captured coastal Chinese Macao in 1577 and took over the carrying trade between China and Japan.

Ottoman Naval Offensive. Islamic Turkey's basically defensive naval posture took an offensive turn in the 1560s. The Ottomans landed an army on Malta for a land-sea siege against the Crusader knights in 1565, only to be driven off with heavy losses. But they retook Tunis in 1569 and landed on Venetian Cyprus and Crete in 1570–71.

Spain allied with Venice to create a combined Spanish-Italian fleet of 210 galleys under the Spanish Mediterranean commander, **Don John,** to assert control in the central Mediterranean. On 7 October 1571, it encountered the 225-galley Ottoman fleet of Ali Pasha at **Lepanto** near the entrance to the Gulf of Corinth. In the last major all-galley naval battle in history the 2 fleets approached one an-

Allied Christian galleys (flying the cross) engage the Ottoman fleet (flying the crescent) during the Battle of Lepanto, 7 October 1571. Fifty cannon on each of 6 galliots of Venice hammer the Turks while galleys of both sides grapple for boarding by seaborne infantry. The crushing Christian victory blunted the last major Turkish naval offensive in the Mediterranean. From a 16th-century Venetian painting. (National Maritime Museum, London)

other in line-abreast crescent formations for the traditional infantry battle at sea. Some 80,000 men on each side fired cannon and boarded as the opposing rams locked the galleys together. Don John's center ships crushed their opposites, killing Ali Pasha, and sank or captured some 150 vessels. The Christians killed over 25,000 Muslims and freed 12,000 enslaved Christian oarsmen against their own losses of 8,000 men and a dozen ships.

The Ottomans built a new fleet, made a separate peace with Venice, and continued to skirmish with the Spanish. They were assisted by the semiautonomous Algerians known to the Europeans as the **Barbary pirates.** The Ottoman-Spanish Mediterranean stalemate resumed by 1580 as both empires concentrated on other fronts.

Rise of England. England first challenged the Iberians in the 1480s, when King Henry VII instigated **Navigation Acts** setting tariffs, subsidized private shipbuilders, and armed several merchantmen as warships of the crown. The real "father of the British navy" was his son **Henry VIII,** who succeeded to the throne in 1509. Relegating the galleys to coast defense, he created a large composite battle fleet of all-sail galleons and supporting flotilla of escorts and scouts. Inspired by Spanish tactical innovations, he issued fighting instructions for fleet actions which exploited broadsides from batteries of cannon forged in English iron foundries. The key to success lay in taking advantage of turbulent Atlantic winds to maneuver into a favorable position for salvo fire—tactics which took centuries to perfect.

Henry's adherence to the Protestant Reformation led to wars with Catholic France and Spain. In 3 short indecisive conflicts between 1512 and 1546 England and France employed galleys and galleons in line-abreast formations, which compromised the use of broadsides until the battle off **Shoreham** in 1545, but even then they had no effect. France captured Calais in 1558, ending England's presence on the continent, but was otherwise preoccupied with internal religious strife. When Elizabeth I became queen of England in 1558 she sent corsairs to weaken Spain's monopoly in America. John Hawkins and **Francis Drake** led the attacks on Spanish shipping in the Caribbean and throughout the world, which Drake circumnavigated in 1577–80.

Dutch Sea Beggars. By the mid-1500s the economic and financial hub of the Spanish empire was the port city of Antwerp in the southern Netherlands, seconded by Amsterdam in the northern province of Holland. The Dutch revolted against repressive Spanish rule in 1568, whereupon Philip II transferred an army from Italy to crush the rebels. Dutch privateers plundered Spanish shipping and in 1572 captured several Spanish-held Dutch ports. They were aided by French Protestant (Huguenot) ships, which attacked Spanish sea communications, and by Queen Elizabeth, who allowed them to operate out of English ports.

Known popularly as the Sea Beggars, these Dutch naval forces developed into a regular fleet which defeated Spanish squadrons on the Zuyder Zee and off Walcheren island in 1573–74. In 1579, the northern provinces—centered on Amsterdam—declared outright independence from Spain as the United Provinces. Philip II, partly to allay the high costs of the fighting, decided to conquer Portugal for its navy, merchant marine, and rich overseas empire.

A Spanish fleet of galleons and galleys under the brilliant naval commander the Marquis of **Santa Cruz** landed and supported 2 armies which overran Portugal in 1580. In response, the Portuguese in the Azores revolted against Spanish rule and obtained French naval support. Santa Cruz ended the uprising with a force of galleons which defeated Franco-Portuguese warships in 2 naval actions off the Azores in 1582–83. These first open-ocean battles in history caused Spain to hasten construction of more galleons and in 1586 to separate the navy from army control.

Spain simultaneously reinforced its army under the Duke of Parma fighting in the Netherlands, enabling it to besiege and capture rebellious Antwerp in 1584–85 and force all non-Catholics to leave the city. Most of them—Protestant and Jewish merchants—emigrated to Amsterdam, where they quickly strengthened the new nation and its navy.

Armada Campaign. Anglo-Dutch attacks on Spanish shipping contributed to King Philip's declaration of war on England in 1585. He seized all Protestant merchant ships in Spanish and Portuguese ports and placed an embargo against further trade. Elizabeth responded by accepting a Dutch invitation to establish a protectorate over the Netherlands and by dispatching Drake with a fleet of 29 ships to plunder Spanish territory. Drake's first victim was Vigo on the coast of Spain, then the Canary and Cape Verde Islands, and—early in 1586—Hispaniola and Cartagena in the Caribbean.

Philip decided to invade England and inspire a Catholic uprising to overthrow Elizabeth. Lacking enough troops to provide an invasion force aboard his "Invincible Armada," Philip charged the Duke of Parma's army in the southern Netherlands with the task, which included building flatboats for the invasion troops and ships to tow them to England. Santa Cruz's armada was to drive up the Channel and protect Parma's crossing from Protestant warships. Santa Cruz assembled his fleet at Lisbon and Cadiz, including ships, troops, and supplies from Italy.

Elizabeth responded with alacrity. Hawkins as treasurer of the navy modernized the English fleet and added more cannon to its sleek galleons. In 1587 Thomas Cavendish plundered Spanish shipping in the eastern Pacific. Drake audaciously sailed 23 warships into the harbor at Cadiz to sink or capture 24 sail and 14 galleys of the Armada and burn all the barrels being dried to preserve its food and water. He then attacked Spanish shipping off Cape St. Vincent and seized and blockaded Portuguese coastal points. The Dutch Sea Beggars simultaneously blockaded and neutralized Parma's invasion vessels in Dutch waters.

These events prevented the Armada from sailing in 1587, but neither they nor the untimely death of Santa Cruz early in 1588 broke Philip's determination. To command the Armada he appointed a landsman with absolutely no experience at sea, the Duke of Medina Sidonia, and obtained crews by drafting men who had never been to sea. The Spanish added new long-range guns to their ships but of varying size and quality. Tactically, Spain's navy was still in the midst of a

The Spanish Armada

The 130-ship Armada of Spain, commanded by the Duke of Medina Sidonia, formed the main naval element for the invasion of England. It reached the Western Approaches of the English Channel on 29 July 1588 (19 July, old-style calendar), bound for French Calais for replenishment and linkup with the Duke of Parma's invasion force, towed in flatboats. The Armada was arranged in crescent formation, the heavier galleons on the wings protecting the galleys, supply ships in the center. Whenever the English warships attacked, the Spanish intended to fire, grapple, and board them for the traditional Mediterranean tactic of an infantry battle at sea. Once victorious, the Armada would escort Parma's invasion vessels to the English coast.

Contrary winds initially kept the English fleet— 120 galleons and 70 small, armed merchantmen under the command of Lord Charles Howard—harborbound at Plymouth. This gave Medina Sidonia the option of sailing into Plymouth and destroying the English ships at anchor or simply proceeding up the Channel uncontested. Because the Armada was committed to the role of covering force, he elected to continue on to Calais. On 31 July, the wind shifted, a "Protestant wind" according to the English, who now made sail to exploit the **windward** or **weather gauge**. Each of the 4 English squadrons sailed in columns and fired on the closest Spanish ships, then retired out of harm's way. They inflicted so much damage on 2 large Spanish galleons that these fell behind and were captured the next day.

Like wolves attacking a herd of buffalo, Howard's ships hit and ran over successive days, returning swiftly to nearby English ports to replenish ammunition while the Armada lumbered up the Channel. Medina Sidonia suf-

doctrinal shiftover from the Mediterranean infantry battle at sea à la Lepanto (1571) to the open-sea tactics initiated at the Azores (1582).

The plan called for the Armada's 130 sailing galleons and rowed galleys to cruise up the English Channel in crescent formation, firing on the English fleet while they closed in for a boarding action with their 19,000 troops. Medina Sidonia expected his ships then to be replenished by Parma at the French port of Calais, and the Armada's troops would be used to reinforce Parma's 30,000-man army. The Armada would then escort Parma's transports to the English coast.

The English, by contrast, developed purely Atlantic tactics. Lord High Admiral **Baron Charles Howard** organized his fleet of 120 all-sail warships to engage the Spaniards with heavy broadsides and thereby prevent grappling and board-

fered more losses but finally managed to drop anchor in the roadstead of Calais on 6 August. There he discovered that Parma had failed to accumulate the necessary supplies to complete the invasion flotilla—or to break the Dutch blockade. The invasion could not be carried out. Nor could the Armada retire through the Channel because of contrary winds, not to mention the presence of the formidable and virtually unscathed English fleet.

Howard acted swiftly to neutralize the Armada. Reinforced by the squadron at the Downs watching Parma, he sent 8 fireships—burning hulks—into Calais harbor the night of 7–8 August. As wind-driven sparks licked at the Spanish galleons, Medina Sidonia cut his anchor cables and rode the tide and winds out into the North Sea. Several ran aground, and after daybreak an aggressive attack by Drake drove others into the shore at Gravelines. The Armada had no choice but to head for home via the North Sea and around Scotland and Ireland.

Already defeated in the first naval battle fought solely with guns instead of boarding or ramming, the Armada faced more travails in its flight over the next several weeks. In addition to 20 ships lost in action, dozens of other Spanish vessels now succumbed to heavy seas and coastal rocks off the Scottish and Irish coasts. The health of already weakened and wounded crews worsened because their water and provisions had spoiled in the uncured wooden barrels used to replace the dried ones destroyed by Drake's Cadiz raid the previous year. So even when the surviving ships straggled into Spanish ports in September, many sailed right into the beach for lack of healthy crewmen to pull in the sails. Half the Armada's 130 ships and only one-third of its 30,000 men survived the campaign and voyage. The English lost no ships and 100 men. England was saved.

ing. Posting a squadron at the Downs, an anchorage at the eastern end of the Channel, to intercept Parma's invasion transports, Howard took personal command of the 4 squadrons he assembled at Plymouth near the western end. He planned to have each squadron charge the edges of the Armada, fire and withdraw, hoping to inflict enough damage to prevent the Armada from supporting a landing. His squadron commanders, including Drake and Hawkins, and their crews were all skilled and experienced naval fighters.

The Spanish Armada sortied from Lisbon in May 1588, only to be struck by a storm that required a layover for repairs at Corunna. In July it proceeded across the Bay of Biscay, bound for the Channel. Unknown to Philip or Medina Sidonia, the Dutch Sea Beggars had completely frustrated Parma from creating his transport force, while France, wracked by religious turmoil, had no intention of co-operating at Calais. Worst of all for Spain, the threatened invasion had the opposite intended effect on the people of England; instead of encouraging the overthrow of Elizabeth, it inspired the English to rally behind her for the defense of their shores. The result was the destruction of the Armada (see essay).

The English and Dutch immediately counterattacked against the Spanish and Portuguese empires and enlisted the support of France. In 1589 the French and Dutch armies battled Parma's army while an Anglo-Dutch fleet under Drake plundered the Spanish ports and merchant shipping at Corunna and Vigo and attacked the Canary and Azores Islands. In the 1590s Elizabeth launched cross-Channel expeditions to aid the French Huguenots, causing Philip II to occupy French Calais and Brest until a national bankruptcy forced him to withdraw.

English and Dutch merchantmen, pirates, and galleons then challenged the Iberians in the Mediterranean; the Dutch penetrated the Portuguese-dominated Indian Ocean; and in 1595 Drake and Hawkins mounted an expedition against the Spanish Caribbean. They completely destroyed the main Spanish port in Panama before both succumbed to fatal illnesses. Spain belatedly dispatched a naval force thence in 1596, leaving Cadiz exposed to an Anglo-Dutch amphibious attack which put the torch to the city and 82 anchored merchantmen and warships.

King Philip mobilized another invasion armada of 100 ships against England, only to have it broken up by a storm in 1596 and again in 1597, partly the fault of inferior Spanish seamanship. Philip died in 1598, but his successor invaded Ireland in 1601 as a stepping-stone to England. The scheme failed, however, when English galleons destroyed a force of Spanish galleys in the Channel the next year. Elizabeth's death in 1603 virtually ended the fighting.

The Dutch fought on, their army punishing Spain's on the continent, their galleons attacking Portuguese shipping in the Indian Ocean. When Spain outfitted a force of 10 galleons at Gibraltar to dispatch to the Indian Ocean in 1607, Dutch Captain **Jacob van Heemskerck** with 26 armed merchantmen annihilated it before it could sail. The Spanish economy collapsed again, and Spain sued for peace.

Spain and Portugal had enjoyed overseas imperial monopolies as long as they had not been challenged by mature maritime nations and navies. So when the English and Dutch achieved naval supremacy, the Iberians lost the initiative. In the peace agreements of 1604 with England and 1609 with the Netherlands, Spain conceded the right of both nations to colonize regions throughout the world unoccupied by Spain and Portugal, thereby abrogating the Iberian monopoly proclaimed in the 1494 Treaty of Tordesillas. As a result, English settlers founded Jamestown, Virginia in 1607, and Dutch colonists arrived at Jakarta, Indonesia, in 1610. The demise of Spain as a great power was only a matter of time.

5

Dutch Naval Mastery

(1590s–1670s)

THE DUTCH REPUBLIC—officially the United Provinces of the Netherlands—was the first nation-state based on middle-class capitalism. Between the 1590s and 1670s it enjoyed strategic insularity between the North Sea, 4 major rivers, the divided German duchies, and a France preoccupied with internal strife. The superb Dutch army manned the forts behind the rivers which separated the Dutch Republic from the Spanish Netherlands (modern-day Belgium). The republic was perfectly positioned astride the major trade routes over which it dominated the carrying trade of Europe—in the North, Baltic, and Mediterranean Seas—and launched colonial offensives into Asian and American waters. This trade was protected by the strongest navy in the world, augmented by sturdy armed merchant ships of several private joint-stock companies.

International Law. The Dutch justified their attack on the Portuguese trade monopoly in the Indian Ocean by articulating a broad new principle that formed the basis of modern international law. In 1609 the Dutch jurist Hugo Grotius published the treatise *Mare Liberum (The Free Sea)* in which he argued that the oceans are a commercial common shared by all mankind, not to be monopolized anywhere by one nation. Englishman Robert Selden countered with arguments eventually published as *Mare Clausum (The Private Sea)*: because a maritime nation utterly depends upon the use of certain waters for its survival, it has the right to exclude other nations from sharing these waters.

Whichever legal interpretation prevailed depended upon the navy powerful enough to enforce it. During the 17th century the Netherlands, England, and France all formed trading companies, founded colonies, and enlarged their navies to encroach upon the Spanish and Portuguese monopolies—and to compete against one another. The irony was that the Dutch and English soon switched their legal positions. Once the republic overpowered the Portuguese in the Indian Ocean, it attempted to monopolize the region, and England eventually fought for free seas when it challenged the Dutch shipping monopoly in

Atlantic waters. The outcome, by 1700, was the adherence of all seafaring nations to **mercantilism,** colonial ports closed to traders of other nations.

The Dutch Navy. The maritime province of Holland, centered on Amsterdam, dominated Dutch wealth, trade, government, and military forces. The States General of the 7 provinces appointed the ruling stadholder of Holland as stadholder and military commander of the republic. Because his chief interest was the army, and due to provincial differences, in 1597 the government created 5 separate admiralties to coordinate fleet operations and convoys and to raise privateers in wartime. Three of these admiralties were located in Holland, 1 in each of the other 2 maritime provinces, Zeeland and Friesland. In 1650, when the stadholdership fell vacant, its functions were assumed by the grand pensionary of Holland and the republic, **Johan de Witt,** who personally reformed the navy into a standing professionalized national fleet.

The Dutch navy preferred offensive tactics. Dutch galleons sailed in line-ahead, firing their guns while attempting to obtain the *weather* or *windward gauge.* Then they rushed downwind to grapple and board the enemy ships. This doctrine developed from their early small squadron actions and continued until the English contested them in line-ahead artillery duels. Like all navies, they employed frigates and fireships.

In contrast to offensive tactics, Dutch naval strategy remained basically defensive—the protection of merchant shipping. The major initial threats were the corsairs of Muslim North Africa and of Dunkirk and the Flanders coast in the Spanish Netherlands, which the Dutch navy continually blockaded. The state provided a few 400-ton galleons but relied on the 5 admiralties to arm merchant ships and raise local navies and privateers to defend commercial shipping.

In response to Algerian captures and enslavement of Dutchmen, the republic mounted the first European naval expedition against the Barbary raiders, a joint venture with the Spanish that destroyed 11 Algerian corsair ships near Gibraltar in 1617–18. The barbarous slaughter of Dutch crews by the Flemish corsairs gave Dunkirk the reputation as "the Algiers of Christianity." The Dutch retaliated by taking no Dunkirkers prisoner—killing them outright—until the Spanish government halted Dunkirker practices in 1628. By that time Spain had fortified Dunkirk into an impregnable roadstead for 30 warships, which plagued Dutch, English, and French shipping alike. But such attacks did not impede the global trade offensives of the republic.

Dutch Seaborne Empire. Dutch merchantmen and warships penetrated the Baltic Sea, where they took over French trade, drove out the Spanish, and allied with Sweden, helping to build its navy and to humble rival Denmark. The Dutch colonized the middle Atlantic coast of North America (around modern

New York City), several West Indies islands, and Guiana-Brazil, from which out-posts they battled the Spanish and Portuguese on land and sea. Admiral **Piet Heyn**'s fleet of 31 ships struck a blow to Spain's economy in 1628, when it cap-tured the entire treasure fleet of 38 Spanish and Portuguese vessels near Cuba. But the Dutch soon abandoned the fight for Portuguese Brazil as too expensive.

The Netherlands, joined by England, concentrated its major effort on break-ing the Portuguese trade monopoly in the Indian Ocean. From 1607 to 1609 the Portuguese and Spanish repulsed Dutch naval attacks on Mozambique in East Africa, the Malacca Straits, and the spice-producing islands of Indonesia. In 1610, however, the Dutch gained a trade foothold in Java. The same year English traders arrived at Surat in northwestern India and between 1612 and 1618 defeated attacking Portuguese squadrons in 4 naval battles. English and Dutch warships thereafter cooperated with the Persians and Mogul Empire of India to weaken Portuguese power in the Arabian Sea. Then the English established trading sta-tions on the eastern coast of India.

The key to Dutch empire was Indonesia. In 1619 Commodore **Jan Coen** seized Javanese Jakarta, renamed it Batavia, brutally conquered the Banda Islands, and expelled English merchants from what now became the Dutch East Indies. In 1630 Dutch warships began the blockade of Portuguese Malacca, forc-ing all local trade through Batavia. In a relentless naval campaign, 1638–45, **Antonio van Diemen** brought an end to the Portuguese commercial empire by isolating Goa, assaulting and capturing Malacca, and occupying coastal positions in Ceylon.

The Dutch sealed their control over all commercial traffic between Europe and Asia by occupying the Cape of Good Hope at the southern tip of Africa in 1652. They established settlements on Chinese Taiwan (Formosa) in the 1620s and, although driven out by the last Ming ruler in 1661, continued to trade at Canton with the new Manchu dynasty. Dutch traders became the sole Europeans to remain (at Nagasaki) after Japan expelled the Portuguese in 1638. The latter retained Chinese Macao, and Spain held the Philippines against several Dutch attacks before 1650, but the Asians preferred trading with Dutchmen. Three an-nual convoys between Batavia and Amsterdam brought the only Asian spices to Europe.

Thirty Years' War. The Netherlands—and England as well—could sustain distant overseas commercial offensives because both were spared the devasta-tion suffered by continental Europe in the long war of 1618–48. The Dutch peace settlement with Spain in 1609 had actually been a formal 12-year truce, after which, in 1621, the 2 nations resumed fighting. The Dutch simultaneously declared war on Catholic Hapsburg Austria, then trying to crush the Protestant

Germans, who now rushed troops to the defense of the Netherlands. Because Dutch trade lanes through the Mediterranean had to be protected from Spain (and the Algerians), the republic instituted a system of 2 annual escorted convoys to markets in Italy and the Ottoman Empire. This successful convoy system lasted 175 years.

When Venice joined the general attack on Spanish shipping in the Mediterranean, it hired 12 armed merchantmen built, equipped, and manned for it by the enterprising Dutch. An Anglo-Dutch raid on Spanish Cadiz in 1625 ended in disaster, due largely to the deterioration of the English fleet under the new Stuart dynasty. In the Baltic, however, Sweden's King Gustavus Adolphus drew on Dutch naval support for his fleet to engage Hapsburg armies that reached the coast in 1628 and to transport the superb Swedish army for a successful counteroffensive into Germany in 1630.

When Catholic France joined the Protestant fight against Spain and Austria in 1635, the Spanish navy immediately seized French islands near Marseilles in the Mediterranean for a naval base, only to be driven out by a French amphibious force in 1637. Cardinal Richilieu, mastermind of the resurgent France, developed a fledgling navy which he used to attack a 28-ship Spanish force near San Sebastian on the Franco-Spanish Atlantic border in 1638. With 18 galleons, the French employed fireships to crush their foe.

In 1637 the Dutch Republic appointed **Maartin Harpertszoon Tromp** to its highest naval rank, lieutenant admiral of Holland, and charged him with reorganizing the home squadrons into a disciplined battle fleet. This proved timely because Spain constructed a new armada with which to drive the Dutch from the English Channel and land 20,000 troops in Flanders to help fight the French and Dutch armies. Tromp therefore kept part of his fleet on constant patrol in the Channel.

In mid-September 1639 Spain's armada of 77 galleons under Admiral Don Antonio Oquendo suddenly appeared. Tromp, with only 31 ships, immediately attacked. Superior Dutch gunnery and maneuvering convinced Oquendo to run up Channel and anchor at the Downs on the English coast, hoping for England's support. An English squadron did put in to the Downs, but under orders to preserve England's neutrality. Tromp and Admiral **Witte Corneliszoon de With** meanwhile blockaded the Downs for a month, during which their fleet was reinforced to 95 galleons and armed merchantmen. The **Battle of the Downs** ensued on 21 October. The Dutch sent in fireships, forcing the Spanish to cut their anchor cables and attempt to flee. The Spanish ships that did not burn or run aground were destroyed or captured by the Dutch. Oquendo escaped with only 12 vessels; Tromp lost 1.

The Dutch victory had important strategic consequences. It gave the Netherlands undisputed command of the Channel with which to suppress pirates and assist the French army. It completely discredited Spain and its navy. France transferred warships into the Mediterranean to support its army before Spanish Barcelona and to neutralize Spanish naval squadrons. It encouraged Portugal, supported by the Dutch fleet, to throw off Spanish rule in 1640. And the inaction of the English fleet to prevent the Dutch attack in its own waters at the Downs so weakened the Stuart crown as to hasten the outbreak of the English Civil War in 1642. The Dutch were now free to intervene in the Baltic with warships and admirals, helping the Swedes to destroy Danish naval power in 1644–45 and thereby attain commercial supremacy. Most welcome to all Atlantic shippers was the French capture of Dunkirk in 1646, ending Flemish piracy.

The end of the Thirty Years' War in 1648 left the Dutch Republic more powerful than ever, its navy supreme. France kept fighting Spain, which recaptured Dunkirk in 1653 and even turned to the Netherlands as its principal merchant carrier.

Cromwellian England. Soon after assuming the throne of England in 1603, the pacifistic Stuart King James I laid up most of the fleet, exposing the English coast and shipping to Dunkirker and Algerian pirate attacks. His successor, Charles I, began his reign in 1625 with a 5-year naval war against Spain and a joint raid with the Dutch on Cadiz. In 1627 he sent a fleet to support rebelling French Huguenots at La Rochelle, where it was defeated by its own incompetent leadership and by the French. He enlarged the navy by taxing the people for "ship-money" in the 1630s, which enraged Parliament, then failed to prevent the Dutch from violating English waters at Battle of the Downs in 1639.

Although inferior in numbers to the Dutch, the English navy progressed in warship design, epitomized by *Sovereign of the Seas,* the model European ship-of-the-line for the future. She displaced over 1,100 tons and was a "3-decker"—100 guns mounted on 3 gun decks—although the preferred line-of-battle ship was the 1,000-ton 2-decker with 60 to 80 guns. The English fleet also standardized its warships into 6 separate rates, each designated by the number of guns and size of each gun crew. Shipboard living conditions and pay were so dismal, however, that the 35-ship navy sided with Parliament against the king at the outbreak of the Civil War in 1642.

With the fleet isolating the Royalists from outside help, Parliament created the New Model Army under Oliver Cromwell, which defeated the crown in 4 years of fighting. In 1648 the fighting resumed, leading Cromwell and the army to break with Parliament and much of the navy. The next year Cromwell appointed 3 of his army officers "generals at sea" to command the enlarged navy of the new

English Commonwealth. One of them, the superb **Robert Blake,** drove the surviving Royalist warships of **Prince Rupert** into the Mediterranean and protected convoys against the privateers and warships of an alarmed France.

In 1651 Cromwell became military dictator of England and immediately moved against the Dutch. He was affronted by Dutch control of international trade, their expulsion of English traders from the East Indies, and their American colonial presence separating New England from English Virginia. Late in 1651 he had Parliament pass a Navigation Act forbidding merchant ships from entering English ports unless they were English vessels or from the country of origin—not intermediate carriers, meaning Dutch ships. The law also insisted on the right of English warships to search neutral vessels and confiscate any military cargo—a direct slap at the neutral Dutch carrying trade. With new and enlarged shipyards, Cromwell doubled his fleet to 41 new men-of-war for enforcing his dictum.

This could only mean war, or a series of wars, inasmuch as 2 nations now claimed hegemony at sea. It would be a fight to the finish, because only one nation could dictate—and enforce—its interpretation of international law. As purely naval wars—no armies were involved—they would be the bloodiest in history, whale versus whale as it were. The humiliation of defeat would be lasting: a warship of the losing nation had to dip its ensign to a man-of-war of the victorious navy—rendering honors to the other's flag in recognition of that nation's supremacy.

The Dutch responded to Cromwell's challenge early in 1652 by authorizing construction of 150 more warships. The republic was at the pinnacle of its power. But its navy was committed to escorting convoys of between 100 and 400 merchantmen to and from the Baltic and Mediterranean. Except for the North Sea route, all shipping had to pass through the Channel and the Straits of Dover— the "bottleneck of Europe." Here the main Dutch fleet would meet these convoys, and here Cromwell meant to attack them. Though the English assumed the strategic offensive and the Dutch the defensive, both practiced aggressive naval tactics.

First Anglo-Dutch War (1652–54). War was precipitated when, on 29 May 1652, Admiral Tromp entered the Straits of Dover with 40 sail and General Blake sortied from the Downs with 25. When they met, Blake demanded that Tromp render honors first, an ultimatum he underscored with several cannon shots. Tromp replied with a broadside that began the Battle of Dover, resulting in the sinking of 2 Dutch ships. The Netherlands declared war and signed a treaty with Denmark closing the Danish Sound and Baltic waters to English shipping. Cromwell's navy instituted a campaign against Dutch shipping that eventually succeeded in capturing perhaps 1500 prizes.

In August, Admiral **Michiel Adriaenszoon de Ruyter** with 30 sail drove a larger English force back into Plymouth to protect an outbound convoy. On 8 October, de Ruyter and de With attacked Blake at **Kentish Knock** at the North Sea approaches to the Thames River. The evenly matched fleets of some 65 sail each broke their formations for individual combat until the Dutch withdrew. On 10 December, Tromp covered a 300-ship outbound convoy by using 73 sail to defeat 42 under Blake off **Dungeness** near Dover. Few ships were actually sunk or captured in such savage gunnery duels, but damage and casualties ran high.

Early in 1653 Cromwell streamlined the Commonwealth navy in order to facilitate a decisive fleet action and issued the first formal Fighting Instructions. They ruled that only galleons—and no longer the less-efficient armed merchantmen—would form in line-ahead to fire broadsides against the enemy. The fleet was divided into 3 squadrons—van, middle, and rear, respectively designated White, Blue, and Red. The rank of admiral replaced "general at sea," the foremost of whom were the brilliant Blake and **George Monck.**

The Dutch made similar and simultaneous innovations under the dynamic leadership of Grand Pensionary de Witt. Sixty new line-of-battle ships were authorized to replace the armed merchantmen in the line for a completely professional navy. With each ship-of-the-line at 600 tons and mounting just under 60 guns, they were no larger or more heavily armed than previous Dutch galleons and therefore smaller than England's 1,000-tonners, but their shallower drafts enabled them to operate in coastal waters. Swift frigates were also developed for escorting convoys.

The leading Dutch admirals, Tromp and de Ruyter, could not dissuade the several bickering provincial admiralties from tying down the fleet to a convoy in any Channel fight. Thus, on 28 February 1653, Tromp's 70 sail began the **Three Days' Battle** against Blake's fleet of equal strength by defending a homeward-bound convoy in a running fight up the Channel. One by one, most of the Dutch ships ran out of ammunition, enabling Blake to sink or capture 11 warships and 55 merchantmen. Though most of the convoy survived, Tromp now convinced the States General to keep the merchant ships in port until he could fight the naval battle. In mid-March the Dutch Mediterranean squadron crushed and drove its English counterpart from the sea, followed by Tromp's destruction of English shipping at the Downs and near the Danish Sound.

With both 100-ship fleets now committed to seeking the weather gauge for a line-ahead slugfest, Monck and Tromp clashed at **Gabbard Bank** north of Dover on 12 June 1653 until Blake arrived with English reinforcements next day. The English, at the cost of 1 ship, sank or captured 20 Dutch vessels and killed 1,400 men as the shallow-draft Dutch ships retreated to shoal waters. Blake clamped a blockade on the Dutch coast that stopped all trade until Tromp and

At the height of the Battle of Scheveningen (or Terheide), 10 August 1653, the English flagship of Admiral George Monck, *Resolution* (*right center*), engages the smaller Dutch flagship *Brederode*. The latter's admiral, Maartin Tromp, has already been killed, and its mainmast is broken. Both fleets suffered heavy losses and damage, but the English won the battle. From a painting by J. A. Beerstraten. (Rijksmuseum, Amsterdam)

de With broke out to engage Monck in the first true line-ahead battle in history. The English won the Battle of **Scheveningen** (or Terheide), 8–10 August, by claiming 14 Dutch ships and the life of Tromp. But so heavy were damage and casualties that the English had to abandon the blockade, thereby missing a 400-ship inbound convoy.

England emerged victorious in 1654. The peace treaty forced the Dutch to accept the Navigation Act forbidding Dutch-carried foreign goods in English ports, to allow the English into the Indian Ocean trade, and to render honors to English ships as recognition of England's naval supremacy in the Channel. The issue was not settled, however, as long as both nations maintained equally strong navies and commercial goals.

Imperial Naval Struggles. Cromwell immediately declared war on the weaker Spain, still trying to recover Portugal and to preserve its monopoly over the Caribbean. In 1655, the Spanish repulsed an English naval attack on Santo Domingo in the West Indies, but the English seized Jamaica for a base there. In the Mediterranean, the Dutch instituted annual forays of up to 20 ships-of-the-line to punish the North African corsairs. Blake and 24 sail destroyed Barbary ships at Tunis in 1655, then anchored off Lisbon for a distant blockade of Spanish Cadiz. He captured part of the incoming plate fleet in 1656 and in 1657 audaciously destroyed 22 Spanish galleons at anchor in the Azores. But he died soon after.

England joined forces with France and in 1658 provided a fleet and troops to help the French army recapture Spanish Dunkirk, which France ceded to England. Spain sued for peace in 1659, recognizing French supremacy on the continent but continuing its fight to subdue Portugal. Meanwhile, the Dutch sent a fleet to assist Denmark in another war against Sweden for control of the Baltic. It relieved the Swedish siege of Copenhagen in a furious naval battle in the Sound in 1658, although Admiral de With was killed. The Baltic status quo ante-bellum was then restored.

The death of Cromwell in 1658 hastened the restoration of the Stuart dynasty under King Charles II 2 years later. Determined to continue England's aggressive maritime policies, he recognized the critical importance of the navy by naming it the Royal Navy, chief military agency of the crown. The army, symbol of Cromwell's dictatorship, received no such honor. Charles II appointed his own brother James, Duke of York, as Lord High Admiral; ennobled Monck as Duke of Albemarle; and reinstated the exiled Prince Rupert to high naval command. The king strengthened and reformed the navy under the able and increasingly powerful administrator and eventual secretary of the Admiralty **Samuel Pepys.**

When Charles helped Portugal repulse the Spanish in the 1660s, a grateful Portugal ceded North African Tangier and Indian Bombay to England. Then de Ruyter, new lieutenant admiral of the Netherlands, and a Dutch fleet cooperated with the English in crushing the Barbary corsairs. In 1664 King Charles created a specialized sea-based infantry regiment to assist in landing operations; it evolved into the **Marine Corps,** and, eventually, the Royal Marines.

Charles sold Dunkirk to France in 1662, an untimely move because France and the Netherlands now formed an alliance in response to England's incursions into the Mediterranean and India. France promptly turned Dunkirk into a base for its privateers. Anglo-Dutch relations deteriorated when a force under Sir Robert Holmes captured Dutch West African outposts in 1664, only to have them retaken by de Ruyter's Mediterranean squadron. The same year, an English squadron assisted North American colonists in capturing Dutch New Amsterdam,

Four Days' Fight

In terms of mutual skill, arms, experience, offensive tactics, and sheer determination to win and retain command of the sea, the Dutch and English fleets fought such a furious 4-day battle, 11–14 June 1666 (1–4 June old-style calendar), that it may be regarded as unparalleled in history. The tactical doctrines of the United Provinces navy and Royal Navy were virtually identical: to sail in line-ahead on parallel tacks to the other, regardless of wind advantage, and use their guns, fireships, and boarding to pound the other into utter destruction. Both fleets eagerly sought out the other, neither one being compromised by the need to protect merchantmen, transports, or armies ashore.

Lt. Adm. Michiel Adriaenszoon de Ruyter anchored the 84-ship Dutch fleet off Dunkirk on 11 June. Its operations on the North Sea side of the Straits of Dover persuaded the Duke of Albemarle to attack with his 58 men-of-war at the Downs; the other 20 sail were away in the western English Channel under Prince Rupert, guarding against possible naval movements by the new French enemy. About noon Albemarle bore down with his center ships against the southernmost Dutch squadron under Lt. Adm. Cornelis Tromp, son of the late Maartin Tromp. The surprise attack placed this Dutch force at a disadvantage in 4 hours of cannonading.

As the 2 lines neared the coast of Flanders, Albemarle had to turn west, his deeper draft ships unable to negotiate shallow waters, unlike the Dutch.

which town the king renamed in honor of his admiral brother, the Duke of York—New York. Then another English fleet attacked a homeward-bound Dutch Mediterranean convoy in the Strait of Gibraltar. Finally, Charles had all Dutch ships in English ports seized. Mutual declarations of war followed early in 1665.

Second Anglo-Dutch War (1665–67). The issues and the stakes were identical to the first war—commercial and naval supremacy. The Dutch instituted construction of 60 enlarged ships-of-the-line—over 80 guns each. De Ruyter imitated the English tactical system of 3 squadrons in line-ahead but with the crucial innovation of concentrating them against parts of the English battle line—by **massing, breaking,** and/or **doubling** on both sides of the enemy line instead of simple one-on-one broadsides. The Dutch also launched a highly effective privateer campaign against English commerce.

His change of direction enabled de Ruyter and Vice Adm. Cornelis Evertsen to catch up, form the Dutch center and van positions, respectively, and deliver superior firepower—guns and fireships—against the outnumbered English. By nightfall, several ships had succumbed on both sides, with Evertsen killed. Next day, Albemarle renewed the attack, although outnumbered 47 to 77 effective ships and unable to exploit an unsuccessful Dutch attempt to mass on his rear. On the third day, Albemarle was down to 30 effectives, so he ran westward away from the Dutch, who nevertheless captured 1 of the English flagships that ran aground.

By dawn of 14 June Rupert had arrived to reinforce Albemarle's line and renew the fight, but Dutch tactics prevailed. With both fleets firing on parallel westward tacks, de Ruyter used the windward gauge to break through the English center, with Tromp swinging to leeward of Rupert's rear squadron. Having "doubled" on the English center and rear, the Dutch poured broadsides from both the windward and leeward sides, finally forcing the English to head for home. De Ruyter followed and instituted a blockade of the Thames estuary. The English lost 5,000 of their 21,000 crewmen killed, 3,000 others taken prisoner, 8 ships sunk, 9 captured. The Dutch suffered 2,000 of their 22,000 men killed and 8 ships lost.

Casualties and de Ruyter's blockade aside, the Four Days' Fight was a tactical draw. Neither fleet suffered irreparable damage. Indeed, both made up their losses and undertook repairs in preparation to meet again.

The 2 fleets met head-on off England's North Sea coast near **Lowestoft** on 13 June 1665. The 103-ship Dutch fleet under Admiral Lord Jacob van Wassenaer of Obdam exchanged fire from its 4,900 guns with the Duke of York's 109 ships and 4,200 larger-caliber guns as they twice passed in well-formed lines ahead. At midday, the English exploited the weather gauge to break through the Dutch line, using fireships as well as boarding parties to destroy 32 ships and kill 4,000 men, including Obdam when his flagship blew up. The victorious English lost only 2 vessels.

In August, an English squadron followed a Dutch convoy to Bergen in Norway, only to be driven off by Dutch ships and Danish shore batteries. De Ruyter's reinforced fleet escorted the convoy home and then protected Dutch convoy traffic by patrolling off the Downs during the autumn. The English did nothing because of the plague then sweeping the country. In the new year, France and

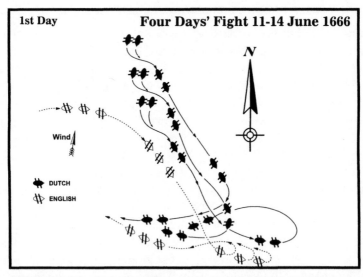

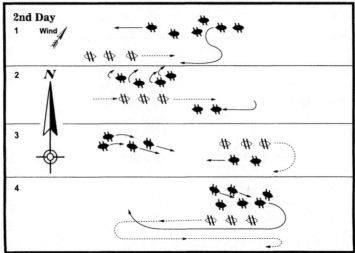

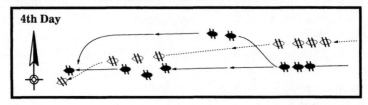

Denmark joined the war against England, causing the fleet to be split between Rupert in the Western Approaches to the Channel and Albemarle at the Downs.

Even the titanic **Four Days' Fight** (see essay) in June 1666 did not alter the basic strategic stalemate. On 4 August (25 July old calendar) the 76 English sail under Albemarle and Rupert attacked the 93 of de Ruyter off the North Foreland near the Downs. This **St. James's Day Fight** lasted 2 days, during which the English outmaneuvered and outfought the Dutch, killing veteran sea fighter Admiral **Jan Evertsen.** The English blockaded the Dutch fleet in the Texel, which Holmes entered with a squadron on the 8th and put the torch to 150 Dutch merchantmen ("Holmes's bonfire").

Then, in September, another fire—the city of London—combined with the plague and costs of the war to force England to lay up its fleet in the Medway near the entrance to the Thames River. When ensuing peace negotiations stalled, de Ruyter sailed 44 warships plus fireships into the Medway in June 1667, destroyed or captured several immobilized ships, and towed away Albemarle's flagship *Royal Charles* to become his own. He then blocked the Thames until England made peace in July.

Again, however, the second war did not resolve the issue of naval supremacy. As victors, the Dutch obtained English recognition of their supremacy in the East Indies and concessions to the Navigation Acts, but they also gave up New York and all claims to North America. Then a new force had entered the strategic picture in the person of King Louis XIV of France. Determined to cement French hegemony on the continent, Louis seized part of the Spanish Netherlands and embarked upon a policy of encircling and crushing the Dutch Republic. In 1670–72 France signed alliances with England and Sweden aimed at destroying Dutch maritime hegemony in the Channel and the Baltic.

Third Anglo-Dutch War (1672–74). After a provocative though unsuccessful English attack on an inbound Dutch convoy early in 1672, England and France declared war on the Netherlands. Louis XIV dispatched his new but untried fleet to join the 71 ships-of-the-line under the Duke of York at **Solebay** north of the Thames. There de Ruyter with 61 of the line plus lesser vessels attacked on 7 June, inflicting sufficient damage to frustrate allied preparations for a seaborne invasion of Holland.

But Louis's army was moving into the Netherlands, forcing the Dutch to give equal attention to their land and sea forces, placing an impossible strain on manpower and finances. The republic's strategic insularity was doomed. The Dutch people overthrew their government in favor of William III of Orange as stadholder. They stopped the French overland attack by opening the dikes to let in the sea and by shifting some of de Ruyter's crews to the army. The English Parliament was so alarmed by the Catholic French attack on the Protestant Dutch that it removed James, Duke of York as Lord High Admiral because of his conversion to Catholicism. The surest way for the Netherlands to survive was to obtain allies on land and sea. It could no longer stand alone.

On the other hand, William III was both a brilliant army commander and an advocate of the navy. To strengthen the navy he turned to the administrative skills of Job de Wildt, secretary of the admiralty of Amsterdam and counterpart of England's Samuel Pepys. Admiral de Ruyter moved aggressively to defend Dutch maritime fortunes. One Dutch squadron crossed the Atlantic to ravage English shipping in the Caribbean and Chesapeake Bay and recapture New York. When Rupert led an Anglo-French invasion force to the Dutch coast in June 1673, the outnumbered de Ruyter attacked and repulsed it twice at **Schoonevelt Bank,** then a third time in August at the **Battle of the Texel.** In each action, the French fleet, comprising one-third the strength of the allied force, proved inadequate. Its poor performance added to growing English opposition to the war, and early in 1674 England made a separate peace with the Netherlands.

In addition to England's friendship Spain and Austria entered the war on the side of the Dutch, forcing Louis XIV to shift his armies to their borders. The Dutch returned New York to England, which in turn granted the right of neutrals to trade with warring nations, a major component of Dutch prosperity. The third Anglo-Dutch war left the Dutch Republic intact, along with its fleet, merchant marine, and colonial empire. But as it fought on against Louis XIV, the republic required the help of neutral England, to which commercial and naval mastery soon passed.

6

The French Naval Challenge

(1670s–1715)

Louis XIV, king of France from 1661 to 1715, challenged both the Dutch Republic and England at sea in order to strengthen French hegemony on the continent. Both maritime powers reacted to his aggressive policies by creating alliances to deter or fight him.

French Seaborne Power. Because France lacked a significant middle class and strong naval tradition, Louis aspired to emulate and succeed the Dutch at sea, whatever the cost. He charged his astute finance minister **Jean Baptiste Colbert** with subsidizing a large merchant marine, building a powerful navy, and establishing an overseas colonial empire. These were immense tasks, given continental France's emphasis on its army. Colbert enlarged the navy from 20 to over 300 ships, a battle fleet of sleek modern ships-of-the-line. He supported it with the aggressive Dunkirker corsairs and other privateers. He constructed naval arsenals along the coast and founded 3 naval academies to provide officers.

The new navy protected French merchantmen on the high seas and administered distant Canadian and Caribbean colonies, including new ones in West Africa, India, and Madagascar. To augment the endless fight against the Barbary pirates and Ottoman Turks, Colbert created the Galley Corps in 1665—officered by seafaring Knights of Malta and manned by convicts, conscripts, and Muslim prisoners (hence the term "galley slaves"). France's overseas enterprises were governed by its own and much admired maritime legal code, the *Ordonnance de la Marine,* created by Colbert in 1681.

The Dutch War (1672–78). After England's separate peace in 1674, Louis XIV fought on, determined to break Dutch power by land and sea and to humble Spain and Austria as well. By the aggressive use of his navy in several quarters he forced the Dutch to split up their fleet. In the Channel and North Sea Dunkirkers like **Jean Bart** led the privateer attack on Dutch merchant shipping, undeterred by the presence of Dutch frigates. The French navy frustrated the Dutch blockade and crushed Spain's Mediterranean fleet near the Lipari

Islands in 1675. The great de Ruyter rushed there to repulse the bold **Abraham Duquesne** at the battles of Stromboli in January 1676 and **Augusta,** Sicily, in April, where, however, de Ruyter lost his life. Two months later, the French navy finished off the Spanish-Dutch fleet at Palermo to achieve command of the western Mediterranean.

France allied with Sweden in its attempt to wrest control of Baltic shipping from Dutch-supported Denmark, resulting in the Scanian War (1675–79). The Netherlands dispatched annual naval squadrons to assist the Danes and Admiral Cornelis Tromp to command their navy. This allied fleet of 31 ships defeated the Swedes at the battle of Oeland in June 1676, and Danish admiral **Niels Juel** repeated the feat at Kjøge Bay 1 year later. But Sweden's victorious army offset these defeats in the end.

All of these basically continental wars ended in virtual stalemates in 1678–79. Louis was learning how to use his navy, which included cooperating with the Dutch and English against piratic "buccaneers" in the Caribbean. But enemies in Europe and overseas created tremendous strains on French navalism by the time of Colbert's death in 1683.

Glorious Revolution. Religion played a major part in naval matters. The Catholic Louis XIV disliked French Protestants (Huguenots) so much that he refused to bestow upon one of them, Duquesne, his best naval leader, the rank of admiral. In 1685 he completely abolished Protestantism in France, and some of its most able naval officers fled to England and the Netherlands to join the fight against him. England's King Charles II was Protestant, and in 1672 Parliament barred Catholics from high office, forcing his newly converted and pro-French brother James, Duke of York to relinquish his post of Lord High Admiral. But in 1677 James's Protestant daughter Mary by his late first wife married William III of Orange, Protestant head of the Dutch Republic.

The marriage added to England's determination to form an alliance with the Netherlands, which it did in 1678, and to strengthen the Royal Navy for a possible confrontation with France. In 1684 James managed to regain his post of Lord High Admiral and the next year succeeded to the throne as King James II upon his brother's death. In 1686 William of Orange mobilized an alliance of several nations against Louis—the League of Augsburg. But James's pro-Catholic stance provoked Parliament to invite William and Mary to occupy the throne of England. They accepted, and James fled to France.

This bloodless Glorious Revolution of 1688 elevated the Parliament to power over the crown and united England and the Netherlands under the same head of state. It also brought their navies together. That November, the main Dutch fleet—built around 48 ships-of-the-line—escorted William and Mary and an ex-

peditionary force from Holland to England, all under the command of an English admiral, Arthur Herbert (later Earl of Torrington). Louis XIV did nothing
with his fleet to prevent the crossing, and when an easterly wind prevented
James's loyal English fleet from leaving its Channel port in England, it surrendered to William.

The Anglo-Dutch union recognized the seniority of England in naval matters.
Because the Royal Navy had some 100 ships-of-the-line to the Dutch navy's 48,
the former agreed to provide about 60 percent of the ships for all joint naval operations and therefore insisted that an English admiral be in overall command.
Conversely, the Dutch would provide the same percentage of troops in joint
army operations with the English, a further reflection of Dutch military resources
being shifted to the army at the expense of the navy.

War of the League of Augsburg (1689–97). Louis XIV declared war on the
Netherlands, England, and Spain, joined by the rest of the league to check the
French invasion of the Spanish Netherlands. In March 1689 a French squadron
landed the exiled James II with an army in Ireland, hoping to restore him to
the English throne. In May, a second squadron brushed aside a smaller force
under Herbert off **Bantry Bay** and landed reinforcements. But English control
of the Irish Sea enabled King William to lead an army to Ireland to fight James.

Although inferior in size to the Anglo-Dutch fleets, the French navy had
newer and often better ships with which Louis intended to invade England, return James II to power, and destroy the Anglo-Dutch union. He united his
Mediterranean and Atlantic fleets at Brest in July 1689, planning to engage and
defeat the allied fleet, enabling invasion transports to cross the Channel. In addition, Jean Bart and over 80 Dunkirker privateers plundered Anglo-Dutch merchant shipping. But the French navy had never fought a major fleet engagement
for command of the sea.

By contrast, the English and Dutch navies shared a common naval tradition
and experience of fighting pitched battles for supremacy at sea—against each
other! They agreed both to prevent the invasion by engaging the French fleet
and to protect their merchant convoys. Their strategy was to **concentrate their
fleets** in the Western Approaches to the Channel, near Plymouth, giving them
the **interior position:** separate squadrons could operate far afield to protect convoys but remain flexible enough to reconcentrate in the Western Approaches and
contest any French invasion attempt.

In June 1690 Louis XIV ordered his able fleet commander, Admiral the Count
Anne Hilarion de Tourville, to engage and defeat the Anglo-Dutch fleet as a
prelude to invading England. The French had superior firepower: over 4,800 guns
in 77 ships-of-the-line, plus 23 fireships. Admiral Lord Torrington (Herbert) had

Fleet in Being

Admiral Arthur Herbert, Earl of Torrington, in command of the Anglo-Dutch fleet early in the War of the League of Augsburg, elected not to engage the French battle fleet in June 1690. This was because he was outnumbered 57 to 77 in ships-of-the-line. Although the French were threatening to invade England, he later explained that as long as "we had a fleet in being they would not make the attempt." That is, he would avoid a naval battle until anticipated reinforcements—another 23 of the line—arrived, enabling him to fight with roughly even odds.

Although Torrington preferred to withdraw the allied fleet to the mouth of the Thames River, he did not envision assuming a static defensive posture. The long naval experiences of the English and Dutch had inculcated in both a fierce tradition of aggressive offensive tactics, in contrast to the less experienced and less confident French navy. With his fleet intact, Torrington could exploit opportunities created by possible French movements to strike out with separate squadrons and weaken his opponent, but to avoid a major one-on-one confrontation until he was reinforced. He was confident that the French would not risk mounting an invasion force as long as his fleet remained active and threatened to interfere.

In the event, Queen Mary ordered him to attack the French fleet in what became the Battle of Beachy Head. Torrington's fleet was indeed defeated in the battle, only to fall back on the Thames as originally planned though now further weakened by its losses. But the French neither pursued his defeated fleet nor dared to attempt the invasion, thereby confirming the wisdom of his bold strategy. The "fleet in being" concept exemplified the Royal Navy's policy of *offensive* tactical operations in spite of its main fleet having been *temporarily* placed on the strategic *defensive*. Once sufficiently strengthened, the fleet commander expected to resume the strategic offensive.

Britain's fleet-in-being stratagem was revived by Admirals Richard Kempenfelt in the War of the American Revolution and Horatio Nelson in the wars of the French Revolution and Napoleon. It was reaffirmed by British and United States admirals during the 20th century. The concept is not to be confused with what naval philosopher Alfred Thayer Mahan described in 1911 as the "fortress fleet," whereby the main fleet remained passively in port as part of static coast defenses. Mahan ascribed such a defensive strategic mentality to the Russian navy, but it was equally applicable to the fleet of any continental nation in history because these navies usually assumed a basically *defensive* posture in both strategy and tactics.

about 3,800 guns in 57 ships-of-the-line, plus 11 fireships. Of these, 22 of the line comprised the Dutch squadron under Admiral Cornelis Evertsen the Youngest.

The only way that Torrington could match Tourville's strength was to recall 2 of his squadrons then absent protecting allied sea lanes: 16 of the line at Cadiz, Spain, and 7 of the line in the Irish Sea supporting King William in Ireland. He convened his admirals in a council of war and all agreed that the fleet should fall back on the mouth of the Thames River until the 2 absent squadrons returned, giving the allied fleet parity with the French.

Torrington believed that as long as his fleet remained intact, battle ready, and undefeated, the French would never dare attempt an invasion. If it did, as in the case of the Spanish Armada of 1588, the French fleet would not only be inhibited by being tied down to its transports but it would be exposed to harassing attacks by Torrington's squadrons. Queen Mary (ruling during William's absence in Ireland) did not appreciate Torrington's stratagem, however, and ordered him to attack Tourville in the Channel. Torrington reluctantly obeyed, but he devised battle tactics designed at least to damage the French fleet sufficiently that it would have to postpone the invasion.

On 30 June 1690, Torrington sortied to engage Tourville at the battle of **Beachy Head** (or Bévéziers) off the English coast near the eastern end of the Channel. He attained the windward gauge, whereupon the 2 fleets closed up in line-ahead, 3 squadrons each. Evertsen's Dutch squadron engaged the French van, and the English and French rear squadrons clashed. But a sluggish Torrington failed to bring his center against the French and go to the aid of Evertsen as Tourville doubled on the Dutch squadron, inflicting heavy damage.

Tourville soundly defeated Torrington, causing the loss of 10 Dutch ships-of-the-line and immobilizing 10 others. The allied fleet retired to the entrance to the Thames, where it anchored. The victorious Tourville, however, did nothing to exploit his triumph, leaving the weakened enemy fleet basically intact, although both Torrington and Evertsen were relieved of command. And within 2 months, the English squadrons from Cadiz and the Irish Sea plus other warships concentrated in the Channel, giving the allied fleet a clear superiority of 90 of the line. Torrington had been correct in his strategy: the French fleet dared not invade England as long as the English and Dutch kept their "fleet in being" (see essay).

The lack of aggressive French naval action can also be partly explained by the nature of France's basically continental strategy. Possible losses in naval battles could not be replaced by expensive new ships, because major funding had to go to the army. Indeed, the day after Beachy Head, 1 July, William's army defeated

James II at the Battle of the Boyne in Ireland, forcing James to return to his exile in France. Louis XIV soon ordered Tourville to avoid another pitched battle and instead to concentrate on attacking enemy commerce (*guerre de course*).

The Anglo-Dutch navies undertook new construction, and by the time Louis mobilized another invasion force in 1692 his enemies were vastly superior. Louis again ordered Tourville to engage and defeat the Protestant fleet, but this time the French Mediterranean fleet failed to arrive from Toulon to reinforce Tourville. The Battle of **Cape La Hougue** (or Barfleur) occurred off the Cotentin Peninsula of France on 29 May 1692. Admiral Edward Russell had 88 ships-of-the-line, including 26 Dutch vessels under Admiral Philips van Almonde, against Tourville's 44 of the line; both sides employed fireships. They engaged in line-ahead, with Tourville's fleet thinly stretched out. Tourville avoided the Dutch in the van by massing on the English rear squadron, but the 2 lines broke up into individual duels. Tourville then withdrew, only to be pursued for several days, culminating in the destruction of 12 anchored French ships-of-the-line on 2 June.

The Anglo-Dutch victory off Cape La Hougue brought an end to France's pretensions to fight for command of the sea—and to James II's dreams of regaining his throne. The 2 allies continued to build more warships while Louis ordered his navy to revert to commerce warfare. In mid-1693 Tourville used his shrinking fleet to capture 92 of 400 Anglo-Dutch merchantmen of a Smyrna-bound convoy west of Cadiz. King William had Russell's fleet winter at Cadiz, away from England, and mount a new campaign in the Mediterranean in 1694. The simultaneous allied blockade of France crippled the French economy.

In America, where the War of the League of Augsburg was known as King William's War, a naval expedition of New England ships attacked but failed to capture French Quebec in 1690. In 1697, however, a French force took Spanish Cartagena on the north coast of South America. The Dutch, dominant in Indian Ocean waters, used 23 vessels to capture French Pondicherry on the coast of India. In the Baltic, England used privateers to attack the arms trade of neutral Sweden to France. But a war weary Europe concluded peace in 1697, Louis frustrated in his continental and maritime ambitions.

Unlike the Anglo-Dutch wars of 1652–74, in which 2 maritime powers had battled for naval supremacy, the War of the League of Augsburg had pitted the Anglo-Dutch maritime coalition against continental France. Louis XIV had been forced by financial constraints to give strategic priority to his army at the expense of the navy. By 1694 he had abandoned his attempt to win command of the sea in pitched battle—*guerre d'escadre*—and turned instead to a policy of *guerre de course.* France's warships and privateers forever after concentrated on attacking merchant shipping in order to weaken the enemy's economy and on protecting French convoys bringing critical supplies to the army.

England, on the other hand, affirmed its naval strategy to dominate the seas by offensively seeking out and destroying enemy fleets in naval engagements, blockading the enemy coast, attacking enemy merchantmen and protecting its own, and capturing overseas colonies. Whenever threatened by a possible cross-Channel invasion, the main fleet would henceforth be concentrated in the Western Approaches to oppose the invasion ships and covering fleet.

The grand strategy of Great Britain—the nation created by the formal uniting of England and Scotland in 1707—now included the tenet that any attempted conquest of the Low Countries (the Dutch and Spanish Netherlands) would be regarded as intolerable, a proverbial "pistol pointed at England." Britain would thereafter create alliances with continental nations in order to make war against the aggressor, namely, France in the 18th century, Germany in the 20th. Britain's continental allies would provide the bulk of the armies to fight these wars on the continent, while the Royal Navy controlled the sea. These armies included the Dutch, whose navy consequently declined after 1697. Britain would always provide material and financial aid to its allies and, if necessary and prudent, a substantial part of the British army.

War of the Spanish Succession (1702–14). King William III, just prior to his death in 1702, forged another alliance to challenge Louis XIV's seizure of the Spanish throne and renewed aggression. William was succeeded by Queen Anne, sister of the late Mary, but Louis XIV resolved to place a Catholic descendant of James II on the throne of England. With France allied to Spain, French armies moved into the Spanish Netherlands, prompting England to sealift an army to the continent under the Duke of Marlborough to cooperate with the Dutch and Austrian armies.

The maritime struggle, subordinated to continental operations, focused on trade. While Dutch squadrons battled the Dunkirkers in the North Sea, the main Anglo-Dutch fleet strangled Franco-Spanish shipping in the Atlantic and Mediterranean. Though repulsed in an attack on Cadiz in the summer of 1702, the Anglo-Dutch fleet under Admiral Sir **George Rooke** annihilated a Spanish treasure fleet and 13 French ships-of-the-line at Vigo Bay on Spain's Atlantic coast in October.

Portugal joined the alliance in 1703, enabling Rooke to base his fleet there for operations in the Mediterranean. After failing to take Toulon and Barcelona, in August 1704 Rooke succeeded in capturing Gibraltar, commanding the entrance to the middle sea. Louis dispatched his own son, Admiral the Count of Toulouse, to recapture that critical base with a Franco-Spanish fleet of 51 of the line. Rooke and the Anglo-Dutch fleet of equal size met Toulouse off Spanish **Málaga** on 24 August. The gunnery duel, fought in strict lines-ahead, ended in a tactical draw and no losses of ships. But the allies won a strategic victory in this only fleet action of the war by retaining Gibraltar and repulsing a French attack on it the following March.

While the main armies battled on the continent Anglo-Dutch landing forces in the Mediterranean captured Barcelona in 1705 and Cartagena in 1706. In 1707 the fleet supported an overland advance by Savoy on Toulon, where the French scuttled their 50 ships-of-the-line in the harbor to avoid capture. In 1708 the allied fleet took Sardinia and Minorca, whose Port Mahon became Britain's main naval base for controlling the western Mediterranean. French naval activity was reduced to privateering, and even this ceased in 1711 in the face of the close allied blockade of the French Atlantic coast.

In the Americas, where the War of the Spanish Succession was known as Queen Anne's War, the navies and expeditionary forces battled over merchant shipping and colonies. The British captured French Nova Scotia in 1710. The French took Nevis and St. Kitts in the British West Indies in 1706 and Rio de Janeiro in Portuguese Brazil in 1711. Overall, the British—due largely to their control of American sea lanes—succeeded in breaking the Spanish monopoly in the Caribbean and the French position in Canada.

The final treaties of 1713–14 affirmed the supreme might of the British Empire. France was allowed to retain its hold over the throne of Spain but had to give up much of Canada and several islands to Britain. And Spain had to cede the southern Netherlands to Austria. Britain retained possession of Gibraltar and Minorca, maintained commercial control over Portugal, and obtained important trading rights in Spanish America. Queen Anne died childless in 1714, ending the Anglo-Dutch joint rule, but the heavy wartime military burden on the Dutch Republic had finished it as a great power.

The Ottomans and Russia. Ottoman Turkey continued its offensive into eastern Europe against Venice. A series of fierce galley battles near the Dardanelles, 1649–57, were followed by an Ottoman naval revival that succeeded in capturing Candia, the main port city of Crete, in 1669. On land, however, the Turks were driven from the gates of Vienna by the armies of Austria and Poland in 1683, whereupon Venice allied with both. In the Morean War (1684–98) Venetian and Turkish squadrons of sailing warships and galleys fought many indecisive naval battles until Venice finally recaptured the Greek mainland.

Imperial Russia meanwhile posed a new challenge to the Ottomans in the Black Sea. Czar Peter the Great tried to Westernize much of Russian life, including lessons in warship construction from Dutch and English advisers. He declared war on Turkey in 1695 and sent galleys down the Volga and Don Rivers in support of his army. The Russians captured Azov on the Black Sea in 1696 and erected a naval base at Taganrog. The war dragged on 4 more years, during which time the Turks retreated from eastern Europe. After 1700 they adopted a general policy of peaceful coexistence, having been contained on land and sea by the European powers.

Meanwhile, the new aggressive king of Sweden, Charles XII, threatened to expand Swedish power throughout the Baltic region, causing Russia, Poland, and Denmark to ally against him by 1699. Because a naval war there would threaten the vital Baltic trade of England and Holland, both countries allied with Sweden to prevent it. When Denmark opened hostilities in April 1700, an Anglo-Dutch fleet under Rooke bombarded Copenhagen, and Sweden invaded Denmark, which sued for peace. The allied warships then withdrew, whereupon Charles sealifted his army to the Gulf of Finland, defeated Peter the Great's army, and invaded Poland.

With the maritime powers locked in the War of the Spanish Succession, the **Great Northern War** (1700–1721) became a continental struggle mainly between Sweden and Russia. Peter constructed galleys and brigantine sailing warships on Lakes Ladoga and Peipus and the River Neva to support his overland advance to the Gulf of Finland, where he founded St. Petersburg in 1702. Charles XII's fleet of 42 ships-of-the-line controlled the Baltic as the Swedish army conquered Poland. Peter, however, fortified the island of **Kronstadt** near St. Petersburg and in 1704 created an elite Galley (or Rowing) Fleet, commanded by experienced foreign naval officers.

Charles XII invaded Russia in 1708, only to be crushed in 1709 by Peter's army, which then liberated Poland. The long-restive Denmark reentered the war, crossed the Sound to invade Sweden, and used its 26 new ships-of-the-line to engage Sweden's 21 indecisively at Kjøge Bay near the Sound in 1710. Two years later, the Danish fleet destroyed half of a 95-transport Swedish expeditionary force near Rügen on the continent. Peter meanwhile developed a Ship Fleet of heavy warships to support his galleys.

Charles diverted Peter's attention by convincing Ottoman Turkey to make war on Russia in the Black Sea region in 1710 and regain territory earlier lost to Peter. The Turks defeated the Russians in 1711 and reclaimed Azov in the peace of 1713. They then made war on Venice, 1714–18, to recover the Morea. The Venetian fleet of some 30 of the line bested the larger Ottoman fleet in battles off Cape Matapan (1717, 1718), but the Turkish army won back the Morea.

The end of the War of the Spanish Succession in 1714 enabled Britain, Holland, and Denmark to build warships for Russia as a counterweight against Sweden. While Peter completed his conquest of Finland and the eastern Baltic, he employed 100 galleys to defeat a Swedish force off Gangut at the entrance to the Gulf of Finland in August 1714. Charles tried to blockade the Russian-held coast and even used privateers to attack British and Dutch merchantmen. An Anglo-Dutch fleet of 30 men-of-war rallied to the support of Denmark and Russia in 1715–16, helping to frustrate Charles's invasion of Danish Norway and to dislodge the last Swedes from the continent.

Charles XII's death in battle in 1718 emboldened Peter to attempt complete mastery over the Baltic region. Giving himself the rank of vice admiral, Peter stepped up his relentless amphibious raids on Swedish coastal towns. Russo-Danish squadrons attacked and decimated several units of the Swedish fleet, which prompted Britain to dispatch a fleet to the Baltic to threaten the Russians in 1720. Peace followed the next year. In it, the powers recognized Russian supremacy in the Baltic, but a British fleet remained on station as a deterrent to further Russian ambitions.

7

British Naval Supremacy

(1715–1775)

GREAT BRITAIN emerged from Europe's wars as the most powerful nation and empire in the world. Its political democracy and capitalist economy were dominated by Parliament, which ensured that the Royal Navy remained supreme in peacetime and war.

International Law. The 18th-century European Enlightenment ushered in a new awareness of the natural rights of individuals and nations. International jurists generally accepted the arguments of Dutchman Cornelis van Bynkershoek in his 1703 book *De Dominio Maris* (*On the Dominion of the Sea*): the sea lanes were open to all nations, except for each nation's coastal waters within the range of coast artillery—"the 3-mile limit." Some jurists argued that, in time of war, ships of neutral nations were free to trade with the warring powers. But in 1737 Bynkershoek rejected this notion of "free ships, free goods" in favor of the previous practice of a belligerent navy seizing as "contraband" any military goods it found on neutral vessels.

Britain accepted Bynkershoek's argument for denying merchant trade to an enemy: a maritime power dependent upon the sea trades for survival must, by right of economic necessity, deny all maritime trade which strengthened its enemies. This included not only the blockade of enemy ports in wartime but also the refusal, in peacetime, to allow any foreign competitors to trade at Britain's colonial ports. Parliament therefore authorized the navy to capture foreign ships attempting to smuggle goods into them. The other European powers also adhered to this policy of peacetime monopoly—**mercantilism**—for their own overseas possessions, although France and Spain still insisted that "free ships" meant "free goods" in wartime. In practice, all the trading powers bent the rules to smuggle goods wherever colonists needed them, which led to wars, declared and undeclared.

The Royal Navy. Over the first 25 years of relative peace, 1715–40, administrative reforms and steady construction transformed the navy into the permanent centerpiece of British power, commanding some 60 percent of the nation's defense budget. The Board of Admiralty maintained a state of naval readiness, and the First Lord of the Admiralty—either the senior admiral or a civilian appointee—sat on the British cabinet as a formulator of government policy. The Admiralty established a naval academy in 1733 to supplement the supply of officers obtained from apprenticed midshipmen. The country's large reservoir of experienced seamen supplied the crews, although harsh discipline and illegal **impressment** of unwilling men and boys into service complicated efficiency.

The strategic missions of the British navy were twofold: (1) maintaining sufficient battle fleet strength to deter its major rivals, France and Spain, from going to war, then defeating their fleets if war came, and (2) policing and protecting the colonies and merchant shipping against pirates, smugglers, and enemy cruisers.

British line of battle ships numbered slightly over 100 until midcentury, then increased during subsequent wars. The French navy declined, but Spain's revived during the 1720s and 1730s; together, they soon matched the British fleet in numbers. Yet Britain's first- to fourth-rate ships-of-the-line were larger and more heavily gunned than those of their opponents, each mounting between 60 and 120 guns. The smaller, swifter fifth- and sixth-rate frigates and unrated sloops guarded and attacked merchant shipping. The galley and fireship gradually passed out of existence.

Naval Tactics. Based on the battles of the Anglo-Dutch wars, the major fleets had settled upon a **formalist** doctrine of engagement using strict line-ahead formations. Opportunities had occasionally been exploited to break through an enemy's line and then mass and/or double on parts or individual ships of the enemy line—creating a **melee.** In 1691, Admiral Russell had issued *Sailing and Fighting Instructions,* which embodied these lessons—always to engage from the **weather gauge** or windward position, with each squadron and ship to lie alongside its opposite number for the gunnery duel. English ships tended to fire on the ship's downroll in order to sink their enemy by punching holes in the hull near the waterline.

But the lack of many fleet engagements after 1691 had caused the Royal Navy to further regiment its tactics by issuing the *Permanent Fighting Instructions* in 1703, which entrenched the rigid formalist line. Individual initiative to create a melee was allowed only if and when the enemy abandoned his line formation and fled. Then a subordinate admiral or captain could order "general chase" to pursue, overtake, and mass his fire on the foe. But that did not happen at Malaga in 1704, and the dearth of fleet actions for the next forty years led to tactical stagnation in the British navy.

The French and Spanish navies were no different, except that they rarely attempted to fight to a decision. Being continental, these fleets preferred to fight defensive actions—engage from the leeward or downwind side; fire at the British sails and rigging merely to immobilize instead of sink their opponent; then disengage at liberty by falling off with the wind to escape. Their primary mission was to support the army and protect merchant convoys; neither country could afford to replace ships lost in pitched battles. French and Spanish ships were supposed to survive a battle in order to fight another day.

European Balance of Power. Britain forged alliances and employed its main fleet to protect the Low Countries (Netherlands) and Europe's maritime trade routes. As it forged a regional power balance in the Baltic, Britain simultaneously countered a Spanish attempt to weaken Austria and Savoy in the Mediterranean. After seaborne Spanish troops seized Austrian Sardinia and Savoyan Sicily in 1717–18, Britain allied with France, Austria, and the Netherlands in the War of the Quadruple Alliance (1718–20). Admiral **George Byng** with 21 of the line destroyed a Spanish fleet of similar size off Cape Passaro near Italian Messina in 1718, then supported the Austrian army in its recapture of Sicily in 1719. British amphibious seizures of Spanish Atlantic ports and a French overland attack brought Spain to the peace table.

When Austria and Russia attempted to enter the commercial maritime field in the 1720s, Britain countered them by concluding alliances with France, Spain, the Netherlands, Denmark, and Sweden. Spain tried to retake Gibraltar by a landward siege but was defeated by the British army and navy. In the 1730s Russia and Austria attacked Ottoman possessions in the Black Sea, but British warships convoyed Ottoman merchantmen as Turkey won the war and became a counterweight against Russia in the European balance of power orchestrated by Britain.

Beyond Europe, North America formed the nucleus of the British Empire, with warships basing at Boston, New York, and the Chesapeake Bay. In 1670 Britain had settled Charleston and the Carolinas for a buffer zone against Spanish St. Augustine, Florida. English privateers had operated from American ports against Spanish and French forces during the wars of 1689 to 1714. With the coming of peace, many of these freelancers turned to outright piracy. Flying the Jolly Roger (skull-and-crossbones flags), "Blackbeard" and other maritime outlaws waged a war of terror against colonial shipping and Royal Navy vessels between 1716 and 1726 until the latter rounded up and executed them by the hundreds.

To stabilize the empire, in the 1730s Britain constructed naval bases at Jamaica and Antigua in the West Indies and founded Georgia and the port of Savannah. Britain's American colonists, often left to their own resources, played an increasing role in defending themselves, always mindful that the Royal Navy remained their principal protector. British warships completely neutralized Spanish Caribbean shipping from Mexican Veracruz to Central American

Panama, forcing Spain to send its ships around South America to supply Peru on the Pacific side.

In addition, English and Dutch merchantmen regularly smuggled goods into Spain's Caribbean colonies. Frustrated Spanish naval patrols sought to make an example of one smuggler they caught in 1731, Captain Robert Jenkins. They cut off his ear! When, 6 years later, the British public learned of this outrage, and Spanish seizures of British vessels increased in American waters, Britain dispatched naval squadrons to the Caribbean and Mediterranean to intimidate Spain. War followed.

War of Jenkins's Ear/War of the Austrian Succession (1739–48). Britain's objectives were to break Spain's trade monopoly in Latin America and the Pacific and to counter the resurgent France of King Louis XV. The maritime War of Jenkins's Ear, begun in 1739, became part of the continental War of the Austrian Succession late in 1740, when Spain, France, and the kingdom of Prussia invaded Austria. Britain allied with Austria and the Dutch Republic to protect the Austrian Netherlands and based a fleet at Minorca to prevent the Franco-Spanish fleet at Toulon from attacking Austria in the Mediterranean. France did not formally declare war against Britain until 1744.

In the Americas, where the conflict came to be known as King George's War for Britain's George II, British and colonial American amphibious forces destroyed Spain's base at Panama but failed in attempts to take Cartagena (1739), Cuba (1740–41), or St. Augustine (1740, 1743). Neither could Spain dislodge Britain's colonists in Georgia (1742). Franco-Spanish and British warships and privateers attacked each other's convoys but never decisively. Britain's greatest blow to Spain's empire occurred when a British squadron under Commodore **George Anson** circumnavigated the globe (1740–44), exposing Spanish weakness in the Pacific. British naval and landing forces seized the French base at Louisburg, Nova Scotia, and repulsed 2 French attempts to retake it (1744–46).

In 1743, France and Spain initiated a 3-part program: invade Britain and place "Bonnie Prince Charlie," heir of the deposed Stuarts, on the throne; conquer the Austrian Netherlands for France; and recapture Italy, Gibraltar, and Minorca for Spain. When Britain's King George II took an army to Holland to check the French ground offensive, France assembled its invasion army at Dunkirk. As its 15-ship escort began to gather there early in 1744, however, Admiral Sir John Norris concentrated his 35 of the line offshore to attack it. A sudden calm enabled the outnumbered French squadron to escape, but it was too weak to support an invasion in any case.

Simultaneously, in February 1744, the 27-ship Franco-Spanish Mediterranean fleet sortied from Toulon to challenge the loose blockade of that port by Admiral Thomas Matthews's fleet of equal strength. On the 22nd, Matthews attacked in line-ahead off **Toulon** but failed to close up his ships sufficiently to decide the issue, thus allowing the enemy fleet to withdraw safely to port. A frustrated Admiralty court-martialed Matthews and 7 of his captains for lack of aggressiveness, making them scapegoats for the navy's stagnant formalist tactics. The British retained control of the sea, but enemy armies held the coast.

A single French frigate landed Prince Charles in Scotland to foment a general "Jacobite" uprising there, followed by an overland attack on England from the north. Admiral **Edward Vernon** concentrated the British fleet in the Western Approaches to thwart another seaborne invasion attempt. He kept several squadrons and privateers active protecting convoys in the Channel and attacking French communications to Scotland. Unsupported, the Stuart pretender to the throne was defeated in 1746. That same year, a French amphibious expedition eluded Vernon's watch and crossed the Atlantic to invade Nova Scotia, but disease among the crews forced it to turn back.

Even as victorious French armies hammered away at the Dutch and Austrian Netherlands, the British reinforced their Western Squadron under the dynamic Admiral Anson to protect friendly shipping, blockade the enemy's, and prevent the invasion. In May 1747, he led 14 of the line to France's **Cape Finisterre,** where he attacked and defeated a smaller French squadron escorting a convoy. By abandoning formalist tactics and ordering general chase, Anson captured 6 of the line and an equal number of merchantmen. The following October, Admiral **Edward Hawke** with 14 of the line repeated the feat. He used the same tactics in the same waters to capture 6 of 8 French line of battle ships. An outbound French convoy escaped, but Hawke dispatched a fast sloop to the West Indies to alert the British squadron there which then captured it.

French arms succeeded in overrunning the Austrian Netherlands and capturing British Madras in India, where armed French merchantmen brushed aside a British squadron off Negapatam in July 1746. But they could not break the British blockade of French Pondicherry. As in the Mediterranean, the Indian theater of war ended in a stalemate when peace was concluded in 1748. France evacuated the Austrian Netherlands, thereby restoring the balance of power, and gave Madras back to the British in return for Louisburg, Nova Scotia.

Colonial Struggles. Britain strengthened its overseas naval bases to counter further French colonial expansion. The English and French East India companies operated their own ground and naval forces to compete for Indian Ocean trade. Better organized than their European and native South Asian competitors, the British had already joined with the Persians in driving the Portuguese out of the Persian Gulf. The sultan of Oman took power in the Gulf, built a fleet, and by 1730 had driven the Portuguese from Mombasa in East Africa. In 1749, the British improved their basing facilities in India by building a drydock at Bombay and established a naval base at Halifax, Nova Scotia, to support the westward expansion of their American colonies.

France and Spain, jealous of Britain, resumed naval construction until their combined fleets roughly paralleled the 117 British ships-of-the-line by 1754. That year, British and French colonial forces and their native American Indian allies clashed in the Ohio Valley. Early in 1755, Admiral **Edward Boscawen** brought a British squadron to Halifax and soon captured 2 warships of a French force hastening to Quebec. When French naval units also moved against the British in the Mediterranean, general war erupted.

Seven Years' War (1756–63). The Anglo-French colonial rivalry was only one aspect of the larger design of France to upset the balance of power on the continent of Europe. France concluded alliances with Austria, Russia, and Sweden in order to eliminate Frederick the Great's Prussia as well as British hegemony in Europe and abroad. The conflict was therefore a global one as Britain struggled to maintain its naval supremacy worldwide. In North America, British colonists called the 7-year conflict the French and Indian War.

Although formal declarations of war occurred at various times, the fighting started when the French navy landed an army on British Minorca and laid siege to Port Mahon in April 1756. The next month, Admiral Byng with 13 of the line attacked the French covering force of 12 sail off **Minorca,** maintained his rigid formalist line to little effect, then sailed away to Gibraltar, with the result that Port Mahon fell. The frustrated British public and government had Byng court-martialed and shot for his ineptitude—an extraordinary punishment due less to Byng than to Britain's overall lack of naval readiness.

Britain declared a blockade of French ports in August 1756 and depended upon the leadership of the aggressive Anson as First Lord of the Admiralty to prevent a French invasion of England, protect British trade from French frigates, and defend New York from a Quebec-based overland attack. Admiral Hawke concentrated the main fleet in the Western Approaches where it prevented a cross-Channel invasion and attacked French merchant shipping. British overseas forces, however, failed to stop the French capture of Fort Oswego on New York's Lake Ontario and were only successful in supporting the East India Company's army in India.

Lackluster British leadership was remedied in June 1757 when George II created a new cabinet dominated by **William Pitt the Elder.** A strategist of genius, Pitt drew upon past British wartime experiences and the suggestions of Frederick the Great to institute what came to be known as **Pitt's system.** It was a **strategy of concentration:** the main **hitting element** was Frederick's army, funded and supported by Britain for a succession of stunning Prussian victories over the armies of France, Austria, and Russia between 1756 and 1760. Overseas, Britain mounted amphibious expeditions to capture France's colonies.

The **holding element** of Pitt's strategy aimed at isolating France by the Royal Navy exercising command of the sea: blockade of the French coast and destruction of the French fleet and merchant marine. Anson used his Western Squadron for an "open" blockade of Brest and Bay of Biscay ports, his Eastern Squadron to control the North Sea as far as the Danish Sound, and his Mediterranean Squadron against Toulon and Minorca. The blockade was both economic and naval because it included the interruption of trade with France by neutrals such as the Netherlands. Parliament formalized this policy as the "Rule of War, 1756," which empowered British warships to stop, search, and seize neutral merchantmen carrying materials of war (contraband) to Britain's enemies.

Pitt spent his first year overcoming deficiencies in ship strength and tactics before his system began to work. Increased numbers of ships-of-the-line and frigates were put in the hands of aggressive commanders willing to depart from the discredited formalism of the Fighting Instructions. Pitt ordered bickering army and navy commanders to cooperate in amphibious raids along the French Atlantic coast and overseas. They succeeded in capturing coastal Cherbourg in August 1758, but Pitt discontinued further raids as indecisive. Admiral Boscawen and 23 of the line crossed the Atlantic with an army that captured Louisburg, Nova Scotia, in the summer of 1758, and British colonial forces burned the French flotilla on Lake Ontario and advanced on Lake Champlain.

1759 became the "year of victory" as Hawke clamped a close blockade on the French Atlantic fleet at Brest, and Boscawen took command at Gibraltar to prevent the French Mediterranean fleet from leaving Toulon for the Atlantic. Pitt was therefore able to mount naval offensives against French overseas possessions. In the Indian Ocean, where British and French squadrons had battled twice without result in 1758, a third engagement off Pondicherry in September 1759 resulted in British victory in India and the withdrawal of the French navy. Simultaneously, a British expeditionary force advanced up the St. Lawrence River to capture Quebec and then all of French Canada. Other British expeditions captured French colonies in West Africa and the West Indies.

A frustrated Louis XV appointed Duke **Étienne François Choiseul** as foreign minister to mount an invasion of England. While the invasion army gathered at Quiberon Bay southeast of Brest, however, Hawke bombarded and destroyed many transports at Le Havre in July 1759. The next month, the French Mediterranean squadron of 12 of the line and 3 frigates departed Toulon and passed through the Strait of Gibraltar. Boscawen, refitting his ships there, gave chase with 14 of the line. On 18–19 August he engaged and destroyed or captured 5 French ships off **Lagos Bay,** Portugal, and blockaded the rest at Spanish Cadiz. When stormy autumn weather forced Hawke to loosen his blockade of Brest, however, the French assembled their invasion flotilla for a crossing to Ireland.

The Marquis Hubert de Conflans sortied from Brest with 20 of the line and 3 frigates to rendezvous with the transports at **Quiberon Bay,** prompting Hawke to depart Torbay with 27 of the line and 6 frigates to intercept him. When Hawke made contact early on 20 November, he ordered general chase as Conflans made for the rocky waters of Quiberon Bay. The aggressive British ships prevented Conflans from forming his line and fought a wild melee in stormy seas that lasted until nightfall. The rocks and gunnery claimed 5 French and 2 British ships, but the rest of Conflans's fleet was scattered or trapped in coastal waters.

The British victory not only scotched the French invasion scheme but also gave the Royal Navy absolute control of the sea. The main fleet, alternating command between Hawke and Boscawen, utilized Quiberon Bay as an anchorage and in 1761 captured nearby Belle Isle for a blockading base. This move threatened Spanish trade to France, as did Pitt's all-out attack on the French West Indies. Fearing a new Franco-Spanish alliance, Pitt deployed fleet units to attack Spanish shipping. When the new pro-peace king, George III, and his ministers opposed these measures late in 1761, Pitt resigned.

But Pitt was correct, for at the turn of the new year Spain declared war on Britain. Pitt's system remained intact as several dynamic admirals extended the close blockade of France to Spanish waters. Spain invaded Portugal to force it into the alliance, whereupon the British landed an expeditionary force in Portugal to engage the Spanish army. In the Mediterranean, Admiral **Charles Saunders** blockaded Franco-Spanish ports. In the West Indies in 1762 Admiral Sir **George B. Rodney** with 22 of the line and amphibious troops captured 4 French islands and Spanish Havana, Cuba, and sank or captured 12 ships-of-the-line there. In the western Pacific, a British expedition seized Manila and the Spanish Philippines.

The only potential weakness in Pitt's enduring strategy was the Prussian alliance. Frederick the Great, beset by mounting costs, faced the growing pressure of Russia and Sweden, whose combined fleets supported their armies in the Baltic region during 1759–61. But early in 1762 Catherine the Great became czarina and pulled Russia out of the war. France and its surviving allies agreed to make peace. British naval supremacy restored Britain's preeminence everywhere, especially Canada, which France turned over to Britain.

Russo-Turkish War (1768–74). Catherine the Great enlarged the Russian navy as part of her designs against neighboring Poland and Ottoman Turkey. To command 40 new sailing warships and 150 galleys, she obtained several British officers and sent Russian naval personnel to train in Britain and Venice. When Russian troops entered Poland in 1768, Turkey declared war, whereupon its subject Greeks and Egyptians revolted. Lacking bases in the Black Sea, Catherine formed a new Mediterranean Fleet from Baltic Fleet units, which sailed to the middle sea in 1770, there to utilize British naval base facilities in order to attack the Turks in the Aegean Sea.

The Ottoman fleet, commanded by the Algerian corsair Hassan Pasha, took up position off the Turkish mainland near **Chesme** and the island of Chios—21 ships-of-the-line staggered in 2 parallel lines, supported by galleys. On 5 July 1770, the Russian fleet, 9 of the line and 3 frigates under Count Alexei Orlov, vigorously attacked the Turks, causing them to cut their anchor cables and drift down into the protected harbor of Chesme. Both flagships caught fire and exploded, though their admirals survived. Shortly after midnight on the 7th, British officers John Elphinstone and Samuel Greig opened a Russian cannonade and fireship attack which completely annihilated the Turkish fleet by dawn. Elphinstone then clamped a blockade on the Dardanelles while the Russian army defeated the Turks along the Danube River.

In 1772 the Russians mounted offensives by land and sea that established Russia as a Mediterranean power. One squadron destroyed 9 Ottoman frigates off Greek Patras, and in 1773 another captured the Syrian port of Beirut. A new Russian Black Sea Fleet supported the army's liberation of the Crimea, which became a Russian protectorate in the peace of 1774. With Turkish naval power broken, Russia gained transit rights through the Dardanelles and dominated all trade between the Black Sea and Ottoman Egypt. The recall of Russia's heaviest warships to the Baltic in 1775 meant that Britain had to court Catherine's favor in order to ensure its vital maritime trade with that region.

Imperial Rivalries (1763–75). France and Spain rebuilt their navies up to parity with Britain's in order to avenge their defeat in the Seven Years' War. In spite of an unsympathetic Louis XV, who placed the French navy under army control in 1772, successive navy ministers Choiseul and **Gabriel de Sartine** built over 70 new ships-of-the-line and an equal number of frigates, improved naval tactics, developed "squadrons of evolution" which tested them, and created a marine corps on the British model. Sartine was supported by Louis XVI, who became king in 1774. In the Mediterranean, France cemented its relations with Austria and obtained Corsica from Genoa to offset the British at Minorca.

Spain, unlike France, still had an overseas empire to defend and used its new naval construction to help extend its American holdings with new colonies in South America and at San Francisco in upper California, while settlers moved into the vast Louisiana and Texas territories. Its colonial naval bases at New Orleans and Buenos Aires augmented Havana as Spain established a permanent fleet of 10 ships-of-the-line in the Americas. Anglo-Spanish relations worsened in 1771 when Britain forced Spain to relinquish its claim to the Falkland Islands in the South Atlantic.

Britain's high cost of fighting the Seven Years' War and protecting the post-war empire led Parliament to pass a new Navigation Act in 1763; it charged the Royal Navy with preventing the American colonists from smuggling with the Franco-Spanish West Indies. Also, for the first time, Parliament taxed these colonists in order to help finance their own defense—acts which aroused opposition because the colonists had no representatives in Parliament to argue their case. In 1763, warships of the North American Station, based at Halifax, Nova Scotia, stopped all smuggling out of New York and Philadelphia and continued to impress colonial sailors into the navy. Colonial protests and opposition to these agents of George III led the navy to land troops at Boston in 1768 to keep order and 2 years later to establish a naval base there. Increased tension and armed clashes led to open colonial rebellion in 1775.

All Europe, but especially France and Spain, watched as mighty Britain attempted to maintain order within the heart of its empire—the 13 colonies of North America. As before, the Royal Navy held the key to preserving British imperial supremacy.

8

War of the American Revolution
(1775–1783)

Early in 1775 Britain deployed army and navy forces to put down the revolt of its 13 North American colonies. But when the United States of America, which declared its independence in July 1776, courted France and Spain for assistance, the Royal Navy had to divide its resources between fighting the revolutionaries and deterring its ancient foes. In 1778 the war escalated into a global conflict, in which the British fleet lacked overall superiority. Because little fighting took place in Europe, the ultimate outcome depended heavily on naval power.

North American Operations (1775–78). Key to Britain's authority in the colonies was Boston, advanced naval base of the North American Station (fleet) and defended by British troops against the rebels. After these "Redcoats" battled colonial Minutemen during the spring of 1775, the rebels' Continental Congress appointed General **George Washington** to command its army. He in turn initiated a navy with 6 schooners that attacked British supply ships off Boston.

An indecisive British government enabled the American patriots to operate successfully on land and sea early in 1776. From Philadelphia, an 8-vessel squadron captured several British prizes and Nassau in the Bahama Islands. Several merchantmen outfitted as privateers, and the defenders of Fort Ticonderoga in upstate New York built a squadron of gunboats on Lake Champlain. Washington's pressure against Boston forced the British to evacuate the city and retire to Halifax, Nova Scotia, in March, enabling Washington to shift the Continental Army to New York. And Congress authorized the construction of frigates for the Continental Navy and Marine Corps.

To crush the rebellion, the British Admiralty appointed Admiral Lord **Richard Howe** to command the 75-ship North American Station with orders to blockade and seize the major American ports and destroy colonial merchant shipping. The Royal Navy sealifted 2 armies of regular British troops and Germanic Hessian allies to America, 1 to defend Canada, the other to assist Howe in taking the seaports. Howe, also instructed to negotiate a peace settlement, elected not to press his blockade of New England throughout the spring of 1776, hoping to convince the Americans to come to terms. The British expedition to Canada, however, relieved Quebec from American troops blockading it, pushing them back to Lake Champlain.

Howe finally acted in June 1776 by sending an expeditionary force to capture Charleston, South Carolina. When defending troops repulsed it at the harbor entrance Howe shifted his efforts to New York, landing troops on Long Island in July. In a series of engagements the British army forced Washington out of New York and into New Jersey in December, only to be driven back when Washington recrossed the Delaware River. The British army from Canada constructed a force of makeshift gunboats on Lake Champlain that destroyed an American squadron of similar size at the battle of **Valcour Island** in October. But with the onset of winter, these Britons withdrew to Canada.

King George III's ministers planned to crush mercantile New England in a grand pincers movement executed by the armies from Canada and New York City. General Sir William Howe (the admiral's brother) would march his 18,000-man army north from New York along the Hudson River toward Albany. It was to meet up with a 9,000-man army under General John Burgoyne coming south from Canada via Lake Champlain, joined by a third force from Lake Ontario. The wide separation of these 3 armies made coordination impossible. Burgoyne easily captured Fort Ticonderoga on Lake Champlain in July 1777, only to discover that the Howe brothers had abandoned their plans to link up with him in order to move by sea against the patriots' capital of Philadelphia. In September, Howe's army drove Washington's from that city.

The British exploited their seaborne mobility to operate from the **exterior position** along the coast, yet Washington had the advantage of the **interior position.** He dispatched troops overland to stop the British advance from Lake Ontario in August and to reinforce General Horatio Gates's militia army facing Burgoyne on the Hudson in September 1777. The next month Gates defeated and captured Burgoyne's entire army at the Battle of Saratoga. The British still held Philadelphia, but the Continental Army controlled the surrounding countryside. This forced Admiral Howe to supply his brother's army at Philadelphia by sea, via the Chesapeake Bay, hindered by Washington's shore batteries and small naval vessels.

By the beginning of 1778 the British held only New York and Philadelphia. The seaward approaches to the latter were threatened by floating mines, the work of inventor David Bushnell, who had also devised the world's first submarine for use against Howe's ships off New York. Both devices had only nuisance value, but they displayed the same Yankee audacity as a small American squadron of 2 brigs and a cutter which operated out of French ports against British shipping during the spring of 1777. The ruling British ministry proved so inept in directing the war that Admiral Howe retired from the navy in disgust.

France saw in the American successes an opportunity to humble the British Empire and in February 1778 concluded an alliance with the United States. It provided open military aid to the Americans and allowed an American sloop-of-war under the command of Captain **John Paul Jones** to operate successfully out of Brest against British merchantmen. The French Mediterranean fleet sailed for America, and in June France declared war on Britain.

Global War. The arrival of France's 12 ships-of-the-line under Admiral **Count d'Estaing** caused the British army to evacuate Philadelphia in late June 1778 and march overland to New York. The deep-draft hulls of the French ships prevented them from passing over the Sandy Hook bar to attack New York, and in August a storm prevented them from dislodging a British garrison at Newport, Rhode Island. D'Estaing thereupon established his base at Boston, and the British fleet remained at New York. General Washington now realized that the key to victory lay in the French navy neutralizing the British fleet in American waters. He fashioned his strategy around that goal.

France, however, viewed the American campaign as only 1 theater of the war and honed its Atlantic Fleet of 32 of the line and 13 frigates at Brest to deny British naval supremacy in European waters. During training exercises off **Ushant** on 27 July this fleet encountered the British Home Fleet of 30 of the line and 6 frigates under Admiral **Augustus Keppel.** For 3 hours the French fired into the rigging of the British ships, while Keppel fruitlessly tried to abide by, then deviate from, the formalist line-ahead tactical doctrine. The French escaped to Brest with minimal damage, and Keppel was court-martialed but acquitted for his failure to win. He, like Howe, elected to retire, frustrated by his country's lackluster naval policies.

Unlike its previous wars, Britain lacked an ally to fight France on the continent and could not take advantage of the absence of the French Mediterranean fleet in America because of the threat of Spain entering the war. The government stepped up naval construction to overcome the combined Franco-Spanish naval superiority, but that took time to accomplish. In the meantime, Britain had to reinforce its North American fleet, especially since the French captured Dominica into the British West Indies in September. The British responded by seizing St. Lucia in November and Savannah, Georgia, the following month. Major naval operations in America thus shifted from the northern colonies to the Caribbean.

Early in 1779 France and Spain initiated plans to invade England, and in June Spain declared war and laid siege to British Gibraltar. Their combined fleets of

66 of the line so outnumbered Britain's naval forces in European waters that the British could not maintain a close blockade of enemy ports. The Spanish fleet easily joined up with the French off Cape Finisterre to cover the invasion transports assembling at Channel ports. As in the past, however, the 2 allies were sluggish in coordinating their preparations, and both were easily intimidated by aggressive British counteractions.

Three successive aged commanders of the British Home Fleet accepted the strategic program of their younger and dynamic chief of staff, Admiral **Richard Kempenfelt.** With the Royal Navy outnumbered, Kempenfelt adopted a "fleet in being" strategy in August 1779: while active frigate squadrons patrolled each end of the English Channel to prevent the invasion transports from concentrating, the Home Fleet of 25 of the line stood ready in the Western Approaches to respond to enemy fleet movements. The Franco-Spanish combined fleet sortied late in the month, seeking battle to clear the way for invasion. But the British fleet avoided contact, instead skillfully maneuvering until the disease-ridden enemy crews became too exhausted to keep up. France and Spain thereupon abandoned their invasion scheme, hoping to resurrect it later.

This was not to be because Kempenfelt's policy remained in force until new construction began to restore British naval superiority. "Flying squadrons" of British cruisers (frigates) attacked enemy merchant shipping while protecting their own convoys, and the Home Fleet actively patrolled the Western Approaches. This open blockade of French and Spanish ports included the Rule of 1756—the seizure of neutral merchantmen—a policy which, however, antagonized other European powers. Kempenfelt simultaneously introduced a new signal system into the fleet which encouraged melee tactics over formalism in naval battles. The Royal Navy obtained additional firepower in the form of a deadly new antipersonnel naval gun—the **carronade.** To improve amphibious capabilities the British converted a merchantman into a shore bombardment vessel mounting 16 guns.

With the active Home Fleet on the defensive in the Channel, Britain conducted offensive naval operations on a global scale. They cleared most of India of the French, kept Gibraltar supplied against the Spanish siege, continued the pressure against the American revolutionaries in New England, and attacked French and Spanish West Indian colonies and shipping. France improved its naval skills under a series of aggressive admirals in American waters, including operations out of Boston to support the patriots. In addition, the dynamic Marquis **de Castries** took over as naval minister in 1780.

West Indies Operations (1779–81). The American campaign of 1779 began with Admiral d'Estaing's capture of the British West Indian islands of St. Vincent and Grenada in early summer. On 6 July his 25 ships-of-the-line frustrated

21 British ships in the naval battle of **Grenada.** When the British prematurely broke up their own line to chase him, d'Estaing maintained his formation, shot away their rigging, and successfully withdrew. A British expeditionary force occupied the shores of Penobscot Bay in Maine in June for a new base. The Americans responded in July with their own expedition of 22 transports escorted by a frigate, 6 smaller warships, and 12 privateers which besieged the British garrison. In August, the British fleet at New York dispatched 7 men-of-war thence which drove the Americans upriver, forcing them to scuttle their vessels. During the autumn, d'Estaing used American troops in a fruitless attempt to dislodge the British garrison holding Savannah.

As 1780 began, Britain detached Home Fleet units for offensive operations in the West Indies and against the southern colonies, coordinated with the defense of Gibraltar and the fleet-in-being stratagem in the Channel. The British correctly counted on the inability of the French and Spanish to exploit their superiority in the Channel for an invasion of England. But the British had other concerns, caused by their blockade of neutral shipping. In February, Russia, Sweden, and Denmark formed the Armed Neutrality and moved their strengthened fleets into the North Sea to protect their merchantmen from being seized by the British. Among several other powers which eventually joined this anti-British coalition was the Netherlands, already actively supporting the American patriots.

Early in January 1780 Admiral Sir **George B. Rodney** took 22 of the line to supply the garrison at Gibraltar before proceeding to the West Indies. He captured a Spanish convoy and its 7-ship escort and on the 16th attacked a Spanish squadron of 12 ships blockading Gibraltar off Portugal's Cape St. Vincent. An advocate of melee tactics, Rodney signaled general chase and captured half the Spanish ships in the so-called Moonlight Battle. He then resupplied Gibraltar before crossing the Atlantic. In February, 11 British warships departed New York and landed an expeditionary force near Charleston to besiege the city and 3 frigates of the Continental Navy anchored there. The city fell in May. Supplied through Charleston and Savannah, General Lord Cornwallis then undertook a lengthy ground campaign in the southern interior.

When Rodney arrived in the West Indies in March 1780, he immediately sought battle with the reinforced French fleet of 23 of the line under Admiral **Count de Guichen.** They clashed off the French base of **Martinique** on 17 April. Rodney ordered the captains of his 20 ships to mass on the rear of the French fleet, but instead they clung to the formalist doctrine of a strict line-ahead. This enabled de Guichen to fire into their rigging and break off the action. Rodney drilled his subordinates in melee tactics and again closed on the

French fleet near Martinique on 15 May, with much the same indecisive result. De Guichen then returned to Europe, escorting a large convoy.

In July another French convoy, escorted by 7 of the line, delivered a French army under General Count de Rochambeau to Newport, earlier evacuated by the British. Although British naval units from New York blockaded the French ships at Newport, the combined Franco-American army under Washington controlled the countryside from the outskirts of New York to Boston. The arrival of Rodney with half his ships from the Caribbean in September, however, frustrated Washington's plans to attack New York. The Continental Army could do nothing until a French fleet could deal with its British counterpart. Rodney returned to the West Indies, where he found that the fleet contingent he had left behind had been decimated by a hurricane and earthquake, thereby restricting his operations.

Fourth Anglo-Dutch War (1780–84). The growth and aggressive leadership of the Royal Navy gave Britain sufficient confidence to declare war on the Netherlands at the end of 1780 for supplying both the French and the Americans. British and Dutch warships then preyed on each other's merchantmen in the North Sea. No fleet action occurred until 5 August 1781, when convoy escorts of both nations collided at Dogger Bank. As in their previous wars, the 7 British ships slugged it out with the Dutch 6 of the line and 6 frigates. The clash resulted in a tactical draw, after which both convoys resumed their courses. The Dutch fleet, unable to contest the British again, thereafter depended on the French navy to protect Dutch trade and colonies.

French Naval Offensives (1781–82). Its navy at peak strength, France organized naval expeditions to America and the Indian Ocean. The former was commanded by Admiral **Count de Grasse,** the latter by Admiral **Pierre Suffren.** The 2 forces sortied together from Brest in late March 1781 while the British Channel fleet was absent escorting a supply convoy to the beleaguered defenders of Gibraltar. Suffren's squadron of 5 of the line separated from de Grasse's America-bound fleet near the Azores. In April Suffren attacked a British squadron gathering at the Cape Verde Islands for a descent on the Dutch colony at the Cape of Good Hope in southern Africa. Though repulsed, Suffren by his audacity convinced the British to abandon their plans for the Cape, to which place Suffren then proceeded and landed troops. He continued on to the Indian Ocean to operate against British shipping.

De Grasse with 26 of the line escorted a large transatlantic convoy to Martinique, main French base in the Caribbean. Upon his arrival on 29 April, de Grasse found Britain's Admiral Sir **Samuel Hood** with 18 of the line standing offshore. Hood immediately opened fire on de Grasse's larger force, but de Grasse elected to do little more than return fire and score some telling hits, content with protecting his convoy and anchorage.

Yorktown Campaign (1781). The arrival of de Grasse's fleet in the Western Hemisphere encouraged Generals Washington and Rochambeau to employ it against the British army. In March 1781 the French squadron of 8 of the line at Newport had sailed toward the Chesapeake Bay to support a French army force under the Marquis de Lafayette in Virginia. It was intercepted off the entrance of the bay by a British squadron of equal strength, which it heavily damaged when they clashed on the 16th. But the British then anchored inside the bay, forcing the French to return to Newport.

General Cornwallis subsequently shifted his British army overland from the Carolinas to Virginia and concentrated around Yorktown on the peninsula formed by the York and James Rivers. Washington and his French allies elected to shift their ground forces from watching New York to attacking Cornwallis in Virginia. They dispatched a ship to de Grasse in the Caribbean urging him to actively participate in their campaign; de Grasse replied by the same vessel in the affirmative.

In mid-August 1781 de Grasse headed north with 28 of the line, taking a longer but elusive course for the Chesapeake where he planned to make contact with Washington's army, then marching south toward Yorktown. In addition, the French 8 of the line at Newport sortied with transports laden with heavy siege guns for Washington's army in Virginia. They took a wide circuitous route in order to avoid the British warships based in New York. In the Caribbean, Admiral Hood, learning of de Grasse's departure, sailed directly from the West Indies to the mouth of the Chesapeake, where his 14 of the line arrived on 27 August. Seeing no French ships inside the bay, he proceeded immediately to New York, where he reported to the new fleet commander there, Admiral Thomas Graves, on the 30th.

The British expected the Franco-American army attack to come at New York or Newport. But because de Grasse had not arrived at either place, and the French squadron at Newport had departed, Graves sailed from New York next day, 31 August, hoping to intercept de Grasse off the Chesapeake Bay. Graves commanded 19 of the line and 7 frigates; Hood led the van squadron. De Grasse's more indirect course to the Chesapeake did not bring his fleet into the bay until 30 August. He dropped anchor just inside the capes and established contact with Lafayette, operating against Cornwallis at Yorktown. On 5 September Graves arrived off the bay and was surprised to see de Grasse's fleet an-

Battle of the Virginia Capes

French naval doctrine of the 18th century centered on supporting army operations on the continent and abroad. In a naval battle with the British fleet,
the French fleet fired into the rigging and sails to disable the enemy's ships,
then withdrew in order to protect the army and the merchant shipping which
supplied it. The British navy, by contrast, aggressively attacked by firing into
French hulls to sink them and thereby win control of the sea and the trade
lanes. During the War of the American Revolution, however, British fleet tactics were still confused: the rigid and ineffective formalist doctrine of maintaining a fixed line of battle versus a growing preference for initiatives by
squadron commanders for a melee—breaking the enemy line and massing fire
on the several parts of it.

Rear Adm. Thomas Graves and the British North American fleet arrived
off the Virginia capes of the Chesapeake Bay the morning of 5 September
1781 and formed the usual conterminous line-ahead. Graves intended to
attack the French West Indian fleet anchored inside the bay supporting
Lafayette's army fighting Cornwallis's British army at Yorktown. The French
fleet commander, Vice Adm. Count F. J. P. de Grasse-Tilly, decided immediately to head out to sea and accept battle, thereby drawing the British fleet
away from Cornwallis and from an anticipated French convoy en route from
Newport. Four of his 28 ships-of-the-line were absent up the bay blockading the river approaches to Yorktown, and many of his crewmen were ashore
assisting Lafayette. An incoming tide prevented his sortie until noon when
the tide changed.

As the 24 French ships cleared their anchorage and formed their line on an
eastward heading into the open sea, Graves signaled all of his ships, then heading west toward the bay, to come about toward the south and reform their line
to parallel the eastward track of the French line. This maneuver caused the 7-
ship van squadron under Rear Adm. Sir Samuel Hood to assume the rear position in the reformed line. With the British attacking from windward, their
lead ships closed with their opposite French numbers. The murderous cannonade began about 4:00 P.M. The firing spread from the vans to the oppos-

ing center squadrons as they came within gun range of each other, whereupon Graves ordered Hood to close up with the enemy in the rear. Hood, however, seems to have deliberately held back (perhaps out of professional jealousy of Graves), so that the larger French fleet massed its withering fire on Graves's van. After 2 hours the British ceased firing, having suffered the heaviest damage, though no ships sank on either side in the indecisive battle.

Next day, both fleets continued their eastward courses, but Graves elected not to renew the fight and soon had to scuttle his most heavily damaged ship. De Grasse maneuvered offshore 4 more days, thereby preventing Graves from relieving Cornwallis at Yorktown and enabling the French convoy from Newport to deliver siege guns to Lafayette. De Grasse then anchored in the bay, where his ships helped transport Washington's army, arriving at the head of the bay from the north, to complete the isolation of Cornwallis at Yorktown. Graves returned to New York to make repairs before he could sail again. In the meantime, Cornwallis surrendered. The naval battle was therefore a strategic victory for the allies, and it guaranteed American independence. It also convinced the Royal Navy to abandon formalist tactics altogether.

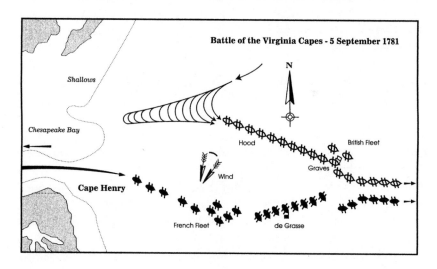

Battle of the Virginia Capes - 5 September 1781

chored inside. The latter was no less surprised, expecting instead the French squadron from Newport. Both fleets nevertheless deployed for action, during which de Grasse defeated Graves in the **Battle of the Virginia Capes** (see essay).

Graves hastened back to New York, consumed several weeks effecting repairs to his battered ships, and sortied on 19 October with 23 of the line, embarking 6,000 troops to reinforce Cornwallis's 8,000 at Yorktown. But he was too late. De Grasse, now reinforced to 36 of the line by the arrival of the Newport squadron, had transported Washington's and Rochambeau's army down the bay— 16,500 troops, strengthened by the siege guns from Newport. Besieged and cut off from seaborne supplies, Cornwallis had no choice but to surrender on the same day as Graves's sortie, the 19th. With its remaining forces hard-pressed throughout the world, Britain granted the Americans their independence.

British Counterattacks (1781–82). The fact that the French naval offensive had helped destroy Britain's North American empire led to a new British cabinet. It recalled from retirement Admiral Keppel to become First Lord of the Admiralty and Admiral Howe to command the Home Fleet. They relied upon aggressive commanders to prosecute naval attacks using melee tactics against the French and Spanish fleets everywhere: Kempenfelt with Howe in western European waters, Rodney and Hood in the Caribbean, and Sir Edward Hughes in the Indian Ocean.

Immediately after the British surrender at Yorktown, de Grasse returned to the Caribbean, aiming to capture Britain's naval bases there and forcing Hood to follow him. In mid-January 1782 de Grasse with 25 of the line landed troops on St. Kitts. But on the 25th Hood with 22 ran past de Grasse's fleet into the road-stead, then repelled its subsequent attack. Next day, with Hood's ships anchored across the entrance of the harbor, de Grasse attacked them. But Hood was able to mass his fire against the leading French ships, which finally withdrew. Hood remained in possession of the harbor until mid-February, when he slipped out to join Rodney, arriving at Barbados from England with 12 of the line. A French convoy reached Martinique, its escort increasing de Grasse's strength to 33 of the line.

On 8 April de Grasse escorted a 150-ship convoy bound for Haiti to join up with a Spanish fleet for the capture of the British base at Jamaica. Rodney, alerted by his scouting frigates, intercepted de Grasse off Dominica next day for an inconclusive gunnery duel. On the 12th, however, Rodney's line of 36 ships was running north on the western side of Dominica on a converging course with de Grasse's 30 moving south near islets known as the Saints. The **Battle of the Saints** unfolded as de Grasse endeavored to maintain his line and the windward gauge. In midmorning, however, gaps developed in the French line, the wind shifted, and Rodney drove his center and van through 2 gaps, while Hood did the same with the rear squadron. Devastating British broadsides, aided by the new carronades, threw the French line into chaos. De Grasse tried to escape but was captured with his flagship and 4 other vessels. Rodney did not elect to pursue the fleeing survivors, yet he had saved not only Jamaica but the British West Indies. He had also proved the efficacy of melee tactics.

The British adopted a strategy of flexible concentration against the coasts of France, Spain, and the Netherlands, whose navies collectively far outnumbered Britain's. With 30 of the line based at Spithead and the Downs, Admiral Howe followed the "fleet in being" philosophy of sending active squadrons north to the Texel and south to Ushant to intimidate enemy naval preparations and to attack shipping. West of Ushant, the 12 of the line commanded by Kempenfelt attacked a 150-ship West Indies–bound convoy in December 1781. The wind held back its escort, de Guichen's 17 of the line, enabling Kempenfelt to capture 15 merchantmen while a storm scattered the rest. Howe spent most of 1782 using the Home Fleet to protect British convoys while avoiding the allied fleets.

Britain's defense of beleaguered Gibraltar was thwarted when the combined Franco-Spanish fleets landed an army on Minorca which laid siege to Port Mahon in July 1781. When the British failed to supply the garrison, it surrendered the following February. In September 1782, France and Spain amassed 49 ships-of-the-line for a land-sea attack on Gibraltar. For 6 days the allied fleet used ships' guns and 10 specially constructed floating batteries to bombard "the Rock." Its defenders fired heated cannonballs and attacked with a force of gunboats to destroy all 10 batteries. The allies called off the attack, although their combined fleets remained on blockade. They did nothing, however, to prevent the arrival of Howe in October with 34 of the line, 12 frigates, and 137 transports and supply ships. Gibraltar held.

Although Britain controlled most of coastal India, Admiral Hughes had to deal with the menace of Suffren's squadron to British shipping in the Indian Ocean. Hughes had the advantage of India's basing facilities, to which he added Trincomalee on Dutch Ceylon by amphibious assault in January 1782. Suffren had only the island of Mauritius as a distant base, but he was a thoroughly aggressive melee tactician unburdened by any need to cooperate with ground forces. Each fleet usually numbered about a dozen ships-of-the-line.

Suffren, hoping to obtain an advanced base along the southeastern (Coromandel) coast of India or at Ceylon, seized the initiative by bringing on battles with Hughes. Suffren doubled on Hughes's rear south of Madras in February 1782 and on his center off Trincomalee in April but without achieving clear decisions. Both fought a standard formalist battle off Cuddalore, France's Indian port, in July, which ended in a draw. Reinforced to 14 of the line, Suffren attacked and captured Trincomalee at the end of August then parried with Hughes off the port early in September. The Dutch gave Suffren succor in Sumatra over the winter. Hughes assisted the British army's siege of Cuddalore until April 1783, when Suffren's fleet arrived and drove him off. News soon reached India, however, that peace had already been concluded.

The treaty restored the balance of power in western Europe and recognized the independence of the United States. In Europe, Britain retained Gibraltar but returned Minorca to Spain. Most Caribbean islands were restored to their prewar owners. The key to a new British empire was India, shared only with a few French posts, and in 1788 it was linked by sea with the new British colony of Australia.

In spite of the lost colonies, Britain and its navy resumed their maritime hegemony in the postwar decade. Britain's new generation of aggressive naval leaders prevailed with the appointment of Admiral Lord Howe as First Lord of the Admiralty in 1783.

United States. Determined to avoid the power struggles of Europe, the new American nation disbanded its army, navy, marine corps, and state forces. The Constitution of 1787 made provision for a navy, but none was created. The United States, interested only in defending its frontiers and overseas trade, depended on tortuous diplomacy during the 1790s to convince the British to evacuate their forts on Lake Champlain and the Great Lakes and the Spanish to withdraw from the eastern shore of the Mississippi River. Even then, Spanish galleys continued to patrol the river from Spanish New Orleans to St. Louis against pirates and native Indian raiders.

The need to protect its overseas trade, however, soon forced the young country to create a navy. With American merchantmen no longer protected by the Royal Navy, Yankee vessels in the Mediterranean were attacked, captured, and their crews held for ransom by the Barbary pirates. The powers of Europe had been paying such ransoms for decades, a lesser expense than punitive expeditions. The Americans used what few funds they had, however, to begin constructing 44-gun frigates for trade defense. Altercations with France then led the government to formally create the U.S. Navy and Marine Corps in 1798.

9

Age of Nelson

(1783–1815)

Britain again dominated the sea when the able **William Pitt the Younger** became prime minister at the end of 1783. Parliament quickly enlarged the fleet to parity with France and Spain. Admiral Sir Charles Middleton (later **Lord Barham**), controller of the navy, made improvements to the ships. First Lord of the Admiralty Howe instituted melee tactics with new signal books. So equipped, a new generation of naval commanders—epitomized by Admiral **Horatio Nelson**—fought and defeated every navy it faced in continuous wars over the next quarter century.

Pitt made certain that Britain would never again stand alone, as it had during the American Revolution, by concluding continental alliances with Prussia and the Netherlands in 1787–88. This and subsequent coalitions provided Britain allied armies as the main hitting element of the **strategy of concentration,** with the Royal Navy as the holding element, control of the sea. Such alliances also served to maintain the balance of the European powers short of war.

Russian Naval Wars (1787–91). Catherine the Great provoked simultaneous wars with Sweden and Ottoman Turkey to extend Russia's borders in the Baltic and Black Seas regions. Her army attacked the Black Sea port of Ochakov, where, in June 1788, the Russian ship and galley fleets under American and German officers, Admirals John Paul Jones and Prince Nassau-Siegen, repulsed the Ottoman fleet. Then Admirals Count Voinivich and **Fedor F. Ushakov** with 12 of the line defeated the 17 of Turkey. The Russian army took Ochakov and control over the northern Black Sea coast while Ushakov soundly defeated the Turkish fleet in 3 battles in 1790–91.

The fighting in the Baltic began when 17 Russian ships-of-the-line repulsed Sweden's 16 plus 7 frigates at Hoglund in the Gulf of Finland in July 1788. One year later Admiral **Vasili Chichakov** outmaneuvered and outfought the Swedish fleet at Svenskund. King Gustavus III personally commanded the 1790 Swedish naval offensive that involved several engagements, culminating in Chichakov blockading the Swedish fleet at Finnish Viborg in early June. On 3 July Gustavus broke out and fell upon the Russian left flank, resulting in a wild battle that claimed 11 Russian and 7 Swedish ships-of-the-line. The Swedes then crushed the Russian galley fleet at Svenskund on the 9th. Such heavy losses convinced both sides to end the war.

Russia's aggression prompted Britain and its allies to support Turkey and Sweden and prevent the Russians from shifting warships between the 2 seas. In the end Catherine controlled the Baltic with 46 of the line, the Black Sea with another 21, making Russia's navy second in strength only to Britain's. She then enlarged the realm by joining Austria and Prussia in carving up helpless Poland.

French Revolutionary War (1792–98). The uprising of France's peasantry against the ruling aristocracy began in 1789 and engulfed the navy's officer corps 2 years later. When the revolutionary regime seized power, it called upon sympathetic junior officers and merchant seamen to fill the vacancies left by the admirals it beheaded or forced to flee the country. The French navy's loss of command expertise was compounded by the assignment to each warship of a political adviser who undermined the authority of the captain. These acts rendered the fleet at Brest impotent, that at Toulon immobile though still controlled by stubborn Royalist officers. In 1792 France invaded Prussia, Austria, and the Austrian Netherlands—the pistol pointed at England.

Britain did nothing until early 1793, when France declared war on Britain, the Netherlands, and Spain. The Pitt ministry immediately added Austria and Spain to its alliance with Prussia and the Netherlands for a continental coalition. These armies invaded France, and Britain declared its traditional blockade of French and neutral merchant shipping. Howe patrolled the Channel with the Grand Fleet, ever ready to concentrate in the Western Approaches. Admiral Lord Hood absorbed the Spanish navy into his Mediterranean Fleet. In August he sailed into the harbor of Toulon, where the Royalist admirals turned over their 30 ships-of-the-line to him. The French army besieged Toulon until December, when its artillery came in range of the anchored fleets. Hood made good his escape but with only 3 French ships, putting the torch to 9 others. He then established his base at Lisbon, Portugal.

Britain depended on the navies of Holland, Russia, Sweden, and Denmark to protect shipping in the North Sea and sent expeditions to capture France's West Indies colonies. The first foray was that of Admiral Sir **John Jervis** (later Earl St. Vincent) to seize Martinique early in 1794. But disease and native uprisings made most of these conquests vulnerable to French recapture. A closer target was the France-bound convoy of 130 ships carrying grain purchased in the United States. Howe sortied to intercept it some 400 miles west of Ushant, as did the French fleet from Brest to protect it.

On the "Glorious First of June" 1794, Admiral Lord Richard Howe's 100-gun flagship *Queen Charlotte* (*left*) exchanges broadsides with Admiral Louis Villaret-Joyeuse's flagship *Montagne,* 120. In the foreground, boats of British sailors rescue survivors of the French 74 *Vengeur du Peuple,* the only ship sunk in the bloody battle. But the victorious British captured 7 ships-of-the-line. From a painting by Philip de Loutherbourg. (National Maritime Museum, London)

Both fleets numbered 26 of the line when they met on 28–29 May, the French line maneuvering away from Howe's attempts to break it. Then, on the **Glorious First of June,** Howe's line closed from windward, and 10 ships' captains obeyed their admiral's entreaties to break through the French line while the other 16 lay alongside. The 10 on the lee side discovered those French gunports closed, enabling Howe's guns to pummel the enemy from both sides. Howe's brilliant doubling maneuver enabled him to capture 7 French ships, although the convoy got through to Brest.

With Britain supreme at sea, the French navy reverted to commerce warfare, *guerre de course:* its Brest and Toulon fleets dared to skirmish with British squadrons only occasionally. French privateers violated the neutrality of the United States by operating out of Charleston, but so did British warships from Chesapeake Bay ports. In August 1794 Hood and Commodore Nelson landed troops on Corsica for an advanced base to blockade Toulon. But the French army moved into Italy, and in March 1795 part of it embarked aboard invasion ships bound for Corsica, only to have its escort of 15 of the line driven back by a British squadron near Genoa.

The French overran the Netherlands and captured the ice-bound Dutch fleet at Amsterdam in January 1795. The Royal Navy clamped a blockade on the Texel and prevailed upon Russia to augment it with a squadron as Holland went over to France. British expeditionary forces then occupied Dutch colonies around the world: Cape Town, Ceylon, and the East and West Indies. The French revolutionary regime began to reform the navy for the aggressive deployment of cruiser squadrons and privateers against British and neutral shipping.

French victories on the continent resulted in the collapse of the allied coalition in 1796. Spain changed sides, and Britain withdrew its squadron from the Mediterranean. The Grand Fleet had such difficulty maintaining its open blockade of Brest that late in the year it failed to prevent a French invasion force from crossing to Ireland, although foul weather soon forced that enterprise to be abandoned. British expeditions, however, captured major Franco-Spanish islands in the Caribbean, inspiring Spanish colonists to develop independence movements.

With Britain standing alone, France and Spain renewed their invasion efforts. Early in 1797 the Spanish fleet sortied from Cartagena in the Mediterranean, 27 of the line under Admiral Don José de Cordoba, escorting a convoy to Cadiz for a projected linkup with the French fleet at Brest. After clearing the Strait of Gibraltar, on 14 February it plodded north in 2 separate groups off Portugal's **Cape St. Vincent** when Admiral Jervis with 15 of the line appeared, heading south. Jervis swept into the gap between the Spanish ships and doubled on the

17 ships in the main group with telling effect. As Cordoba tried to join up with his other ships, Commodore Nelson, commanding the rear British squadron, boldly attacked, supported by Jervis. In the wild melee Nelson personally led boarding parties which seized 2 of the 4 Spanish ships facing him. Two other Spaniards surrendered, and Jervis broke off the action. Cordoba's heavily dam-aged survivors ran into Cadiz, where they were blockaded. The invasion thwarted, Jervis was elevated to Earl of St. Vincent, Nelson knighted and promoted to rear admiral.

The Royal Navy, pressed on all fronts, was handicapped by mutinies over pay and living conditions in the Channel warships based at Spithead and the Noire until concessions and discipline restored order. Nelson suffered a severe defeat attempting to land a force in the Spanish Canary Islands in July 1797, and France gathered an invasion army for Ireland at Dunkirk. The Dutch fleet sortied in October to provide an escort for the crossing, but a blockading squadron of Admiral **Adam Duncan** intercepted it off **Camperdown** on the 11th. With both forces at 16 of the line, the shallow-draft Dutch ships attempted to fall off into shoal water. But Duncan ordered a melee battle: general chase, breaking the enemy line in 2 places, and doubling from the leeward and windward sides, which resulted in the capture of 9 Dutch ships. Deprived of its escort, the French fleet again had to scotch its invasion plans.

Increasingly dominated by Napoleon Bonaparte, France conquered Venice in 1797 and decided to move against Mameluke Egypt. In May 1798 Britain sent Nelson with a squadron from the Grand Fleet to frustrate the sortie of Napoleon's invasion army from Toulon to Egypt. Napoleon's transports had already sailed, however, escorted by 13 of the line and 4 frigates under Admiral F. P. Brueys d'Aigailliers. This force captured Malta in mid-June, landed in Egypt on 1 July, and defeated the Mamelukes. Nelson meanwhile frantically searched the Mediter-ranean with 14 of the line, all the while inculcating his captains with melee tac-tics and personal initiative. Thus did he forge them into his **"band of brothers."**

Alerted to Napoleon's presence in Egypt, Nelson proceeded there, his ships sailing in order of battle. Arriving at the entrance to the Nile midday of 1 August 1798, Nelson found Brueys's ships anchored in a line against the shoal waters as a virtual wall of fixed guns. He nevertheless rounded Aboukir Island late in the day to initiate the **Battle of the Nile.** The captain of his lead ship detected a space between the French van and the shoal water and led the next 4 ships into it, raking the head of the French line with broadsides in the process. Nelson then ran down the seaward side, thereby doubling each French ship in succession. All through the night Nelson's gunners pounded the French into submission; the flagship exploded, killing Brueys. Only the 3 vessels of the rear squadron were able to flee the harbor. Several British vessels received damage, but none were lost in one of the most stunning victories in naval history.

Second Coalition (1798–1801). Nelson's victory encouraged a second coalition of allies late in 1798. Russian and Turkish squadrons helped Nelson blockade Napoleon in Egypt, and, with Austrian warships, clear the Aegean and Adriatic of French forces. Portugal lent ships to the British blockade of Malta, and a British force captured Spanish Minorca. But a French overland offensive forced Nelson to evacuate the allied government of the Two Sicilies from Naples. Britain gained an unofficial ally in the United States, whose new navy of frigates fought the **Quasi-War** (1798–1800) against the French in the Caribbean over attacks on its merchantmen.

As 1799 began, Napoleon pushed the Ottoman army up the Levantine coast as far as Syrian Acre, where he was stopped by Anglo-Turkish defenders and a British squadron. He retreated back to Egypt where he annihilated a Turkish force landed by British ships at Aboukir during the summer. Royal Navy units simultaneously joined the new Bombay Marine of the British East India Company to patrol the Indian Ocean exits from the Red Sea and Persian Gulf. Napoleon, completely checked, boarded a frigate and escaped to France in August, leaving his army behind in Egypt. He was nevertheless welcomed home by being made virtual dictator of France.

The Anglo-Russian fleet blockading Holland landed an expeditionary force on the Helder peninsula in August 1799. It captured the 8 Dutch ships-of-the-line anchored in the Texel for absorption into the Royal Navy. But the amphibious troops failed to advance beyond the beach and had to be withdrawn in October, a defeat that contributed to Russia quitting the coalition. During 1800–1801 Napoleon defeated the Austrian army, destroying the second coalition. British fleets closely blockaded the Franco-Spanish fleet at Brest and captured Malta from the French. But Britain again stood alone, also opposed by the Armed Neutrality of Russia, Sweden, and Denmark.

Although the Pitt ministry fell from power early in 1801, British naval strategy had been set: dominate the Mediterranean and Baltic by eliminating the French army in Egypt and forcing Denmark to quit the Armed Neutrality. Admiral Lord Keith's squadron, based at Ottoman Rhodes, conducted amphibious rehearsals before landing 16,000 troops at Egyptian Aboukir on 8 March. British and Turkish gunboats supported the landing and drive up the Nile, and British reinforcements from India arrived via the Red Sea. The French army in Egypt surrendered during the summer.

A British fleet under Admiral Sir Hyde Parker, with Nelson second in command, solved the Danish menace at the **Battle of Copenhagen,** 2 April 1801. Parker sent Nelson with 12 of the line, frigates, and bomb vessels against the city's anchored warships and shore batteries. When the Danish cannonade damaged several ships, Parker ordered Nelson to break off the attack. Nelson ignored the order, however, pressed on, and brazenly issued a surrender ultimatum to the Danes. They accepted it and withdrew from the Armed Neutrality, which collapsed. The exhausted warring powers made peace early in 1802.

United States Naval Operations. The naval quasi-war between France and the United States (1798–1800) had restored to American merchant shipping the protection of the Royal Navy against a mutual foe. But Napoleon had no desire to antagonize the young republic, and after Spain ceded its vast Louisiana Territory west of the Mississippi to France in 1802, Napoleon sold it to the United States the very next year. But the United States assiduously avoided being drawn into an alliance with either warring power. Attacks on Yankee shipping by the Barbary pirates were another matter. In 1801 President Thomas Jefferson dispatched a squadron of frigates under Commodore **Edward Preble** to the Mediterranean to deal with the North Africans. So aggressively did the Americans attack the warships and ports of Tripoli and Tunis in the **Barbary wars** that both piratic states ceased their depredations against American shipping in 1805.

Soon after the French dictator resumed the European war in 1803 Anglo-American relations deteriorated. As a neutral power, the United States insisted on its right of free trade with both Britain and France, a demand both rejected. When the Barbary wars ended, Jefferson allowed his frigates to deteriorate in preference for virtually useless defensive harbor gunboats. British warships were therefore able to stop American merchantmen and naval vessels to impress U.S. sailors into British service or to confiscate war goods bound for France. The result was naval clashes between individual British and American warships and U.S. frustration.

Napoleonic Wars (1803–15). When the European fighting resumed in 1803 the British resolved to crush Napoleon. Pitt returned to office in 1804, with St. Vincent as First Lord of the Admiralty, succeeded by Admiral Lord Barham in 1805. Britain took 2 years to create the third coalition of continental allies— Russia, Austria, Sweden—and closely blockading the Atlantic coast of Napoleon's empire from Brest to Ferrol in northern Spain. Admiral Keith commanded the Grand Fleet, its active squadrons led by admirals Sir William Cornwallis in the Channel and Sir Robert Calder in the Bay of Biscay. Nelson commanded the Mediterranean Fleet in an open blockade of the French squadron at Toulon. These several British forces remained ever ready to concentrate off Ushant and prevent the expected invasion.

Napoleon, no student of naval warfare, resorted to traditional French naval doctrine: *guerre de course* against British trade and plans for a cross-Channel assault. He assembled an army and 2,000 landing barges at Boulogne and ordered Admiral Pierre Charles de Villeneuve to take the Mediterranean squadron to the Caribbean, thereby luring Nelson away from Europe to follow him. With the British fleet split, Napoleon planned to concentrate the French and Spanish fleets—including Villeneuve, racing back from America—to escort the invasion armada to England. At the end of March 1805, Villeneuve made good his sortie, undetected by Nelson, passed through the Strait of Gibraltar, picked up a Spanish contingent at Cadiz, and crossed to the West Indies with 23 of the line. He captured a British convoy there in May.

Nelson, in what became the Trafalgar campaign, assumed that Villeneuve had headed eastward to support a possible French overland thrust into southern Italy. The victor of the Nile searched the Mediterranean fruitlessly for a month before heading west across the Atlantic with his 11 of the line. Villeneuve, upon learning of Nelson's arrival in the Caribbean in June, set sail for France to link up with the rest of the French and Spanish fleets for the invasion of England. Nelson, alerted 3 days later of Villeneuve's departure, set sail for Cadiz to guard the Mediterranean and dispatched a fast brig for England to alert his superiors. This ship shadowed Villeneuve long enough to ascertain his course for France instead of the Mediterranean, then it hurried home to report in mid-July.

First Lord Barham ordered his squadrons to concentrate in the Western Approaches and prevent the Franco-Spanish invasion. Cornwallis's 17 of the line turned westward to intercept Villeneuve's 20, and Calder's 14 made for Ferrol and the 16 Franco-Spanish vessels there. In the event, the 21 French ships-of-the-line at Brest made no attempt to break out, and Calder encountered Villeneuve off Ferrol on 22 July. Calder attacked Villeneuve's rear but managed to capture only 2 vessels. When Calder failed to renew the action next day, Villeneuve ran into Ferrol. Calder then rejoined Cornwallis off Ushant.

Nelson meanwhile touched at Gibraltar, learned of Villeneuve's movements, and hastened north to rejoin Cornwallis and Calder, bringing the reconcentrated British fleet to 39 of the line plus frigates. Britain's strategy had succeeded, and in August Villeneuve ran south to Cadiz, only to be blockaded there by Calder. Napoleon abandoned his seaborne invasion scheme and instead launched an overland offensive against Austria. The British established their advanced base at Lisbon, where in September Nelson assumed command of the blockade of Villeneuve's fleet at Cadiz. He purposely maintained a loose blockade in hopes of luring out Villeneuve for battle. Nelson was not disappointed, for in October Napoleon ordered Villeneuve to take his fleet back into the Mediterranean to

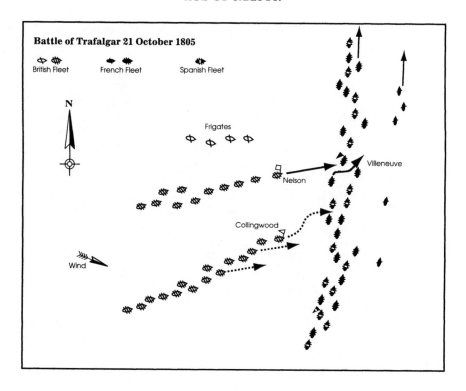

Battle of Trafalgar 21 October 1805

British Fleet French Fleet Spanish Fleet

N

Frigates

Nelson Villeneuve

Collingwood

Wind

support the French army in Italy. When Villeneuve sortied, Nelson met and destroyed the Franco-Spanish fleet in the **Battle of Trafalgar** (see essay).

Napoleon offset the loss of his fleet by defeating the armies of Britain's shifting coalitions from 1806 to 1811 and by developing a new fleet. With it, he planned to break the British blockade of his continental empire and to invade England. In addition, in 1806 he declared a counterblockade, the **Continental System,** in order to prevent his own allies from trading with the British. Unlike the British blockade, however, Napoleon lacked the means to enforce his own system until his new fleet became a reality. To create a navy which outnumbered Britain's 100 ships-of-the-line, he undertook massive naval construction in the ports of France and Spain as well as occupied Antwerp. He hoped to augment his fleet with warships of the nations his army defeated and forced into his empire—Russia, Sweden, Denmark, Portugal, Austria, and Venice.

Britain maintained its strategy of concentration: forging successive continental coalitions, blockading Napoleon's empire, and attacking enemy shipping and

Battle of Trafalgar

During the autumn of 1805 Vice Adm. Lord Horatio Nelson maintained an open but vigilant blockade over the Franco-Spanish fleet of Vice Adm. Pierre Charles J. B. S. de Villeneuve anchored at Cadiz, Spain, on the Atlantic side of the Strait of Gibraltar. Nelson intended to attack and defeat his enemy with 27 ships-of-the-line captained by his "band of brothers." All were honed in melee tactics to exploit tactical opportunities by individual initiative—the "Nelson touch." Villeneuve, the only French admiral to escape Nelson's crushing victory at the Battle of the Nile in 1798, had no desire to fight Nelson, especially after the long chase across the Atlantic. But Napoleon ordered him to sortie for the Mediterranean on threat of being relieved of command. On 19 October Villeneuve weighed anchor at Cadiz, more or less resigned to his fate at the hands of Nelson.

Alerted by scouting frigates of Villeneuve's departure, Nelson allowed the enemy fleet to stand well out to sea on a southern heading before pursuing it, thereby preventing any chance of Villeneuve returning to Cadiz. Then, on the morning of 21 October, Nelson closed for action off Cape Trafalgar. Villeneuve turned north, giving him the lee gauge in traditional French fashion—an opportunity to break away and fall off with the wind, although the Spanish coast could be seen to the east. The 18 French and 15 Spanish ships-of-the-line were intermingled in a ragged line-ahead formation, with Villeneuve aboard his 80-gun flagship *Bucentaure* near the center. Nelson approached obliquely from the west in 2 columns, he leading the 12-ship van

colonial possessions throughout the world. The strategic and tactical policies of the late Nelson and Pitt (who died in 1806) continued in the navy, now thoroughly imbued with the "Nelson touch." When a 7-ship French squadron broke out from Brest to the West Indies, it was destroyed by a British squadron off Santo Domingo in February 1806. British forces attacked Spain's Latin American possessions, where revolutionary movements undermined Spanish authority, and in 1809 the British captured French Santo Domingo and Martinique. Other British naval expeditions took Dutch Cape Town, the Dutch East Indies, and French possessions in the Indian Ocean by 1811.

In and near the Mediterranean, Admiral Lord **Cuthbert Collingwood** kept Toulon and Cadiz closely blockaded, put a landing force into southern Italy, and cooperated with the Russian navy against pro-French Ottoman Turkey. When a British squadron penetrated the Dardanelles in an attempt to seize the

in *Victory*, 100 guns, with Vice Adm. Cuthbert Collingwood commanding the 15 ships of the rear division in the 100-gun *Royal Sovereign*.

Nelson achieved tactical concentration to near perfection. At about noon he and Collingwood pierced the allied center at separate points. The wind prevented the French van from turning about to assist the separated center and rear upon which both British divisions massed and doubled. *Victory* and *Téméraire*, 98 guns, closely engaged and captured *Redoutable*, 74, but not before a French rifleman wounded Nelson in the chest. His division then overwhelmed *Santissima Trinidad*, 120, and *Bucentaure*, taking Villeneuve prisoner. Collingwood's ships simultaneously battered their opponents until most surrendered. The British drove off the French van ships when they were finally towed back into the battle by longboats at day's end.

Nelson learned of his victory just before he died of his wounds late in the afternoon. The British captured 8 French and 9 Spanish ships-of-the-line, sank 1 French vessel, and lost not a single ship. But many vessels in both fleets suffered heavy damage and casualties: dead and wounded numbered about 2,600 Franco-Spanish, 1,700 British, plus some 7,000 French and Spanish officers and sailors taken prisoner. The senior Spanish admiral died of his wounds. Storm-whipped seas claimed 5 more Franco-Spanish ships and many captured prizes over the next 2 days.

At Trafalgar Nelson had achieved British naval supremacy in one of the most decisive naval battles in history, although at the cost of his own life. The prisoner Villeneuve suffered a similar fate; upon being exchanged in 1806 he ignominiously committed suicide rather than face the wrath of Napoleon.

Ottoman fleet in 1807, it was driven off by Turkish shore batteries. A Russian squadron, however, defeated a Turkish force off Mt. Athos, Lemnos, in the Aegean in July. Russia then switched sides, but when its 10 ships-of-the-line in the Mediterranean attempted to return to the Baltic via the Strait of Gibraltar they were blockaded and then captured by the British at Lisbon in 1808. British forces occupied most French-held islands in the Adriatic Sea and defeated a Franco-Venetian squadron off Lissa in 1811.

Britain's control of the North and Baltic Seas required the neutralization of the Russian, Swedish, and Danish fleets as Napoleon tried to appropriate them for his imperial navy. In August 1807 a British fleet landed an invasion army in Denmark and the next month so effectively bombarded Copenhagen with Congreve rockets that Denmark surrendered its fleet of 16 of the line and 10 frigates. During 1808–9 Napoleon's Russian ally defeated Sweden. Britain, more anxious about Napoleon's shipbuilding program at Antwerp, landed an expeditionary force at **Walcheren** Island in August 1809. Supported by naval guns, it destroyed the shipyards at Flushing before being withdrawn in the face of counterattacking French troops. Napoleon's attempt to appropriate the small Portuguese fleet by invading that country in 1807 was frustrated by a British squadron that escorted the Portuguese government and fleet to colonial Brazil.

Napoleon nevertheless persevered with naval construction and invaded Spain in 1808 to place his brother on the throne and absorb the 28 Spanish ships-of-the-line. The people of Spain and Portugal revolted, prompting Admiral Collingwood to rush warships and troops to their assistance at Cadiz and Lisbon, capturing Spain's fleet in the process. But Napoleon personally led a counterattack overland which forced the British to withdraw from Spain early in 1809. Britain, however, continued to blockade the continent from Gibraltar, Lisbon, and the Western Approaches. When a French squadron escaped from Brest to Rochefort in April, the blockading fleet attacked it with fireships in Aix Roads at night, destroying only 2 ships-of-the-line but bottling up the rest in port.

Although Napoleon's armies defeated Austria in 1808–9, the British turned their Iberian foothold into a major theater of operations known as the **Peninsular War.** Supported by the fleet at Lisbon, the British army under General Sir Arthur Wellesley (later Duke of Wellington) initiated a series of overland thrusts along the Tagus River in the spring of 1809. It repeatedly drove the French army back into Spain, then withdrew behind Portuguese fortifications, leaving French land communications and supplies to be attacked by Spanish guerrillas. This stratagem so weakened Napoleon's army in Spain that Wellington was finally able to mount a major ground offensive that captured Madrid in the summer of 1812. In the meantime, Russia refused to follow Napoleon's dictates, so he invaded Russia that same summer.

The defeat of Napoleon's armies in Spain and Russia enabled Britain to forge its final coalition: Russia, Prussia, Austria, and Sweden. British warships escorted the Russian fleet to England, thence to the Mediterranean to assist Austria and the Italians. In 1813–14 Wellington drove into France from Spain, and the allied armies finally crushed Napoleon, forcing his surrender. Britain's strategy of concentration had finally succeeded: victorious coalition armies and absolute control of the seas everywhere. The only unexpected wrinkle in the final struggle was the American declaration of war against Britain in June 1812.

War of 1812. The United States was the largest neutral trader in the world but with a navy too weak to protect its merchant shipping against the British and French blockades. President Jefferson's regime enacted self-imposed embargoes against any American trade with either belligerent in 1807 and 1809, a policy which nearly ruined the American economy. In addition, British warships continued to impress U.S. seamen into the Royal Navy, and British and American troops clashed along the Canadian border. The next president, James Madison, and anti-British elements in Congress opted for war in 1812 in order to end these outrages and attempt to annex Canada.

The Royal Navy convoyed troops from the West Indies to check American ground offensives into Canada and conducted the same economic war on the United States as against France: blockade and independent cruisers. Several American frigates, however, defeated British counterparts in individual duels, and with Yankee privateers they waged *guerre de course* on British shipping. During 1813 the British extended their blockade from New England all the way to New Orleans on the Gulf Coast, and both sides built men-of-war along the Canadian frontier for operations on Lakes Ontario, Erie, and Champlain.

In September 1813 Captain **Oliver Hazard Perry** and 9 light American warships defeated and captured a squadron of 6 British vessels in the **Battle of Lake Erie,** then transported an army force that drove the British from Detroit. With Napoleon's demise early in 1814, the Royal Navy completely sealed off eastern U.S. ports and landed troops which burned Washington, D.C. in August, although its attack on Baltimore was repulsed. That same month British troops invaded New York State from Canada, supported by 4 sailing ships and 12 galleys until these were defeated and captured by a makeshift U.S. squadron in the **Battle of Lake Champlain** in September. The British withdrew to Canada, leaving the border unchanged.

To protect the Spanish Florida frontier and pacify active southern Indian tribes allied to the British, General Andrew Jackson captured Pensacola in November 1814. He then shifted to New Orleans where a British invasion force from Jamaica landed in December. Unaware that the diplomats had concluded peace, the British attacked Jackson's army in January 1815, only to be soundly defeated. With Canada intact, Britain agreed to stop impressing U.S. seamen and to restore the vitally important commercial relations between the 2 countries. The War of 1812 otherwise accomplished nothing for either side.

The 2 English-speaking nations each affirmed the restoration of international law and order in separate conflicts during the spring of 1815. When Barbary Algerian corsairs resumed their attacks on U.S. shipping, Commodore **Stephen Decatur** led a 9-ship squadron to the Mediterranean, where it defeated the Algerian navy and blockaded Algiers, which then submitted to U.S. demands. In France, Napoleon suddenly seized power and raised another army, forcing Britain to assemble a coalition army which defeated him at Waterloo. Britain restored the balance of power in Europe and exiled the French dictator to St. Helena Island in the South Atlantic, where the Royal Navy kept him imprisoned for the rest of his days.

10

The British Pax

(1815–1860s)

BRITISH GLOBAL HEGEMONY followed the defeat of Napoleon—a century
of general peace, pax, between the great powers. Britain's naval superiority prevented the outbreak of major wars and enforced international law on the sea
lanes of the world. The **Pax Britannica** fostered humanitarian principles, notably Britain's abolition of the slave trade in 1807 and slavery in 1833, laws which
its navy had to enforce. Economically, it adopted free trade by abolishing the
Navigation Acts in 1849 and stimulated industrial capitalism in Europe, America, and Asia. The world ran on London time from 1815 to 1914, with no major
challenge to Britain's naval supremacy until after the 1860s.

British Naval Policy. Naval power served as an instrument of diplomacy at
the able hands of prime ministers Viscount Castlereagh until 1822, George
Canning to 1830, then Viscount **Palmerston,** usually foreign secretary or prime
minister until 1865. Castlereagh and Canning relied on the Admiralty and Navy
Board to make policy as in the past. But the reform-minded ministry of 1830 gave
Palmerston this role in order to control expenditures; it abolished the Navy
Board and reduced the power of the Admiralty to a managerial role.

A sound fiscal policy became essential with the introduction of new and expensive technologies into the fleet—steam propulsion to augment sail power,
using side paddle wheels from the 1830s and underwater screw propellers from
the 1840s; iron hulls for some vessels from the latter decade and iron-plated hulls
in the 1850s; more powerful guns—rifled as well as smooth bore; the introduction of the explosive shell and the contact mine; and the construction of steam
gunboats for global service in the 1850s. In spite of reluctant admirals weaned on
sailing warships, steam engineers were given officers' commissions in 1847, and
the lot of crewmen—the Lower Deck—was steadily improved (see essay).

British naval strategy and tactics did not change. In 1817 Castlereagh identi-
fied a potential Franco-Russian alliance as the only possible naval threat, thus the
"2-power standard" by which to set fleet strength. The Home Fleet operated

between the North Sea and Mediterranean and dispatched ships to reinforce colonial stations. It remained ready to reconcentrate in the Channel or Western Approaches for deterring an invasion and did so during several political and diplomatic crises with France between 1844 and 1853. Tactically, the navy perpetuated its offensive Nelsonian character except that no occasion arose for fighting a fleet engagement.

The French navy reverted to its traditional strategy of *guerre de course* but maintained a modern battle force to intimidate Britain and confront lesser navies. The Russian fleet was divided between the Baltic and Black Seas for coast defense against Sweden and Ottoman Turkey, respectively. British tacticians therefore welcomed steam power for wartime use—the blockade of and aggressive attacks on enemy seaports and naval bases, and the offensive destruction of commerce raiders as a substitute for defensive convoys.

The British used a combination of older warships, gunboats, and occasional newer fleet units to protect and patrol Britain's ever-expanding colonial empire. A unique global network of bases developed which provided convenient coaling stations for the new steamships. Bases at Lisbon, Gibraltar, and Malta enabled the navy to police the western Mediterranean. Domination of the Indian Ocean was facilitated by naval bases at Calcutta and Bombay in India, Trincomalee in Ceylon, Mauritius Island, and Cape Town, South Africa. As Britain pushed into Southeast Asia and the western Pacific, it acquired major colonies and bases at Malayan Singapore (1819) and Chinese Hong Kong (1842). The sun never set on the British Empire or its naval forces.

Western Europe (1815–50). For the postwar balance of power, Britain arranged the unification of the northern and southern Low Countries—the Netherlands and Belgium—to prevent future French designs on the region, the proverbial pistol pointed at England. Belgium, however, proclaimed its independence in 1830, which the major powers accepted, whereupon the Dutch invaded Belgium and captured Antwerp in 1831. The British fleet sailed up the Scheldt to blockade Antwerp, and the French attacked by land, restoring Belgian independence.

Britain intervened in a Portuguese civil war with a landing force in 1827, but rebel leader Miguel collected a fleet which expelled the monarchy. Queen Maria rallied naval forces from colonial Brazil and Anglo-French volunteers to recapture the Azores and repulse Miguel's fleet there in 1828. British naval forces under Admiral Sir Charles Napier landed Maria's army in Portugal in 1832 and the next year defeated Miguel's fleet off Cape St. Vincent, recapturing Lisbon. Miguel surrendered in 1834.

Prussia instigated a revolt of 2 Danish duchies against Denmark's rule in 1848. Britain and Russia immediately mobilized naval forces to support the Danes,

The Lower Deck

The lot of the common sailor living and toiling on the "lower decks" of warships differed markedly from that of the officers stationed on the upper decks. In the age of the galley, seamen remained at the oars when cruising, fighting, and sleeping—feeling the lash if they happened to be slaves. In the age of fighting sail, crewmen climbed the yards to handle sails aloft in all types of weather. Barechested and barefooted, they worked the cannon in close quarters on the gun decks. Accidents could claim life or limb, and bloodshed was so rife during battle that gun decks were painted crimson to minimize the psychological effect. Few warships carried medical personnel, although hospital ships tended those in need. Throughout the age of sail, some wives of enlisted men (and officers) lived and fought alongside their spouses at sea, unofficially and without pay. In the 1690s the Royal Navy did enlist nurses and laundresses for its hospital ships.

For the crews of up to 1,000 men in a line-of-battle ship, living spaces were situated among the guns—cramped and crowded for "messing" (eating) and sleeping, the men strung up in hammocks. They relieved themselves in a space near the bow of the ship—at the beakhead (hence "head" for latrine). Seamen's health suffered from the damp, unventilated, and vermin-infested spaces, leading to disease. Inadequate diets were another cause, because fruits and vegetables could not be preserved at sea; crews lacked ascorbic acid (vitamin C) and succumbed to scurvy. Beef and pork were preserved by salting until hard as mahogany. Hot pea soup was a favorite, but oatmeal nauseating. The unattractive hard sour biscuits bred weevils and maggots but could also be burned and boiled to make "Scotch coffee." Once drinking water became brackish, it was combined with rum to create grog for a daily ration, supplemented by beer, wine, and brandy—warming to the body but a source of alcoholism and dulled senses that led to accidents.

Discipline took precedence over morale, especially when seamen were coerced into service by "press gangs" or drawn from the criminal element to fill depleted crews. Disobedient and unruly sailors faced trial—"before the captain's mast." Mutinous acts resulted in hanging, although flogging with the cat-o'-nine tails was the standard punishment for lesser crimes. A simple deterrent to misdeeds was tyrannical officers and the masters-at-arms responsible for discipline. One duty of shipboard marines was to protect the officers and prevent mutinies. The adoption of standardized officers' uniforms cemented the gulf between officers and crews of the British navy in 1746, followed by noncommissioned ratings' uniforms in 1787. But when the most reliable enlisted men—those drawn from the merchant service—felt brutalized, as in 1797, they mutinied, forcing the Admiralty to mend it ways.

Reforms to improve the lot of the Lower Deck of the Royal Navy were already in the wind. The medical research of naval physician James Lind led to improved health at sea during the late 18th century: lime and lemon juice rations for vitamin C, the scrubbing of decks and airing of hammocks, clean clothes, the initiation of vaccinations against smallpox in 1798, and the issuing of soap from 1810. Between 1814 and 1825 the British adopted canned foods; made fresh beef, vegetables, and bread standard issue; and replaced wooden water casks with iron tanks. Chocolate, tea, and sugar followed when the daily grog ration was cut in half in 1825 and the beer ration ended in 1831. Salted beef survived until 1906, salt pork to 1926, by which time refrigeration had revolutionized shipboard food preservation. The U.S. Navy abolished shipboard grog in 1862 and all alcohol in 1914, but grog remained a British staple until 1970.

Britain's lead in 19th-century humanitarian social reforms extended to its navy, often the result of civilian pressure as well as practical expediency. Press gangs were discontinued after 1815 except for merchant sailors caught smuggling. The haphazard practice of 5- to 7-year terms of enlistment yielded to a permanent manning system. Enlisted men received standardized uniforms in 1824, and the need for literate sailors to understand modern guns led to the teaching of reading and writing, plus shipboard libraries, in the 1830s. Pensions were now provided for 21 years' enlisted service, culminating in 1853 with the continuous career policy of 10-year initial enlistments plus pay during leave and sickness. Pay was increased and issued punctually.

The United States paralleled Britain in protecting the rights of its enlisted naval personnel. Congress outlawed flogging in 1850, followed by Britain's limiting the practice to a court-martial punishment in 1859 and virtually abolishing it in 1879. Discipline remained rigid, to be sure, but the old abuses were dramatically minimized. General health improved in iron-hulled ships over wooden ones, while medical personnel were gradually introduced at sea. The advent of steam propulsion forced both navies to give specialized training to enlisted men on board permanently docked training vessels instead of having them merely learn on the job as on sailing ships. By 1860 the British and American navies had created professional careers for ratings. Except in wartime, these men were usually volunteers, unlike most continental navies, which depended heavily on conscripts—and suffered major mutinies—well into the 20th century.

leading to restored Danish rule in 1850. Denmark was so weak, however, that it could no longer enforce payment of the Sound tolls by foreign merchant ships. After the United States simply refused to pay them in 1855 they were abolished.

Mediterranean Wars (1815–50). So vital was the middle sea to European stability and world trade that Britain positioned its major fleet there after 1815. France, Austria, Russia, and the United States also employed naval forces to protect their expanding maritime commerce against the Barbary states and Ottoman Turkey.

In August 1816, Admiral Lord **Edward Exmouth** led an Anglo-Dutch force which bombarded and destroyed much of piratic Algiers and its entire fleet. He not only freed 1,200 Christian slaves but also forced the dey of Algiers to renounce any future enslavement of Western Christians. The U.S. Mediterranean Squadron, based at Port Mahon in Spanish Minorca, demonstrated against Algiers when it broke the treaty terms in 1822, as did the British fleet in 1824 and against Moroccan Tangier in 1828.

A French naval revival and diplomatic offensive ended the Barbary problem. After blockading Algiers from 1827 to 1829, the French fleet landed a 38,000-man army in 1830 which conquered the city and annexed Algeria to France. Protracted pacification operations included naval bombardments of Tangier and Mogador in Morocco in 1844. France's actions, however, aroused British fears of a possible French threat to Britain's sea routes to the Middle East and, via the Persian Gulf, to India.

The bloody **Greek War of Independence** broke out against Ottoman Turkey in 1821. Two Greek fleets raided and skirmished with the Turkish navy, none more dramatically than that under Konstantin Kanaris. In separate fireship attacks at Chios and Tenedos during 1822 his fleet destroyed 2 Turkish flagships with their admirals. In 1824 the Turks called upon the modernized navy of subject Egypt to raid the Greek islands and invade mainland Morea. The Ottoman reconquest of the Morea culminated in the successful siege of Missolonghi on the Adriatic coast in 1826, although the Greeks remained successful at sea.

The European powers, aroused by the plight of the Greeks but also anxious over indiscriminate Greek piracy, intervened to force the Ottomans out of the Morea. In mid-1827 British, French, and Russian naval forces converged on the Bay of **Navarino** in the Adriatic Morea, along with the Greek fleet, now commanded by Admiral Lord **Thomas Cochrane** and other British officers. On 20 October, Admiral Sir Edward Codrington with 11 allied ships-of-the-line and 9 frigates attacked the anchored Ottoman fleet of 3 and 19 respectively. In just one hour allied gunnery annihilated the Turkish-Egyptian fleet in the last major sailing ship battle in history.

In 1828 the allied fleet blockaded the Morea and crushed Greek piracy, and Turkey declared war on Russia. The French landed an army in Greece and supported the Greek navy in taking Missolonghi and Lepanto in 1829. Turkey granted Greece its independence but turned against Russia in the Black Sea. That summer Russian ground forces, supported by the Rowing Fleet, moved down the coast while another Russian fleet arrived from the Baltic via British Malta to blockade Constantinople from the Aegean side. Pressed from both directions, the Ottomans sued for peace, giving up the mouth of the Danube River and other Black Sea territories to Russia.

The Ottoman defeat exacerbated Britain's larger strategic goal, deterring France and Russia. Both nations exploited chaotic conditions in the Middle East to weaken British hegemony in the Indian Ocean. Warring Arab principalities and pirates so ravaged commercial shipping between the Persian Gulf and Bombay that East India Company warships began policing the Gulf in 1819. Russia crippled Persia in a border war, 1825–28, giving Russia naval control of the inland Caspian Sea. Russia's defeat of Ottoman Turkey in 1829 triggered the revolt of Egypt against Ottoman rule, supported by France. Russia was also expanding overland into Central Asia, threatening India.

Palmerston had good reason to fear an Ottoman collapse and subsequent peril to British trade routes to the East. The navy's preoccupation with the Belgian and Portuguese crises prevented its use against Egypt's conquest of Ottoman Syria in 1831–33. With the resolution of these crises, however, Palmerston created a buffer zone of Turkey, Persia, and Afghanistan against French and Russian involvement in the region. To deter Egyptian moves into the Persian Gulf and Red Sea, in 1838–39 he sent British warships into the Gulf and established a permanent base at Aden, entrance to the Red Sea. Turkey's army attacked the Egyptians, but was defeated; its fleet defected to Egypt, which France supported. Palmerston rallied Russia, Austria, and Prussia behind Turkey and sent an Anglo-Austrian naval force to Syria. It landed Turkish troops and bombarded Acre into submission, forcing Egypt and France to quit the region.

Palmerston countered Russia in 1841 by convincing the powers, including Russia, to restrict warships of any nation other than Turkey's from making passage through the Dardanelles and Bosphorus in times of peace. This new rule of international law prevented easy Russian naval access to the Mediterranean at that time, and it has remained generally intact down to the present (reaffirmed by the **Montreux Convention** of 1936).

Concurrently with shoring up Ottoman Turkey against Russia, Palmerston intervened in Persia and Afghanistan. In 1835 the East India Company convinced the warring sheiks of the Persian Gulf to observe a maritime truce during the summer pearling season, enforced by British warships. This **Trucial System** soon became permanent, policed by the company's Indian Navy until 1859, then by the Royal Navy until the system was terminated in 1971. Although Russia wrested more territory from Persia, it had no designs on conquering Persia, Afghanistan, or India, only in expanding eastward through Central Asia to the Pacific.

By 1850, British India was secure. British trade hastened unchallenged through the Mediterranean and Red Seas, via overland transit across the Suez isthmus, through which a canal began to be constructed in 1859.

Suppressing the Slave Trade. The British navy was the major agency attacking the slave trade even after other nations abolished it because many were reluctant to hunt down slavers. The major source of slaves was prisoners taken by African tribes, the major customers being Middle Eastern Muslim states, Portugal, and the southern United States (which outlawed the slave trade in 1807). The easiest access to thwarting the nefarious trade was from bases in the coastal African colonies of the European nations.

Palmerston launched an all-out offensive against the slavers in the 1830s by assigning over 100 antislaving cruisers to the squadrons operating on the sea lanes which served Africa: Lisbon, the Mediterranean, North America, the West Indies, South America, West Africa, and the East Indies. In addition, treaties of cooperation were negotiated with African tribal chiefs, and coastal raids were carried out against slaving facilities. Joined by French, Portuguese, and U.S. warships, the Royal Navy succeeded in ending the West African slave traffic by 1850. East Africa was more difficult because the coast was controlled by maritime Oman as far south as Mombasa, then to Zanzibar after 1828, and Oman's major income came from slaves. Although the closest British naval bases were distant Bombay and Cape Town, Britain's cruisers ultimately proved effective, especially after Ottoman Turkey, Oman-Zanzibar, and Persia began to cooperate with them in the 1840s.

A revival of southwestern African slaving occurred in the 1850s to serve the southern states of the United States through Spanish Cuba. The growing sectional cleavage between the American North and South was reflected by Southern-born U.S. Navy captains who often avoided intercepting slave-carrying ships. And Congress refused to allow foreign warships to challenge any vessels flying the American flag, however doubtful their true national registry. The outbreak of the American Civil War in 1861 ended this traffic, however, when Congress allowed British warships to run down all suspected slavers. Indian Ocean slave traffic continued until 1890, when an international conference agreed that all nations would suppress the slave trade, though smuggling in slaves survives to this day.

East Asia. Trade offensives by the Western powers into the waters of the South China Sea, East China Sea, Yellow Sea, and southwestern Pacific required naval support and protection, with Britain at the forefront. Its dominant East Indies Squadron cooperated with the Dutch in Indonesia, the Spanish in the Philippines, the French opening up Indochinese Vietnam, and the United States, which created its own East India Squadron in 1835. The main missions of these naval forces were (1) protecting merchantmen against native pirates, (2) pacifying native peoples who resisted outright European colonization, and (3) forcing reluctant Asian rulers to open their markets to Western traders.

Early in 1819 Britain occupied **Singapore,** the island off the tip of Malaya, in order to break the Dutch monopoly over European trade with East Asia. Singapore commanded the critical Malacca Straits through which all merchant traffic passed between the Indian Ocean and China, making it the strategic pivot and major naval base for Britain's trade offensive. Security of the straits was so essential that when local Malay pirates plundered shipping in the straits in the 1830s, the British established naval patrols which crushed them. In the 1840s British, Dutch, and Spanish naval forces eliminated major pirate activities throughout Indonesia and the South China Sea.

The demise of Spain's monopoly over Pacific Oceania beyond the Philippines occurred as European competitors established their own colonies, especially Britain. No native resistance was more ferocious than that of the New Zealand Maoris utilizing guerrilla tactics against the British. Britain's Australasian Squadron, based at Australian Sydney, fought the **Maori wars** of 1843–48 by bombarding the coast with naval guns and Congreve rockets and landing colonial troops to pacify the natives. Such tactics were typical of the limited wars fought by the British and other Western powers against tribal native peoples everywhere over the entire century.

The need for political stability in eastern waters led to British intervention in purely Asian wars. When the kingdom of Burma attacked its neighbors, including India, the British mounted an expeditionary force from the Andaman Islands up Burma's Irrawaddy River in 1824. The ground forces, supported by sailing warships, a steamer, and armed rowboats firing rockets, captured Rangoon, defeated the Burmese army and galley fleet, and forced Burma to cede its northern territory to Britain. When fighting erupted again in 1852–53, another British amphibious force recaptured Rangoon and annexed southern Burma.

Britain intervened in China when its weak and declining Manchu (Ch'ing) dynasty refused to expand its trade with the West beyond the East India Company's enclave at Canton and Portugal's at Macao. Palmerston therefore terminated the company's monopoly in 1834 and promoted the trade of illegal opium from India into China in search of profits. This threat to China's government prompted the Chinese to seize Canton in 1839. Britain instituted a naval blockade of the Chinese coast, and late in the year 2 British warships drove a force of 29 armed junks from Canton to begin the **First Opium War.**

Covered by 3 battleships, the British landed 20,000 troops at Chusan and entered the Yangtze River in mid-1840. When China refused to yield, British naval and landing forces spent 1841 capturing or recapturing key Chinese coastal cities—Hong Kong, Canton, Amoy, Chusan, and Ningpo. Turning Hong Kong into an advanced base, the British East Indies fleet of over 70 vessels captured Shanghai in June 1842. Moving up the Yangtze to Nanking in August, it sealed off the canal supplying the capital, Peking. China submitted, opened up trade with the British, and ceded **Hong Kong** to Britain, which made it home base for the new China Station in 1844. Similar treaties opened Chinese trade with France and the United States.

China reeled internally from its defeat, including an outbreak of widespread piracy. China stubbornly refused British naval aid against the pirates until 1848, at which time Britain allied itself with the navy of Vietnam to destroy a large pirate fleet in 3 battles during 1849. The outbreak of the Taiping Rebellion against Manchu rule in 1850 inspired further piracy. Notable among Western navies which rallied to Britain's side against China's pirates and belligerent warlords was that of the United States.

U.S. Naval Policy. Because of the War of 1812 and postwar concerns about British naval power, Congress in 1813 and 1816 authorized the construction of 12 74-gun ships-of-the-line. Only half saw eventual duty, however, because both democracies basically cooperated after 1815 as maritime trading partners. Fearing the emergence of a British-style naval elite, however, Congress vested naval authority in the civilian Secretary of the Navy instead of a senior naval officer. Rather than an Admiralty, in 1815 it created the Board of Commissioners of 3 senior captains to advise the secretary and even refused to create the rank of admiral. As in most navies, the senior captain commanding several U.S. warships held the honorary rank of commodore. The missions of the U.S. Navy during the long Pax Britannica were simply to protect American trade and the coastlines, augmenting the army's fortifications.

Despite opposition by new states of the interior to naval construction, it became necessary because of U.S. territorial expansion to the Gulf and Pacific coasts and the concurrent growth of American global trade that had to be protected. Several permanent naval squadrons were gradually established—the Mediterranean in 1815; Eastern Pacific, 1818; West Indies and Caribbean, 1822;

Brazil, 1826; East Indies, 1835; the Home Station, 1841; and Africa, 1843, the latter primarily for antislaving operations.

The advent of steamships and modern ordnance (guns) forced Congress to institute naval administrative reforms. In 1842 the Board of Commissioners was replaced by a system of bureaus, whose heads reported directly to the secretary. In 1845 the U.S. Naval Academy was established at Annapolis, Maryland, to instruct officers in steam engineering. The global reach of the navy led to the adoption of the formal rank of flag officer in 1857, superseded by that of rear admiral in 1862 for the Civil War navy. But the United States had no interest in establishing overseas colonies. Continental and commercial growth were sufficient national goals for the young Republic, always shielded from potential European enemies by the British navy which continued to dominate American waters.

Latin American Revolutions (1815–30). Both Britain and the United States supported Latin American independence movements in order to humble Spain and create trade opportunities for themselves. In 1815 Spain dispatched an expeditionary force to the Caribbean, where piracy and privateering flourished. When pirates based at Amelia Island in northeastern Florida attacked shipping, U.S. warships and landing forces seized the place in 1817, an event that contributed to an enfeebled Spain ceding all of Florida to the United States in 1819. When the pirates shifted to Galveston in Spanish Texas, U.S. naval patrols forced them out by 1820. General Simón Bolívar recruited a Dutch Creole as admiral of his South American revolutionary fleet of privateers. It defeated the Spanish at sea and mounted seaborne invasions to liberate Venezuela and Colombia from 1816 to 1823. General José de San Martin did the same in Argentina, Chile, and Peru, 1815–26, using American and British naval volunteers, in particular his admiral, Lord Cochrane of Britain.

In 1822–23 the United States and Britain formally recognized the new Latin American republics and announced the doctrine named for President James Monroe expressly forbidding the intervention of any European nation (and navy) in the Western Hemisphere. The major vehicle of its enforcement was the Royal Navy, which joined the 2 new regional U.S. squadrons in a successful antipiracy campaign in Latin American waters. The **Monroe Doctrine** also encouraged the Mexican and Central American colonies to revolt successfully from Spanish rule and colonial Brazil from Portugal. In 1823 Lord Cochrane at the head of the Brazilian navy drove away Portugal's warships to secure independence. From 1825 to 1829 Spain attempted to recover its Caribbean possessions but was countered by the Mexican navy commanded by former U.S. Navy Commodore **David Porter.**

By 1830 only Cuba and Puerto Rico remained as colonies of Spain in America, enabling Britain and the United States to dominate the trade of the new Latin American nations. Civil strife had already broken out, however, and would become endemic to the region, causing occasional naval responses by the powers. In 1833 Britain improved its naval position by annexing the Falkland Islands off the coast of Argentina. In 1838–39 a French squadron bombarded and temporarily occupied the Mexican port of Veracruz to protect French nationals. For similar reasons, an Anglo-French naval force blockaded and occupied part of Uruguay during its civil war in the 1840s. The U.S. Navy helped the army to pacify Florida's Seminole Indians, equipped with arms from Spanish Cuba, during the **Seminole War** of 1835–42.

The major Latin American problem which affected the United States was the revolt of American settlers in Texas against Mexican rule, 1835–43. Both Mexico and the republic of Texas raised small navies; the latter eventually defeated Mexico's to ensure Texas independence. Although Britain and the United States supported Texas, they argued over the Canadian border and possession of the Oregon territory. Fearing war with Britain, the United States created its Home Squadron in the Gulf of Mexico in 1841. And in 1842 the commander of the U.S. Pacific Squadron temporarily occupied Monterey in Mexico's upper California in order to deter British designs on the region. The boundary question and division of Oregon were settled by treaties, but the U.S. annexed Texas in 1845 lest it fall prey to Britain. The boundary between Texas and Mexico was not settled, however, precipitating war between the United States and Mexico in May 1846.

Mexican-American War (1846–48). Though the initial fighting occurred near the disputed territory, U.S. objectives were enlarged when upper California revolted from Mexico in June 1846 and proclaimed itself a pro–United States independent republic. Furthermore, an invasion of Mexico became necessary to force Mexico to come to terms. The U.S. Navy therefore undertook its first offensive war and very much in the British tradition. The Home Squadron, based at Pensacola, Florida, instituted a blockade of Mexican Gulf Coast ports, while the Pacific Squadron seized San Francisco and Monterey and ferried rebel Californian ground forces south to San Diego for operations against Los Angeles. Two U.S. sloops-of-war attacked shipping and blockaded Mexican ports in the Gulf of California.

The small Mexican gunboat navy posed no threat, but 3 American landing expeditions failed to seize its anchored vessels up 2 rivers on the Gulf of Mexico coast until the autumn of 1846, when Tabasco and Tampico were finally taken. Despite difficulties caused by stormy seas and tropical diseases, the blockade was maintained and Tampico developed into a staging base for the eventual invasion of Mexico. Simultaneously, an army column marched overland from Missouri to San Diego where it linked up with Commodore **Robert F. Stockton**'s Pacific Squadron to defeat the Mexican army defending Los Angeles early in 1847. Stockton's ships established an advanced base at La Paz near the tip of lower (Baja) California in April and spent the rest of the year blockading the western coast of Mexico.

The ultimate American objective was the capture of Mexico City, making U.S. strategy basically a continental one. The task of the navy was to land General Winfield Scott's army on the eastern coast near Veracruz, Mexico's main seaport, invest it by a land-sea siege, then use it as the army's base of operations for the overland campaign. The U.S. Army and Navy cooperated closely in planning and executing the **Veracruz landing.** The army provided troop transports and specially designed rowed assault boats, and the navy purchased and built shallow-draft, steam-driven schooners for close-in fire support and for passing over coastal sandbars. The assault took place on 9 March 1847 and was a complete success (see essay).

The Home Squadron under Commodore **Matthew C. Perry** then ranged the Mexican Gulf Coast while Scott's army fought its way into Mexico City in September, and the Pacific Squadron captured Mazatlán on the western coast in November 1847. Yielding to American demands in the 1848 peace treaty, Mexico not only gave up its claims to Texas north of the Rio Grande but also ceded all its territory between Texas and California to the United States.

Whatever imperial designs the United States had were purely continental, satisfied by its territorial gains from Mexico, with the U.S. Navy reverting to trade protection. The Caribbean continued to be dominated by the British North American squadron, commanded from 1848 to 1851 by Admiral Lord Cochrane, late of the Chilean, Brazilian, and Greek navies. Both countries agreed to share any future transisthmian canal across Central America and renounced future territorial acquisitions in Latin America. They had greater concerns in the Pacific, not only over trade opportunities but also concerning the expansion of Russia, which already owned Alaska.

Crimean War (1854–56). Imperial Russia undertook another war against the weak Ottoman Empire in the autumn of 1853. The Russian Black Sea fleet, after blockading a 12-ship Turkish squadron at Sinope on Turkey's northern coast, annihilated it using the new exploding shells on 30 November. Britain and France rushed a combined fleet to the defense of Turkey, followed by formal declarations of war on Russia early in 1854. This conflict, the only major war between

Assault on Veracruz

The first major amphibious operation in U.S. naval history occurred in March 1847, when the Home Squadron landed a 12,000-man army near Veracruz for the invasion of Mexico. Early in the year the expeditionary force was combat-loaded on board army transports at Lobos Island near its staging base of Mexican Tampico. Working in close cooperation, Commodore David Conner and Major Gen. Winfield Scott, the respective navy and army commanders, together reconnoitered the coast from the sea and selected the landing beach. At the beginning of March specially constructed army assault "surf boats" were loaded on to army transports and supply ships which then rendezvoused with the fleet off Anton Lizardo, south of Veracruz.

At dawn on 9 March the fleet's steam frigates and other large ships began bombarding the landing beach and the castle of San Juan de Ulloa, the heavily armed Mexican fort in the harbor of Veracruz. The 40-feet-long double-ender surf boats were lowered into the water from the transports and towed by steamers to Sacrificios Island, $2\frac{1}{2}$ miles off the target beach south of Veracruz. Scott's troops transferred from their transports to the heavier men-of-war anchored off Sacrificios. These vessels loaded them into the surf boats, one 90-man infantry company per boat. All this maneuvering consumed the entire day, at the end of which—6:00 P.M.—the first wave of 4,500 men pushed off.

Covered by the "Mosquito flotilla" of small gunboats providing close-in fire support, the assault craft were rowed to the sandbar where the troops

European powers during the century-long Pax Britannica, focused on the Crimean peninsula in the Black Sea, although Palmerston used the opportunity to weaken Russian naval strength in the Baltic. The British fleet captured the Baltic Aland Islands in August and in 1855 destroyed Sveaborg at the entrance to the Gulf of Finland, cutting off Kronstadt from the sea.

To protect Turkey the allies decided to capture Russia's Crimean naval base at **Sevastopol.** The mostly steam-driven Anglo-French-Turkish fleet, basing at Varna, bombarded Russian Odessa in April 1854 and sealifted the 50,000-man invasion army to Sevastopol in September. The 4-day landing operation took place north of the city. The army's overland advance forced the Russians to scuttle many of their warships and thereby block the harbor entrance. As the armies

jumped out and waded waist deep 100 yards to shore. Fortunately, they encountered no opposition, partly because the Mexicans were expecting instead an assault on the harbor fort, still under fire by the guns of the fleet. Meanwhile, the surf boats returned to the embarkation ships as the next wave approached the bar. The army established a defense perimeter on the beach and by 10:00 P.M. had 10,000 men ashore. Next day, General Scott brought in the last troops along with his artillery. Horses and mules swam ashore, tethered to boats.

Commodore Conner, having completed the landing, now turned over command of the fleet, as planned, to Commodore Matthew C. Perry, who transported heavy naval guns ashore to assist in the siege of Veracruz. The well-coordinated and expeditious operation included the precaution of not crowding too many transports into the roadstead for fear that a sudden Gulf storm might hit. Unfortunately, in their zeal to get provisions and siege guns ashore, the transports became congested, only to be ravaged by a "norther" which sank 26 of them. The disaster did not seriously impair the siege, however, and after 3 weeks Veracruz and its harbor fort surrendered.

Taking advantage of navy pontoons for a river crossing, Scott sent an army column overland to take Alvarado in early April, forcing the Mexicans to scuttle their last gunboats there. Perry's ships then captured Tuxpan up the coast, thereby securing Scott's rear for his cross-country advance on Mexico City. The Veracruz campaign was a model amphibious operation, albeit against a weak enemy, which gained invaluable experience for junior officers destined for positions of high command in the American Civil War.

encircled Sevastopol, the fleet established an anchorage at the harbor of Balaklava south of the city. An ill-conceived army assault on Sevastapol was repulsed on 17 October, and several allied bombardment ships were severely damaged by coast artillery. After a winter siege, the fleet, under Admiral Sir Edmund Lyons, forced the Russians to abandon Kerch in the eastern Crimea, enabling it to destroy Russian supply routes in the Sea of Azov during the summer of 1855. Sevastopol fell in September, as did Ochakov in October after a devastating bombardment of Fort Kinburn by 90 ships, including 3 French armored steamers.

Palmerston now moved to weaken Russia permanently in the Baltic. Early in 1856 he ordered massive construction of modern steam gunboats, mortar boats, armored vessels, and supply ships for a seaborne invasion of Kronstadt, gateway to St. Petersburg. Russia sued for peace, its Baltic fleet obsolescent, its Black Sea fleet scuttled. In the settlement, dominated by Britain, the entire Black Sea was demilitarized, with Russia and Turkey having to give up all naval forces and defenses there. The Danube River basin was opened to commerce of all nations, thereby crippling Russian influence in the region. Russia was also weakened in the Baltic by the demilitarization of the Aland Islands.

The powers used the occasion to issue the 1856 **Declaration of Paris.** It outlawed privateering, permitted neutral shipping with warring powers (except for contraband of war), and ruled that a blockade had to be effectively enforced by warships in order to be legal and binding on neutral shippers. Despite the fact that the United States refused to sign because of its need for privateers to augment its weaker navy, the Declaration became a generally accepted tenet of international law. Its enforcement, like that of the demilitarized Black Sea and Aland Islands, depended on Britain's naval supremacy.

The Crimean War had ramifications for Britain's Indian Ocean empire because Persia, expecting a Russian victory, had invaded Afghanistan in 1855. Late in 1856 the East India Company's navy landed an expeditionary force in the Persian Gulf, although Britain negotiated peace in 1857. That May, however, the Great Indian Mutiny broke out. Britain crushed it by mid-1858, and the crown replaced the East India Company's rule—and army and navy—in India. The security of India and the Afghan frontier remained essential because of Russia's overland expansion toward the Pacific.

Pacific Rivalries (1850–1860s). With Britain embroiled in the affairs of China, Russia and the United States developed trade offensives for Pacific markets. Both nations dispatched naval squadrons to force long-closed Japan to open its markets to the Western powers. The Russian expedition left the distant Baltic late in 1852 but lost out to the Americans when Commodore Perry's 4 powerful steam warships entered Tokyo Bay first, in July 1853. Japan yielded to American demands for open trade and soon granted similar privileges to Russia and the other powers. Realizing their technological inferiority, the Japanese quickly turned to Western advisers to teach them modern naval practices.

Chinese trade was exacerbated when rebelling Taiping armies captured Nanking for their capital in 1853 and threatened to overthrow the Manchu dynasty. Manchu frustrations with fresh British trade demands led the Chinese to seize British merchantman *Arrow* at Canton in October 1856, resulting in the **Arrow War** (or Second Opium War) with Britain. The British fleet under Admiral Sir Michael Seymour immediately attacked Canton's forts, one of which made the mistake of firing upon boats belonging to the neutral American squadron present. The Americans responded by forming a naval brigade which, under cover of ships' guns, assaulted and captured all 4 barrier forts below the city. In addition, the Russians, advancing eastward along the Amur River, in May 1857 forced China to cede its Pacific provinces north of the Amur to them. The murder of a French missionary led France to join the British in the naval bombardment and capture of Canton in December.

When the Chinese refused to make peace, the British fleet bombarded the Taku forts at the entrance to the Peiho River in May 1858, forcing their evacuation. With the approaches to Peking threatened, China agreed to negotiate and reoccupied the forts. Then the murder of a Spanish missionary in Vietnam caused a Franco-Spanish fleet to bombard and capture Vietnamese Tourane during the summer. The French proceeded to establish a naval base at Saigon to begin the conquest of Vietnam. China reneged on its concessions in 1859 and successfully repelled an Anglo-French assault on the Taku forts in June. The Anglo-French fleet thereupon landed a 20,000-man army for a land-sea attack which recaptured the forts and moved on to take Tientsin in August 1860. It captured Peking in October and dictated the peace.

Britain now dominated the external affairs of China as well as the waters of eastern Asia. Its gunboats assumed the task of protecting trade on China's major rivers, and American and British military adventurers helped the Manchus destroy the Taiping army by 1864. To contain Russian expansion into the Pacific, an Anglo-French squadron operated out of San Francisco and Vancouver, British Columbia, during the Crimean War. But when the Russians founded the town of Vladivostok on the Asian Pacific coast near Korea in 1860–61, they simultaneously occupied Tsushima Island, situated in the Korea Strait between Japan and Korea. Aimed at challenging Britain, the move prompted a British naval demonstration in Japanese waters that convinced the Russians to evacuate Tsushima late in 1861. Russia abandoned its interest in the eastern Pacific by selling Alaska and the Aleutian Islands to the United States in 1867.

Britain encountered stiff commercial competition from the United States, whose merchant fleet nearly surpassed Britain's in the 1850s. A boundary dispute in British Columbia's Puget Sound led to the establishment of a new British naval base at Esquimalt on the Sound in 1859. In 1862 the British moved their Pacific Squadron headquarters from Valparaiso in Chile to Esquimalt as a hedge against American assertiveness. Both countries also cast covetous eyes on the Hawaiian Islands, an independent kingdom dominated by Western shippers.

All the powers depended on the Royal Navy to command coalition forces against Asians who threatened Western lives and trade. So in 1864, during the

Japanese civil war, the British led 9 of their own warships, 4 Dutch, 3 French, and 1 American in bombarding and occupying Yokohama. From 1867 to 1869 warships of 7 Western navies under overall British command waged a concerted campaign against Chinese pirates.

Ironclads. European naval operations during and after the Crimean War revealed the need for technological change in warships. The combination of steam and sail became the accepted system of propulsion, and the old line-of-battle sailing ships were quickly phased out. Their obsolescence was equally hastened by the vulnerability of wooden hulls to powerful, new long-range and rifled guns using exploding shells.

France therefore constructed the world's first iron-plated wooden warship, 5,630-ton *Gloire,* from 1858 to 1860, with 13 more to follow by 1865. Britain, regarding these ships as a threat to its naval supremacy, especially in the Channel, responded with an even more superior vessel, the first iron-hulled and iron-plated warship. Displacing 9,180-tons, *Warrior* was built in 1859–61 and followed by 10 more by 1865, plus 8 new and converted wooden-hulled ironclads. French industry and finances could not keep pace in this arms race, especially since France's wooden ironclads and its only 2 all-iron vessels were downright inferior to Britain's. No other navy could even compete.

The naval operations around Mexico, the Crimea, and the barrier forts of China also demonstrated that inshore operations—naval bombardments of coastal and riverine defenses as well as amphibious assaults—had replaced fleet engagements for the foreseeable future. Gunboats, mortar vessels with high-trajectory fire, and coast-assault ships were required to augment heavy-gun ships in reducing forts and to support landing forces. This change was demonstrated again when a Sardinian naval bombardment overpowered the city of Gaeta near Naples to climax the 2-year war of Italian unification early in 1861. Such new offensive naval realities also had the opposite effect on all nations having coastlines, including Britain and France, namely, the need to strengthen coastal fortifications.

By the 1860s Britain's global peace was enforced by the world's strongest navy, some 2 dozen overseas naval bases and stations, and 45,000 regular troops deployed throughout the Empire. Of the navies which cooperated worldwide with the Royal Navy none did so more closely than the U.S. Navy. That cooperation was suddenly diminished in March 1861, when all but 3 American warships overseas were recalled home to fight the Civil War.

11

American Civil War

(1861–1865)

DURING THE WINTER AND SPRING OF 1860–61 the states of the American South proclaimed their independence from the Federal Union of the United States and formed their own nation, the Confederate States of America. The Civil War began in April 1861 when Southern troops bombarded and captured Fort Sumter, the U.S. coast defense installation in Charleston harbor. The Union, comprised of the industrialized states of the North and West, fought to reunify the nation and adopted an offensive strategy of invasion by land and water. The agricultural Confederacy, seeking only independence, assumed a defensive posture. Although fundamentally a land war, military operations were shaped in important ways by the seacoasts and rivers of the South.

Union Naval Strategy. President Abraham Lincoln ordered a naval blockade of the 2,700-mile-long Confederate coastline—from Chesapeake Bay in Virginia to the mouth of the Rio Grande in Texas. He charged the Secretary of the Navy, **Gideon Welles,** with enlarging the small U.S. Navy into a huge wartime force to close off or capture the South's major ports and to attack Southern merchantmen and warships.

The blockade carried the diplomatic risk of Great Britain becoming involved, because under the **Declaration of Paris** (see chapter 10) neutral merchant ships could trade freely with a warring nation's ports as long as those ports were not actively patrolled by the blockading navy. Lincoln's navy, in fact, never got large or effective enough to enforce the blockade completely and thereby have it considered legal under this prevailing tenet of international law. But the British government never challenged the blockade simply because it did not want to set a legal precedent that could backfire one day when Britain might be at war and the United States neutral—as would indeed be the case in World War I.

Although the United States had not signed the Declaration of Paris, the Union accepted its provisions. This included the outlawing of privateering, which the Confederacy practiced briefly during 1861. Britain wanted Southern cotton suf-

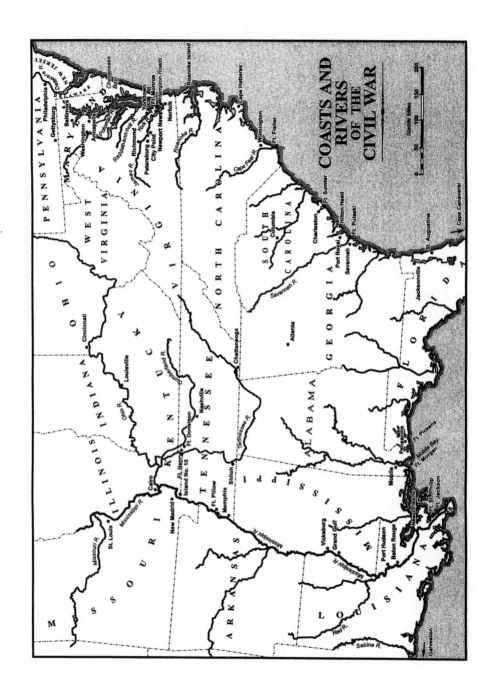

COASTS AND
RIVERS
OF THE
CIVIL WAR

Statute Miles
0   50   100   150   200

ficiently to allow blockade running merchant ships to operate out of British Bermuda and the Bahamas to run British products into the loosely blockaded ports and to bring out cotton. The Palmerston government also turned a blind legal eye to shipbuilders who constructed warships in Britain for sale to the Confederacy.

Many diplomatic incidents occurred as the Union responded by violating official British neutrality on the high seas. The most celebrated case was the **Trent affair.** In November 1861 U.S. steam frigate *San Jacinto* forcibly removed 2 Confederate diplomats from British passenger ship *Trent* in Caribbean waters. Britain rushed troops to Canada and transferred warships from the China Station to British Columbia, but Lincoln wisely released the diplomats.

Along with the blockade, the Union employed the navy to support the army. The aged General Winfield Scott in May 1861 recommended his so-called **Anaconda Plan,** a strategy compared to a giant snake squeezing its prey to death. While the navy blockaded the South's Atlantic and Gulf coasts, said Scott, a large army should move down the Mississippi River and establish forts along its shores, making it into a third blockaded coastline. Its seizure would cut off supplies from trans-Mississippi Texas and Louisiana to the eastern Confederacy. Union leaders, hoping for a short war, rejected the scheme as too time-consuming, although in fact it was implemented out of necessity as the conflict became prolonged.

The Mississippi was not the only river regarded as crucial. In 1862 the Union named all its armies for the rivers along which they invaded the Confederacy—the Army of the Potomac into Virginia, the Army of the Tennessee and those of the Ohio, Cumberland, and Mississippi into the middle South. Furthermore, the army provided its own troop transports for all river and coastal operations.

Administratively, the Union navy depended on Secretary Welles and Assistant Secretary **Gustavus V. Fox** to provide steam warships and ordnance for attacking coastal and river bank forts and for supporting the armies. By early 1862, 5 major naval commands had been created—the North and South Atlantic and East and West Gulf Blockading Squadrons and the Mississippi Squadron. The rank of flag officer, inadequate for these senior commands, was replaced that year by the ranks of rear admiral and commodore. **David G. Farragut** became the first rear admiral and in 1864 the only vice admiral in the U.S. Navy.

Confederate Naval Strategy. The Confederacy used its makeshift navy in typical continental fashion—coast and river defense and commerce raiding (*guerre de course*). President Jefferson Davis appointed **Stephen R. Mallory** Secretary of the Navy to authorize privateers, man and equip cruisers outfitted at home and in Europe, and build gunboats for defense of the harbors and rivers. Privateers proved only marginally effective early in the war, unlike the few sail-steam frigates obtained from European shipbuilders. With construction of warships hampered by an inadequate industrial base, Mallory promoted new technologies for his harbor and river squadrons: steam-powered (without sails) ironclad rams, steam launches, and hand-powered submarines carrying "torpedoes"—mines released from an underwater spar device. The senior Confederate naval rank was flag officer, except for admiral bestowed on **Franklin Buchanan** in 1862 and rear admiral on **Raphael Semmes** in 1865.

Regional armies and coastal districts reflected the Confederacy's defensive continental strategy and the subordination of naval forces to army commanders. By 1862 the Army of Northern Virginia defended the capital of Richmond, supported by the James River Squadron. The army's Department of South Carolina, Georgia, and Florida defended those coasts, augmented by the Charleston and Savannah River Squadrons. The Mississippi River Squadron helped defend New Orleans, the Mobile Squadron that port. Warships also operated on the North Carolina and Texas coasts and on several inland rivers.

Atlantic Blockade. The Union navy suffered a severe loss in April 1861, when Virginia troops suddenly forced it to evacuate Norfolk Navy Yard and scuttle several warships there. But the Union army held on to Fortress Monroe at the eastern end of the Virginia peninsula—the land between the James and York Rivers—and it easily recaptured nearby Newport News on the James. Captain **Samuel F. DuPont** recommended that joint army-navy expeditions capture coastal positions along the Southern coast to serve as coaling stations for the steam vessels of the blockading squadrons. Secretary Welles, reluctant at first, agreed, and Union amphibious expeditions captured Hatteras Inlet, North Carolina, in August and Port Royal (Hilton Head), South Carolina, in November 1861.

Not only did these conquests disrupt Confederate coastal shipping from Norfolk to Savannah but raised the specter of a possible Union invasion of the Confederacy from the sea. General Robert E. Lee was given command of South Carolina, Georgia, and eastern Florida coastal defenses in November 1861 to meet this threat. Because the main Confederate armies were concentrated in northern Virginia and Tennessee, Lee had insufficient manpower to protect all of the coast under his jurisdiction. He therefore decided on a defense-in-depth strategy, keeping his troops at selected inland places ready to concentrate wherever the enemy invaded the coast. Even then, Lee planned to give battle well behind the beach in order to remain beyond the range of Union naval guns.

Lee, however, misjudged Union intentions and naval capabilities. The North's strategy was to invade the South via Virginia and Tennessee, and its navy lacked the ships to mount and sustain a major seaborne invasion as far away as the Carolinas or Georgia. Union coastal seizures were designed only to establish advanced fortified bases for its blockade ships. So, between January and April 1862, the North Atlantic Blockading Squadron under Flag Officer Louis M. Goldsborough landed troops and provided gunfire support for the capture of Roanoke Island and adjacent North Carolina coastal towns. This included a gunboat flotilla under Commander **Stephen C. Rowan** which eliminated the defending Confederate squadron. In February and March Flag Officer DuPont and the South Atlantic Blockading Squadron, based at Port Royal, isolated Savannah by bombarding and capturing Ft. Pulaski, Georgia. It also occupied Amelia Island and St. Augustine, Florida, places that Lee by his strategy had elected not to defend.

Although Lee had been wrong about a seaborne invasion so far south, the senior Union general, George B. McClellan, did elect to invade Virginia via the Chesapeake Bay. To prevent it, the Confederate navy converted former U.S. steam frigate *Merrimack* into formidable ironclad *Virginia*. Its mission was to recapture Newport News on the James River and destroy the vulnerable wooden warships in Hampton Roads blockading Norfolk. Although this revolutionary coast defense vessel was unsuited for operations beyond inshore waters, McClellan and his naval commanders feared that it would destroy their fleet, take Newport News, drive all blockaders from the Southern coast, and even steam up the Eastern seaboard to bombard New York City!

The Union navy therefore rushed its own experimental ironclad *Monitor* to completion to counter the ex-*Merrimack*. The latter, commanded by Flag Officer Buchanan, sortied from Norfolk on 8 March 1862 and began sinking wooden Yankee steam frigates. The *Monitor* arrived next day and succeeded in defending the Union fleet (see essay). The *Virginia* returned to Norfolk, where by its mere presence it deterred further Union naval activity on the James. One week later, however, McClellan began moving his 100,000-man Army of the Potomac in 400 army transports and supply ships down the Chesapeake to Fortress Monroe in preparation for his advance against the rebel capital, Richmond. Because the Union navy refused to relax its watch on *Virginia* at Norfolk and thus to support McClellan's planned advance up the James, he choose instead to direct his attack on Richmond up the York River and without naval support.

Lee, transferred from the Carolinas to orchestrate the defense of Richmond, was assisted by McClellan's sluggish advance in this Peninsular campaign. McClellan laid siege to Yorktown in April, giving Lee time to shift his forces into position. Norfolk had already been isolated by the Union conquest of the Hatteras coast, so on 10 May Lee had Norfolk evacuated and *Virginia* blown up; its draft was too deep to enable it to retire up the James with the shallow-draft

Monitor and Merrimack

The battle between the *Monitor* and ex-*Merrimack* in March 1862 climaxed the technological revolution from wood, sail, and smoothbore solid-shot broadside batteries to iron, steam, and rifled shell-firing pivot guns. Steam-driven screw propellers gave a ship the maneuverability it lacked when dependent upon the wind for its sails. High-powered guns fired exploding shells that easily penetrated wooden hulls before exploding inside enemy ships, spreading destruction.

The USS (United States Ship) *Merrimack* was commissioned in 1857 as a 3,200-ton wooden frigate, powered by a 3-masted sailing rig and auxiliary steam engine with screw propeller. She was armed with a broadside battery of 40 rifled guns, mostly 9-inchers (the diameter of the muzzle and shell). Scuttled by the U.S. Navy during the evacuation of Norfolk in April 1861, the *Merrimack* was raised and rebuilt by the Confederate navy as ironclad ram CSS *Virginia*. Lieutenant John M. Brooke designed her to carry no sails and rely completely on a steam engine.

The *Virginia*'s main deck was enclosed by a slanting wooden structure overlaid with 4-inch-thick iron casemates forged from railroad track. Gunports were evenly spaced around the deck for 10 guns firing explosive shells: 1 bow and 1 stern 7-inch rifled pivot gun, 2 6-inch rifles and 6 9-inch smoothbores placed for broadsides. She was fitted with a 4-foot-long iron ram that projected from the bow just below the waterline. (Her exact reconfigured tonnage is unknown.) The *Virginia* was commissioned at Norfolk on 17 February 1862. The captain of her 90-man crew was Flag Officer Franklin Buchanan.

The USS *Monitor* was a 987-ton all-iron, steam-powered turret ship designed by Swedish naval architect John Ericcson, a pioneer in the development of screw propellers for warships. At the time the U.S. Navy let the contract, October 1861, a similar turret ship was being constructed in Britain on a design of Captain Cowper Coles, Royal Navy. The *Monitor*'s single revolving cylindrical turret, constructed of 8-inch-thick iron plate, housed 2 improved 11-inch Dahlgren smoothbore guns and rose over a flat low-freeboard deck. One observer likened the vessel unto a cheese box mounted on a large floating shingle. Worked by a crew of 47 men, *Monitor* was commissioned at New York Navy Yard on 25 February 1862, Lieutenant John L. Worden in command. She departed for Hampton Roads, Virginia on 6 March and had to be towed part of the way. The *Monitor* and "*Merrimac*" (by which the rebel ship was known and spelled during the war) were both on their maiden voyages, with unproved equipment and untried crews.

The *Virginia* and 5 small gunboats steamed out of Norfolk toward Newport News at high tide early on 8 March and immediately attacked the anchored 30-gun Union sailing sloop *Cumberland*. While shot and shell from *Cumberland*'s broadsides and pivot guns deflected off *Virginia*, the latter's fire bludgeoned the 20-year-old wooden ship. Buchanan then rammed *Cumberland*, sending her to the bottom with 121 of her crew. He turned on 1,800-ton 40-gun sailing frigate *Congress* (on which his brother was an officer), which ran aground in an attempt to maneuver. Set ablaze, with her broadside guns unable to bear on *Virginia*, *Congress* struck her colors. Union shore batteries, unaware of *Congress*'s submission, poured a heavy fire on *Virginia* and 2 Southern gunboats approaching to accept possession. Buchanan was severely wounded by this cannonade and responded by having *Virginia* unleash incendiary shells which completely destroyed *Congress*. She lost 120 men, including her captain.

Lieutenant Catesby ap R. Jones, executive officer, assumed command of *Virginia* and moved her toward 50-gun steam frigate *Minnesota*, sister ship of the original *Merrimack*. The *Minnesota* fired her pivot guns and broadsides and suffered several casualties before *Virginia* withdrew, unable to penetrate the shallow waters to destroy her. The *Virginia* anchored for the night, having lost her ram in the attack on *Cumberland*, with her armor plate loosened by repeated hits and her smokestack riddled, reducing engine power. Jones intended to finish off *Minnesota*, which had run aground, next morning. During the night *Monitor* steamed into Hampton Roads and took up position near *Minnesota*.

After daylight on the 9th, *Virginia* closed in for the kill, only to be intercepted by *Monitor*, supported by *Minnesota*'s fire. For 6 hours the 2 ironclads slugged it out, their shells exploding on each other's armor at close range. The *Monitor*, with only a 12-foot draft, proved more maneuverable because of the shallow waters; the *Virginia*'s 22-foot draft forced her to remain in a deeper but narrow channel. Just before noon a Confederate shell struck *Monitor*'s small pilot house, temporarily blinding Captain Worden. Fearing serious damage to his vessel, he withdrew *Monitor* to shallow water, whereupon Jones returned *Virginia* to her anchorage. The battle was over, a tactical draw. But because the Confederates decided not to renew the action, *Monitor* had succeeded by saving the wooden Union blockade fleet.

As a result of this epic duel, the Union navy began building more monitors, and both navies developed more ironclads for coastal and riverine operations. In Britain, the Royal Navy immediately cut down a 131-gun 3-decker wooden ship-of-the-line into an armored vessel with 4 turrets. It also laid down an iron-hulled coast defense ship. Freeing armored ships from the coasts for high seas operations under steam power alone was only a matter of time: 1869, when the British designed their first seagoing 9,330-ton turreted battleship without sails.

gunboats. Goldborough's Union gunboats pressed upriver, only to be driven back by shore batteries at Drewry's Bluff on the 15th. Union reinforcements were ferried down the Chesapeake to McClellan who, however, instead of pressing on against Richmond, fought his way back across the peninsula against Lee from the York to the James at the end of June. His exhausted army, covered by the navy, retired back down the James to Fortress Monroe.

The Union blockade intensified from the coastal enclaves at Norfolk, the Hatteras area, Port Royal, and Florida ports as far south as Cape Canaveral. The major obstacle was Charleston, through which blockade runners operated with impunity. In December 1861 and January 1862 the Union navy sank stone-filled hulks (the so-called stone fleet) to block the harbor entrance, but they quickly disintegrated in the tidal currents. The port was virtually impregnable due to intersecting arcs of defensive fire from Fort Sumter and 5 other harbor forts. Another obstacle developed with the construction of ironclad rams for the Charleston Squadron, 2 of which dashed out of the harbor in January 1863 to capture 1 blockader and disable another. Admiral DuPont's fleet was thereupon reinforced by 9 new coastal monitors.

When the navy ordered DuPont to use these monitors to attack the Charleston forts in April 1863, 1 was sunk and the rest repulsed. Admiral **John A. B. Dahlgren** relieved DuPont and landed troops on Morris Island at the southern entrance to the harbor during the summer. They captured it after heavy fighting, but the blockading ships were then plagued by rebel submarines. One of these, *Hunley*, sank a Union steam sloop off the harbor entrance in 1864. Because the blockade tightened around Charleston, many runners shifted to less risky Wilmington, North Carolina. As long as they got through with arms, Lee's army remained well equipped.

Western Rivers. Unlike the Virginia front, where the main armies remained stalemated through a succession of land campaigns from 1862 to 1864, the Western theater developed into a war of movement as the Union fought to seal off the Mississippi River and Gulf Coast. Its major objectives were the port city of New Orleans and the fortified river town of Vicksburg, Mississippi, where batteries prevented Union riverine warships from cutting Confederate supply routes to Texas. The vast distances of the region enabled armies to be moved, supplied, and supported by river steamers and railroads.

With superior resources and manpower, the Union early in 1862 undertook simultaneous campaigns down the Mississippi, Tennessee, and Cumberland Rivers and against Gulf Coast ports, forcing the Confederacy to shift its limited forces between these areas to try to stop all these advances. The U.S. Navy built a river gunboat flotilla on the western waters, and the army fashioned a fleet of rams to protect its transports. The heavy warships of the Gulf blockading squadrons patrolled and attacked Gulf coast ports. The C.S. Navy fashioned a makeshift gunboat squadron to patrol the entire Mississippi and built assorted warships on rivers which fed into it.

Flag Officer Farragut assembled his West Gulf Squadron and expeditionary forces at Ship Island off New Orleans to attack that city. Simultaneously, Flag Officer **Andrew H. Foote** gathered river gunboats and transports near Cairo, Illinois, on the Ohio River for the Union offensives along the Southern rivers. In February 1862 Foote's gunboats bombarded and captured Fort Henry on the Tennessee. Days later they supported General U. S. Grant's capture of Fort Donelson on the Cumberland, although Foote was badly wounded. Outflanked, the rebels abandoned Nashville on the Cumberland and sent their gunboat squadron to support the army's defense of Island No. 10 on the upper Mississippi. Grant and Foote penetrated up the Tennessee as far as Shiloh (Pittsburg Landing).

The Confederacy transferred army garrisons from Pensacola and Mobile on the Gulf, plus troops from New Orleans, to northern Mississippi for a surprise attack on Grant's army at Shiloh on 6 April. Two gunboats helped prevent a Union disaster and enabled Grant's reinforced army to drive back the Confederate army next day. Union army-navy forces simultaneously captured Island No. 10 on the Mississippi, whereupon the gunboats pressed on to Fort Pillow, which guarded the approaches to Memphis. This threat convinced Secretary Mallory that the main Union attack on New Orleans would be downriver, via Memphis, rather than from the sea. He therefore ordered the 8 gunboats of the Confederate Mississippi Squadron to defend Memphis instead of returning to New Orleans, in spite of the fact that Farragut began his bombardment of New Orleans's barrier forts on 18 April.

Stripped of major ground and naval forces, **New Orleans** lay virtually helpless against Farragut's fleet. Two dozen heavy warships and 19 mortar boats — each mounting 1 13-inch mortar for high trajectory fire — bombarded Forts Jackson and St. Philip below the city for a week. After midnight on 24 April Farragut ran the fleet past the forts and easily destroyed the few defending Confederate warships after dawn. Next day he occupied New Orleans and pressed up the Mississippi as far as Vicksburg, where his vessels were stopped by Confederate shore batteries. The fall of New Orleans caused the rebels to evacuate undefended Pensacola, which Farragut made his base of operations for blockading Mobile, Alabama.

Meanwhile, on the upper Mississippi, the Confederate squadron attacked and damaged Union gunboats and mortar boats bombarding Fort Pillow on 10 May, but the Union army rushed its ram flotilla to the aid of the navy. These riverine forces bombarded the fort until it was evacuated on 4 June. The Union squadron then moved on to Memphis, where it destroyed the Confederate squadron in a brief battle on the 6th. It pressed downriver as far as Vicksburg, whose guns stopped it. Later in the month Farragut's fleet ran the Vicksburg batteries from the south side but, lacking troops with which to invest the city, had to return to New Orleans. The supply link between the main Confederate states and the trans-Mississippi West had been reduced to the 125-mile strip of river between Vicksburg, Mississippi, and Port Hudson, Louisiana. In October 1862 Farragut needed only 5 warships to bombard and capture the port of Galveston, Texas, only to have it retaken by the rebel army 3 months later.

While the Confederate army maintained a stalemate in central Tennessee, Grant built up his forces along the Mississippi in order to capture **Vicksburg.** The army transferred its rams and gunboats to the navy's Mississippi Squadron, now commanded by the aggressive Admiral **David D. Porter.** In addition, an elite army Mississippi Marine Brigade was organized, employing specialized landing craft and supply vessels to police the rivers against raiders and guerrillas. Porter's gunboats supported army transports which landed 32,000 troops above Vicksburg at the end of December 1862, but the navy guns could not be brought to bear against the defensive shore batteries on the heights, forcing the Yankees to withdraw.

Grant and Porter spent the early months of 1863 trying to negotiate the Mississippi's swampy shores and fluky river levels to get the army around Vicksburg's commanding guns. In one attempt Porter's vessels became so mired in the wooded swamps that the army had to cut them free. In March, the Army of the Tennessee landed on the western shore above Vicksburg and constructed a road over which it moved to a point 50 miles below the city. The night of 16 April 12 of Porter's gunboats ran the gauntlet of Vicksburg's guns, which sank 1 of them. Transports and supply barges repeated the feat with some losses the night of the 29th. Next day Porter's squadron covered Grant's crossing to the east bank of the river south of the city, after which Grant struck out overland to encircle and besiege Vicksburg from the land side.

Porter convoyed reinforcements and supply ships to Grant's siege lines around Vicksburg and continuously bombarded the city from the river. Meanwhile, beginning in March 1863, Admiral Farragut supported the Army of the Gulf as it moved upriver from New Orleans as far as the Red River and besieged Port Hudson on the east bank of the Mississippi. These joint land-river operations finally starved both places into submission. Vicksburg surrendered on 4 July, Port Hudson 5 days later. The Union navy now had complete control of the Mississippi River, thereby blockading the eastern Confederacy from its Texas supply source. To further isolate that state, Farragut kept Galveston blockaded and in November landed an army force near Brownsville to tighten the blockade at the mouth of the Rio Grande.

High Seas Operations. The Confederacy attacked the North's economy by waging *guerre de course* against Yankee merchant shipping on the high seas. Aside from its brief use of privateers, which destroyed 17 merchantmen during 1861, the South commissioned navy cruisers for the purpose. Two of them were converted sail-steamers which departed Southern ports in 1861 to attack Union shipping in European waters. One, a sidewheeler, destroyed 2 rich merchantmen in the English Channel. The other, screw steamer *Sumter* under Captain Raphael Semmes, took 18 prizes in the West Indies before escaping across the Atlantic to Gibraltar, where it was trapped in port by Union pursuers and had to be sold. Both vessels were thereafter employed as blockade runners. A few smaller ships were converted into raiders which operated along the northeastern seaboard. The Confederacy needed genuine warships, however, which it purchased in Europe.

The U.S. Navy realized early that the South could never employ more than a few raiders to impair the North's overseas trade. It therefore elected to utilize seagoing steam frigates to hunt them down offensively rather than creating defensive convoys. On the other hand, Yankee shipowners were so terrified by the danger of rebel cruisers—and the soaring marine insurance rates that they caused—that the majority transferred their national registry from the U.S. to the British flag. Because this amounted to 800,000 tons of merchant shipping, it wrecked the U.S. merchant marine. But these same ships still carried the same Union goods and now under the protection of the Royal Navy. Yankee shippers who stayed with the U.S. flag lost 262 vessels totaling 110,000 tons to Confederate warships.

Five British-built rebel cruisers plundered Northern shipping, the most successful being screw sloop *Alabama*. Built by John Laird and Sons company in Britain, the 8-gun raider was commissioned off the Azores under the command of Captain Semmes in August 1862. She operated in the North Atlantic and West Indies and sank a Union blockading ship off Galveston in 1863. After sinking more merchantmen in the South Atlantic, *Alabama* made for the East Indies via Cape Town, South Africa for further depredations. She then returned to Europe for repairs at Cherbourg, France in June 1864, where she was challenged by Union steam frigate *Kearsarge*. Ignoring the fact that a commerce raider must never engage a more powerful warship, Semmes gave battle. The *Kearsarge* sank *Alabama* in the last sailing ship gunnery duel in history, after the raider had destroyed 69 Yankee merchantmen with a total value of almost $6 million.

Britain's clear violation of neutrality by condoning rebel warship construction peaked when the Confederacy contracted the Laird company to build 2 1,800-ton seagoing armored rams. Powered by sail and steam, these powerful ships were designed to mount 2 9-inch rifled guns in each of 2 turrets. However, in June 1863 General Lee's Army of Northern Virginia invaded Pennsylvania, only to be defeated by the Army of the Potomac at the epic Battle of Gettysburg on 3 July. Next day, in the West, Vicksburg surrendered. With Union military fortunes dramatically improving, Britain yielded to the demands of U.S. diplomats to seize the Laird rams. British as well as French companies continued to build warships for the Confederacy, however, and their blockade runners kept supplying weapons to the Southern armies throughout 1864.

Union Offensives of 1864. As strong as the Union navy was by the beginning of 1864, its blockade had failed to close Wilmington, Charleston, Savannah, Mobile, and Galveston—and many smaller bays and inlets used by the runners. Grant had succeeded in driving the Confederate army from Tennessee late in 1863, and Porter's squadron kept the Mississippi under Union control. But riverine operations were still hazardous, as Porter discovered when his vessels supported an abortive Union army drive up the Red River into western Louisiana during the spring of 1864. He lost several vessels to enemy artillery and nearly the whole flotilla to low water before it managed to extricate itself.

Lincoln elevated Grant to supreme command of the Union army in March 1864 for simultaneous offensives to defeat the Confederacy. Headquartered with the Army of the Potomac, Grant, supported by the navy in the Chesapeake Bay, planned to drive Lee's army back on Richmond. General William T. Sherman would push from Chattanooga to Atlanta and thence to the seacoast to link up with the blockade fleet. To deprive Lee's army of vital supplies, admirals Farragut and Porter would endeavor to close and even capture Mobile and Wilmington. Because Charleston and Savannah could not be captured from the sea, Sherman would take them from the land side.

The campaigns against Richmond and Atlanta commenced in early May 1864. In the Wilderness Campaign, Grant repeatedly attacked Lee and each time extended the left flank of his larger army around the right of Lee's. This kept Grant's back to the navy in the Chesapeake and his own base on the Rappahannock River. The Army of the Potomac fought its way to the James River, which it crossed in mid-June, and threw up siege lines south and east of Richmond and Petersburg, now occupied by Lee's army. Grant established his base at City Point on the James, where the navy supplied and supported the siege. Lee sent one-third of his army up the Shenandoah Valley and across the Potomac for a descent on Washington in early July. But Grant sealifted an army corps from City Point

Admiral David G. Farragut's Union fleet closes in on Confederate ironclad ram *Tennessee* at the Battle of Mobile Bay, 5 August 1864. Closest to her are wooden screw sloop *Ossipee* (*left center*), 2 double-turret monitors, and wooden steam frigate *Hartford*, Farragut's flagship (note his 2-star rear admiral's flag). Repeatedly hit by cannon balls and rammed, rendering her unable to maneuver, the *Tennessee* was surrendered by her admiral, Franklin Buchanan. (R. U. Johnson and C. C. Buel, eds. *Battles and Leaders of the Civil War*)

and another from New Orleans to drive back the rebel force from Washington and down the Shenandoah during the summer and fall.

In the Atlanta campaign, Sherman drove back the opposing Confederate army until the city fell in September 1864. The rebel army tried to lure him away from Atlanta by invading Tennessee, but other Union forces concentrated by river steamer and railroad at Nashville to destroy it there in December. Sherman, virtually unopposed, cut his overland communications and marched from Atlanta to the sea. His army took Savannah from the land side in mid-December and restored his logistics with Dahlgren's blockading fleet.

Meanwhile, on 3 August, Admiral Farragut landed an expeditionary force on the Alabama coast to assault the 2 barrier forts at the entrance to **Mobile Bay.** Two days later he fought a naval battle against Admiral Buchanan's small squadron inside the bay. Farragut's 14 wooden ships and 4 monitors ran past the forts and through a field of underwater torpedoes (mines). One of these sank a monitor, but Farragut in steam frigate *Hartford* attacked, rammed, and forced the surrender of the rebel flagship, ironclad ram *Tennessee*. Taking control of the bay, Farragut supported the army's capture of the barrier forts 2 weeks later. Without sufficient troops, he could not attack the city of Mobile, but he had closed it to trade.

Wilmington tenaciously defied the blockade. What was more, between August and November 1864 a Confederate cruiser, converted from a blockade runner, twice sortied from Wilmington to capture no fewer than 39 Yankee merchantmen in middle Atlantic and New England waters. Grant appointed Admiral Porter to command of the blockading squadron in October with orders to capture **Fort Fisher** at the entrance of the Cape Fear River leading to Wilmington. The assault, carried out by troops from City Point in December, was bungled by the inept army commander. Porter repeated the attempt in mid-January 1865 with the largest fleet yet assembled in the U.S. Navy's history—over 60 ships, including 5 ironclads and totaling 627 guns. The preassault barrage expended 22 tons of shells on the fort; 2 shells hit per second. Some 10,000 well-led troops, sailors, and U.S. Marines then overran Fort Fisher on the 15th.

Grant and Sherman orchestrated the final campaign by exploiting their waterborne mobility. Grant sent a division by sea from City Point to hold Savannah, thereby releasing Sherman to invade the Carolinas from the south. Late in January 1865 the navy transported half of Sherman's army from Savannah to the Port Royal blockading base as a feint against Charleston, while the other half advanced overland to capture Columbia in mid-February. In so doing, Sherman outflanked Charleston, Lee's last source of foreign supplies, forcing its evacuation. Simultaneous with Sherman's movements, part of the Union army in Nashville was transported by steamers up the Tennessee and Ohio Rivers to Cincinnati, by rail to Annapolis, Maryland, and by sea aboard army transports to Fort Fisher. It occupied Wilmington in late February and then linked up with Sherman's army pushing into North Carolina. As the vise closed on Lee, he abandoned Richmond but was overtaken by Grant's pursuing army. Lee surrendered on 9 April, just as a final army-navy assault captured Mobile, Alabama. The Confederacy collapsed, ending the war.

Naval power had played a critical role in the long struggle, although the Union blockade had never been completely successful; runners continued to use Galveston until it surrendered on 2 June. The 4 blockading squadrons had employed some 300 warships to capture 5 times as many blockade runners. Indeed, the blockade may have been run successfully as many as 8,000 times. Well-defended coastal forts had proved difficult to capture with less than 10:1 superiority in naval guns and assault troops. Union mobility on the inland rivers had been vital, however, and innovations in technology on both sides—ironclad rams, turreted monitors, high-powered rifled guns, submarines, and mines—transformed naval warfare.

Enforcing the Monroe Doctrine. The European powers took advantage of the Americans' preoccupation with the Civil War to exert their influence in the troubled affairs of Latin America. Civil war in Mexico resulted in unpaid debts, leading to the joint occupation of Veracruz by warships of Britain, Spain, and France in December 1861. After the others departed the following April, France attempted to enlarge its empire by declaring war on Mexico. Its squadron blockaded both coasts and landed a 40,000-man army that captured Mexico City in 1863 and established a former Austrian admiral as puppet ruler. The same year, Russia's Baltic Fleet visited New York, and the new Pacific Fleet visited San Francisco. Both visits, ostensibly shows of friendship, were actually designed to prevent the Russian navy from being blockaded at home during a diplomatic crisis with Britain.

These events—and Union victories after Gettysburg— convinced Palmerston to cooperate with the United States in matters regarding Britain's Franco-Russian naval rivals. During 1864 U.S. and British warships patrolled the Pacific coast from Esquimalt to Valparaiso as the Russians visited Hawaii and the Spanish seized the Chincha Islands claimed by Peru. To fight Spain, Peru and Chile mobilized their small navies, whereupon British, French, and U.S. warships intervened to prevent hostilities early in 1865. That September, however, the Spanish navy blockaded Valparaiso, leading Chile and Peru to declare war on Spain. The United States protested Spain's violation of the Monroe Doctrine by dispatching a 4-ship squadron round Cape Horn to join the British force in the eastern Pacific. Neither navy, however, could deter Spain from destroying Valparaiso by naval bombardment in March 1866. When the Spanish fleet approached Callao, Peru in May, however, British-built Peruvian ironclads and gunboats drove it off with heavy losses.

The United States restored its overseas naval squadrons, exerted diplomatic pressure on France to quit Mexico in 1867, and negotiated Spain's withdrawal from South America. Brazil, Argentina, and Uruguay fought a long war, 1864–70, against an aggressive Paraguay. River flotillas fought several actions until Brazil employed ironclads and monitors to destroy Paraguay's fleet. The United States mediated the peace.

Anglo-American tension simultaneously mounted over British fears of a possible American annexation of Canadian territories and U.S. displeasure over the damage inflicted by the British-built Confederate cruisers during the Civil War. Both nations desired compromise, which was achieved in the early 1870s, when Britain agreed to pay reparations over the so-called *Alabama* claims. By that time, the United States had reduced its 700-vessel wartime navy—the largest in the world in sheer numbers—to a mere 52. It then concentrated on industrial and internal growth while the British navy continued to police the world.

12

Naval Strategists and Arms Races
(1866–1914)

IN THE SECOND HALF of the Pax Britannica oceanic travel was quickened by steam technology and completion of the great canals at Suez (1869) and Panama (1914). Between 1860 and 1871 the reunification of the United States coincided with the unification of 3 major new nations during regional wars: Italy, Japan, and Germany, with Austria-Hungary joined in a dual monarchy. As they and the older powers grew jealous of Britain's might, they sought to emulate it—with merchant fleets, overseas colonies, and navies. The result was a new era of European imperialism and naval arms races that culminated in World War I.

Material Strategy. Technology transformed warships so rapidly that navies had to keep pace by constant discussion, experimentation, and changes in weapons, ship design, and training. This was especially expensive for Britain, because it meant altering and ultimately replacing the very ships which had guaranteed British naval supremacy. France and Russia did not try to keep up, concentrating instead on their armies. Nor did the United States, geographically isolated from real enemies on land or sea. But the new nations—Germany, Italy, and Japan—and several small states started navies from scratch, their construction based on the newest innovations.

All naval development focused on hardware—high-technology machines of war—rather than on the tried and true strategies and tactics of the past. The result was **technological determinism** or **material strategy:** the belief that weapons determined strategy, rather than the reverse. Lessons learned from the historical experiences of preindustrial times were minimized. **Quantitative** yardsticks rather than qualitative considerations defined naval policy: the numbers, sizes, speeds, and defensive armor of battleships and the long ranges, accuracy, and striking power of their guns. Tactical panaceas were also sought in alleged miracle weapons designed to neutralize the battleships—notably underwater mines and automotive torpedoes delivered by small torpedo boats and, after 1900, by submarines.

The material revolution was reflected in new specialized schools for advanced training in steam engineering, naval architecture (ship design and construction), ordnance (gunnery), and torpedo warfare. Naval officers and technical specialists debated the merits of each innovation in new professional journals such as the U.S. Naval Institute *Proceedings* (1873) and *Brassey's Naval Annual* (1886) of Britain. Within each navy traditionalist senior officers tried to resist the transformation demanded by younger machine-oriented specialists, especially engineers, whose struggle for acceptance into the regular line lasted until the end of the century.

The 1860s. Britain and France used the lessons of the American Civil War and 2 small European wars to build turreted "breastwork monitors" and ironclad "armored frigates" with 9-inch armored belts around the waterline and barbettes protecting each gun. Top speeds increased from 14 to 17 knots but did not progress much beyond 20 knots by 1900 due to the increased weight of ever-larger battleships. Most navies also adopted the underwater ram from the Civil War experience, led by Austria, whose navy helped Prussia wrest a coastal province from Denmark in a short war in 1864.

In the Seven Weeks' War of 1866 Prussia and newly unified Italy attacked Austria. When the Italian navy attempted to land an army on the Austrian island of Lissa in the Adriatic, it was driven off by coast artillery. Then, on 20 July, the Austrian fleet of Admiral **Wilhelm von Tegetthoff** attacked the Italians off **Lissa.** In the first fleet action between ironclads, Tegetthoff employed line-abreast tactics with his 7 ironclads to ram the 11 of the Italians, sinking 2 and putting the rest to flight. The Prussian army won the war, but Lissa convinced all navies to equip their battleships with rams until the turn of the century. Also, Tegetthoff's use of forward-firing guns led to their adoption over broadside batteries.

The 1870s. British engineer **Robert Whitehead,** working for Austria, in 1866 invented the **automotive torpedo**—a torpedo (mine) propelled through the water at 6 knots by a small motor. The Austrian and other small navies built coast defense torpedo boats to attack battleships, forcing the larger navies to follow suit. The most efficient torpedo boats were fast (19 knots) in order to run in and out to launch their torpedoes at battleships, yet sufficiently small (32 tons) to avoid being hit by big guns. Naval architects responded by giving the battleships machine guns and even more effective 4.7-inch "quick-firing guns" to shoot at torpedo boats as well as electric arc searchlights to spot them at night. Italian naval designer Benedetto Brin initiated cellular compartments with watertight bulkheads (walls) below the waterline on Italy's new battleships. Should a battleship be struck by ram or torpedo, capsizing could be prevented by counter-flooding compartments on the opposite side of the ship.

Brin's battleships reflected evolving naval technology: 12,000 tons, top speed 18 knots, and 17.7-inch guns in turrets armored with 24-inch plates of wrought iron, homogeneous steel, or compound iron and steel. The British followed suit, but France—defeated in the Franco-Prussian ground war of 1870–71—and the retrenching U.S. Navy could not. They replaced their steam frigates with virtually useless compromise ships: unarmored "cruising vessels," lightly armored "protected cruisers," and "armored cruisers." Intership communications were improved with the augmentation of signal flags by searchlights shuttered with venetian-blind blinkers flashing Morse code. Navies employed "squadrons of evolution" in tactical exercises that tested the new technologies.

The ultimate trial was actual battle. Russia built a new fleet of ironclads, monitors, and torpedo boats to weaken the Ottoman Empire in the **Russo-Turkish War** of 1877–78. Off Turkish Batum Lieutenant Commander **S. O. Makarov** employed spar and towed torpedoes before launching Whitehead torpedoes to sink a large Turkish warship. Russian riverine craft supported the army's drive up the Danube to permanently liberate Balkan Rumania, Bulgaria, and Serbia. Turkey then ceded Batum to Russia. In the **War of the Pacific** between Chile and allied Peru and Bolivia in 1879–81 both sides used British-built armored battleships but no underwater weapons. The Chilean fleet blockaded their enemies' coasts, sank the Peruvian ironclad which tried to break out, and launched invasions by land and sea. In the end, Bolivia surrendered its entire coastline to Chile.

The 1880s. The ever-improving battleship remained the backbone of the British navy. Russia's success against Turkey in 1878 and its pressure against Afghanistan in 1885 led Britain to dispatch fleets to the Black Sea in the former crisis and the Baltic in the latter. More intimidating to the Russians in both instances, however, was Britain's mobilization of coastal assault forces, adoption of antitorpedo nets for its ships, and experiments in mine warfare. This clear message of possible British amphibious attacks on Sevastopol in the Black Sea and Kronstadt in the Gulf of Finland forced Russia to back down.

The French navy challenged Britain's "blue water" battleship fleet with its own material alternative. The *jeune école* (young Turks) reformers of Admiral Théophile Aube argued that the torpedo boat had neutralized the battleship. Also, while French cruisers waged *guerre de course* on the high seas, torpedo boats could cross the Channel to attack British dockyard installations and anchorages. Although French torpedo boats never performed adequately, these arguments generated fears in Britain of a swift French invasion. The "bolt from the blue" school of thought in Britain advocated keeping the fleet at home to augment coastal fortifications in lieu of overseas blockades and naval battles. This argument was sustained by no fewer than 4 "invasion scares" between 1888 and 1900.

Mahan and Corbett

The leading philosophers of naval power in the years around 1900 were the American Alfred Thayer Mahan (1840–1914) and the Briton Julian S. Corbett (1854–1923). Both were self-taught historians. Mahan (rhymes with "the man") was son of Dennis Hart Mahan, West Point professor who had educated the entire generation of Civil War army leaders in the art of land warfare. An 1859 graduate of the U.S. Naval Academy, Mahan served on blockading vessels during the Civil War, after which he commanded 2 separate ships before being promoted to captain and appointed president of the U.S. Naval War College in 1886. Corbett graduated from Cambridge University with a law degree in 1875 but rarely practiced. His affluent family enabled him to travel widely and write undistinguished novels until 1889 when he turned his attention to naval history.

Both men studied the history of Britain and its navy in the age of sail in order to discern strategic and tactical principles of naval warfare. Mahan's magnum opus, *The Influence of Sea Power upon History, 1660–1783,* was published in 1890 and translated into several languages, followed by similar volumes on the wars of the French Revolution and Napoleon and biographies of Nelson and Farragut. After commanding protected cruiser *Chicago* he retired from the Navy in 1896 in order to concentrate on his prolific writings. These also included works on the Civil War, the small wars and contemporary issues of the day, and a book on theory, *Naval Strategy,* in 1911. Corbett wrote 5 books between 1898 and 1910 in chronological order from Drake (1580s) to Trafalgar (1805). He combined history and theory in his magnum opus of 1911, *Some Principles of Maritime Strategy,* in which he also examined the small naval wars of 1854 to 1905.

Mahan held that in order for a nation to become a "sea power" it required (1) an economic manufacturing base, (2) overseas colonies, and (3) a flourishing merchant marine—all protected by a powerful navy able to exert "command of the sea." History showed him that a superior fleet of battleships

In reality, France had greater strategic concerns on the continent. In 1881–82 Germany, Austria-Hungary, and Italy formed the Triple Alliance; its combined military strength obliged France to give greatest attention to the army. Italy increased its naval strength in the Mediterranean so dramatically that France retaliated with an economic offensive and construction program of superior battleships that nearly wrecked the Italian economy. Battleships were simply too expensive for any country to hope to match Britain's. All other navies—includ-

achieved naval supremacy by defeating enemy fleets in battle. He minimized the importance in history of commerce warfare and trade protection (convoy), blockade, amphibious operations, and limited wars. He virtually ignored modern naval technology.

Corbett shared Mahan's disdain for commerce protection, especially the threat to shipping from torpedo boats and crude submarines. But he criticized the big-battleships/big-battle determinism of Mahan and studied the subtle importance of blockade, amphibious warfare, and the relationship of the navy to army objectives. Corbett argued that only great naval powers such as Britain could develop a coherent maritime strategy. This was because only they were capable of (1) commanding the seas with a navy strong enough to deter war in Europe and protect the homeland, and of (2) isolating disputed overseas objectives—islands and peninsulas—from outside naval interference or supply, which enabled the navy to support ground forces engaged in pacifying the targeted territory. From his evidence Corbett was advancing a theory of fighting limited wars.

Neither Mahan nor Corbett could overcome the prevailing school of material strategy—modern machine weapons exemplified by the big-gun armored battleship and including the mine, torpedo, and submarine. Also, both men were dead wrong about the insignificance of commerce warfare, especially the utility of underwater weapons for attack and the need for countermeasures against them. But the advice of each man was actively sought by their superiors—Mahan's by the U.S. Navy in the Spanish-American War of 1898 and by big-navy advocate President Theodore Roosevelt; Corbett's by the British Admiralty before and during World War I, in which Corbett served as official historian of the Royal Navy. Mahan's theories contributed to the imperialism and arms race that led to World War I. Corbett's theories on limited war proved untimely, because his book of 1911 appeared only 3 years before the outbreak of the total war of 1914–18; his ideas would have greater relevance in the limited wars after 1945. Mahan was promoted to rear admiral on the retired list in 1906; Sir Julian Corbett received his knighthood in 1917.

ing the United States—concentrated instead on coastal defenses, torpedo boats, gunboats, and monitors. They also experimented with the submarine, which had not survived the American Civil War for lack of suitable engines and underwater stability. Technological improvements in Sweden and the United States during the 1880s, however, began to surmount these shortcomings.

Despite such alternative weaponry Britain reaffirmed its material blue water strategy in the Naval Defense Act of 1889. This legislation restored the 2-power standard against Britain's most likely enemies—France and Russia. At a minimum the Royal Navy's battleship strength should equal the combined number of Franco-Russian battleships, but ideally it should outnumber them 5:3. The law authorized the construction of 10 new battleships, 42 cruisers to support them, and 18 torpedo gunboats over the next 5 years.

Historical Strategy. In spite of the technological determinism, advanced strategic thinking had been developing in the armies of Europe, inspired by Prussian theorist Karl von Clausewitz early in the century. Such military philosophy was rooted in historical events of the preindustrial era, especially the wars of Napoleon. American Commodore **Stephen B. Luce,** a reformer in naval education, founded the U.S. Naval War College in 1884 to develop naval philosophy. He appointed Captain **Alfred Thayer Mahan** to the faculty for a series of lectures on the uses of navies in history. In 1890 Mahan published these lectures in book form—*The Influence of Sea Power upon History, 1660–1783.*

Mahan's book took Europe and the United States by storm, initiating a golden age of naval philosophy that lasted until the year of his death, 1914. The British government, navy, and people were especially struck by Mahan's insights which not only glorified Britain's naval past but also provided a justification for its contemporary naval power. He argued that British command of the sea with a superior fleet of line-of-battle ships had accounted for British prosperity and power during the age of sail.

One of Mahan's reasons for expressing these ideas was to convince his own country to follow Britain's example. Not only was he relatively successful, but he unintentionally inspired most other nations to embrace his theories uncritically. The major powers—France, Russia, Italy, Japan, Germany—not only accelerated battleship construction but also embarked on overseas imperial conquests. Many small nations that could not build battleships purchased them from Britain. Certain British pundits and historians had been writing in a vein similar to Mahan since the late 1860s, most importantly **Julian Corbett,** who produced his pivotal book in 1911—*Some Principles of Maritime Strategy.* Other nations created war colleges on the U.S. model, and new naval philosophers joined the discussion dominated by Mahan and Corbett (see essay).

History at the hands of amateur scholars—politicians, admirals, and patriots—is always in danger of being misused or distorted to suit particular agendas. Their appropriation of the writings of Mahan, Corbett, and others at the turn of the century was no exception. Historical arguments were employed by continental nations to justify expensive battle fleets and overseas imperialism. The result was a naval arms race and series of regional rivalries and conflicts which helped bring about World War I. In naval warfare—in which even Mahan was often wrong—the material strategists followed Britain's historical example to place their faith almost entirely in modern battleships at the expense of the commerce warfare and amphibious operations so important in the past.

The 1890s. Britain's new battleships achieved a standardized formula which other navies imitated: 12 to 14 inches of face-hardened steel armor and 2 main battery turrets mounted fore and aft along the center line. Each turret had 2 breech-loaded 12-inch guns which fired steel-capped, armor- and semi-armor-piercing exploding shells. The rule of thumb became 1 inch of gun caliber had to equal 1 inch of armor. Broadside firing returned with the wide arcs of fire from the turrets, augmented by secondary batteries of 6-inchers and quick-firing guns. Long-range gunnery duels were now possible between 2,000 and 6,000 yards. Accuracy was improved by the addition of a gyroscope to compensate for the roll of the ship, resulting in "continuous aim" at the target. The battleships and their supporting cruisers could attain speeds up to 15 knots in battle. But rigid formalist line-ahead tactics were imposed after a fatal collision during maneuvers in 1893 sank the fleet flagship, taking the life of the innovative Admiral Sir George Tryon.

The menace of torpedoes led to the development of a new type vessel—the "torpedo boat destroyer," equipped with quick-firers and its own torpedoes. Powered by the first steam turbine engines, it could attain speeds in excess of 30 knots to attack torpedo boats. Because of its own torpedo capability it soon assumed the designation of simply "destroyer" and became part of the flotilla of cruisers protecting the battle line. By 1899 the submarine had developed into the major underwater menace thanks to improved stability and electric storage batteries which charged an internal combustion engine (and later the oil-driven diesel engine). The sub could cruise 500 miles on the surface at 10 knots or submerged at 6½ knots, firing torpedoes of 30-knot speed at targets 800 yards away.

These material improvements to navies, combined with Mahan's historical arguments for fleets and colonies, dramatically affected the international balance of power. In 1890 Kaiser Wilhelm II initiated an aggressive German foreign policy aimed at Russia and France on land and Britain at sea. This prompted France and Russia to conclude a defensive alliance in 1894. At the same time, the United States embarked on a program of battleship construction potentially dangerous to British hegemony in the Caribbean. French and Russian battleships—the objects of Britain's 2-power standard—remained inferior to Britain's, although the new allies pressed ahead with submarine and torpedo development, forcing the British to do the same. Very soon, however, the high quality of German and U.S. battleships convinced Britain to redirect its 2-power standard away from the Franco-Russian fleets to match the theoretical combination of Germany and the United States.

German Navalism. Kaiser Wilhelm had a canal dug from Kiel across the base of the Jutland peninsula, enabling his new warships to shift quickly and safely between the Baltic Sea and Germany's naval bases on the North Sea coast. In 1897 he appointed as naval minister the forceful Admiral **Alfred von Tirpitz,** who lost no time in developing his "risk theory" against Britain. Because the British fleet was scattered throughout the world protecting the Empire, he calculated that Britain would not dare risk war if the main German battle fleet, concentrated in the North Sea, numbered two-thirds the size of Britain's total battleship strength. Tirpitz therefore had the Reichstag (parliament) pass 2 naval bills in 1898 and 1900 to achieve this goal. Britain responded by increasing its inventory to some 40 battleships by 1905.

The Anglo-German naval arms race was on, not only in numbers of battleships but also in the technical features of each. Lightweight steel covered the entire vessel, steam turbines increased speed, and wireless maritime radios enhanced intership communications. Shipboard electricity and telephones enabled gun director personnel to coordinate the turrets for salvo fire at ranges up to 15,000 yards. The culmination of these technological improvements was HMS (His/Her Majesty's Ship) *Dreadnought,* designed by Admiral Sir **John Fisher,** First Lord of the Admiralty, and built over 1905–6. This 21-knot battleship displaced 18,000 tons; mounted 10 12-inch guns in twin turrets on or near the centerline; carried no secondary batteries except for 27 4-inch quick-firing anti-torpedo-boat guns; and included 5 18-inch torpedo tubes below the waterline. Similar vessels were already under construction in Germany and the United States. The *Dreadnought* design became the standard for all navies, rendering existing battleships nearly obsolete as "predreadnoughts."

Imperial Rivalries. By contrast, the humble gunboat formed the backbone of Western naval forces supporting colonial expansion in the Middle East, Africa, East Asia, and the Pacific islands. In the Mediterranean, Egypt proved incapable of operating the Suez Canal, prompting Britain and France to take control of it in 1876. In 1881 naval bombardments of Tunisian ports initiated a French protectorate over the entire country. In 1882 Italy pushed down the Red Sea to annex Eritrea, and an Egyptian army revolt led Britain to dispatch a fleet and troops from Malta to Alexandria and gunboats to occupy the Suez Canal. In July, ironclads joined the gunboats in shelling the Egyptian forts prior to their capture by assault. Britain turned Egypt into a British protectorate, with Alexandria serving as the key intermediate base between Gibraltar and India.

Beginning with Belgium's conquest of the Congo in 1877, the European powers carved up Africa. In 1882 France used warships and landing forces to pacify Madagascar which it made into a protectorate. From 1883 to 1885 Germany employed gunboats and marines to establish colonies in East, West, and Southwest Africa. Britain occupied the coast of Kenya in 1889 and created a protectorate over Zanzibar in 1890. A fanatical Arab uprising in the Sudan caused the British to send gunboats up the Nile to capture Khartoum in 1884–85 and support the conquest of Sudan from 1896 to 1898.

The Dutch-descended Boer farmers of South Africa tried to throw off British rule, resulting in the **Boer War** (1899–1902). With absolute control of the surrounding seas the British navy landed and supported a large army in South Africa and blockaded German contraband supplies to the Boers at neighboring Portuguese Mozambique. When the Boer army besieged Ladysmith in the interior, 3 British naval brigades participated in the relief expedition. Britain won the war but granted South Africa dominion status, retaining only the vital naval base at Cape Town.

Britain and the navy thwarted Turkish expansion into the Persian Gulf region by annexing Bahrain and enlarging the Trucial System in the 1880s and 1890s. When Royal Navy patrols failed to suppress piracy in the Indian Ocean, Britain annexed the entire Malay peninsula. Among the Pacific island groups claimed by the powers was Samoa, disputed by Britain, Germany, and the United States. They all dispatched warships there only to have them destroyed by a hurricane in 1889. The island was thereafter jointly administered by Germany and the United States. The latter also established a coaling station at Pearl Harbor, Hawaii, in 1887.

British naval forces policed the Western Hemisphere, to which the United States acquiesced until the 1890s when Spain brutally suppressed an uprising in Cuba, 2 German warships forced economic concessions from Haiti, and Britain disputed the border of Venezuela and British Guiana. A desire to free Cuba from Spanish rule gripped the American people, and early in 1898 the United States sent the battleship *Maine* to riot-torn Havana to protect American lives. But in mid-February the *Maine* mysteriously exploded and sank, taking the lives of 260 crewmen. Suspecting Spanish treachery—a floating mine (probably true)—and influenced by other factors, the United States declared war in April.

Spanish-American War (1898). The U.S. Navy, administered partly by Assistant Secretary **Theodore Roosevelt,** already had 2 fleets in place to attack the Spanish Empire. One of them, centered on 4 cruisers under Commodore **George Dewey,** had been dispatched to British Hong Kong. It attacked and destroyed the antiquated Spanish squadron anchored at Manila Bay in the Spanish Philippines on 1 May, sinking 7 ships. The other was the main Atlantic fleet under Admiral William T. Sampson. Before it could act, Spanish admiral Pascual Cervera crossed the Atlantic with 4 armored cruisers and 3 destroyers and slipped into Santiago harbor on Cuba's southern coast. These were immediately blockaded by the squadron of Commodore W. S. Schley. Sampson soon arrived with the main force, built around 4 new battleships, and seized Guantanamo Bay 40 miles to the east as his advanced base.

The Americans mounted a ragged amphibious assault with their volunteer army at Daiquiri and Siboney in late June, fighting their way 20 miles up the coast to Santiago. Once their artillery reached the heights over the harbor Cervera had no choice but to flee. As the Spanish warships cleared the harbor on 3 July Schley (then Sampson, who arrived late in the battle) destroyed each one by sinking or running them aground. Later in the month another landing force took Puerto Rico, and in August Admiral Dewey's fleet bombarded and captured Philippine Manila then landed army forces to occupy it. Spain immediately capitulated by ceding its remaining colonies to the United States: the Philippines, Guam in the Mariana Islands of the central Pacific, Puerto Rico, and Cuba. The latter was soon given its independence as a virtual American protectorate, with Guantanamo Bay leased as a permanent U.S. naval base. Spain sold the rest of the Marianas as well as the Caroline Islands to Germany.

With the additional occupation of uninhabited Wake Island and annexation of the Hawaiian Islands in 1898–99, the United States had some semblance of an overseas empire, though quite minor by European standards—the Philippines and a few scattered islands throughout the Pacific (including Alaska's Aleutian group) and in the Caribbean. The native Filipinos, despite the promise of eventual independence, revolted in 1899. U.S. gunboats and a brutal antiguerrilla army campaign ended major resistance in 1902, although the Philippine Insurrection dragged on the rest of the decade. Spain picked up a few crumbs of empire by occupying West African Guinea and Rio de Oro, 1902–7.

Rise of Japan. The Japanese civil war, which involved rival naval forces, ended in 1868, whereupon the government of the Mejii Restoration created the Imperial Japanese Navy and turned to Britain for technical assistance. The army, however, dominated Japanese strategic policy, essentially because continental China remained at the center of Asian affairs. The navy supported the army in countering Western intrusions into politically chaotic China and adjacent countries. This included French and U.S. naval bombardments and assaults on aggressive forts at the entrance to Korea's Han River in 1866 and 1871 and an 1873 French naval expedition which fought "Black Hand" Chinese pirates on Vietnam's Red River and captured Hanoi. In 1874 Russia established a naval base at Vladivostok near the Korean border. China began to strengthen its navy during the decade, largely with French help, partly as a defense against Japan.

Japan employed warships to extend its seaward defenses against Russia and China. In 1874 the Japanese mounted a punitive expedition against pirates of Chinese Formosa (Taiwan). In 1875 Japan occupied the Kurile Islands to the north and the Bonin Islands to the south. In 1879 Japanese forces seized the Ryukyu Islands (principally Okinawa) opposite Chinese Shanghai and in 1891 the Volcano Islands (mainly Iwo Jima) to the south. In the 1880s the pro-German Japanese army caused the navy to replace its British advisers with Germans and French, whose *jeune école* advocates convinced the navy to obtain swift cruisers and torpedo boats. Japan's most direct concern was Chinese Korea, pointed like a pistol at Japan but temporarily protected when a British naval demonstration prevented Russia from taking possession of Korea's Wonsan Harbor.

China employed a northern and a southern fleet to guard its long coastline but continued to support the Black Hand pirates against the French in Vietnam. In 1883–84 French ironclads recaptured Hanoi and bombarded Hué, forcing the Chinese out of Vietnam. The **Sino-French War** ensued. In August 1884 a force of 8 modern French cruisers plus torpedo boats annihilated a squadron of 11 wooden Chinese warships at Foochow. The same force attacked Formosan ports in October and destroyed a relief expedition the following February, ending the war. In 1887 France created the colony of Indochina out of Vietnam and Cambodia. A French naval demonstration off Bangkok in 1893 forced Siam to cede Laos to France. China had to submit to Russian demands for concessions along Manchuria's Amur River. But China also purchased 2 German-built battleships and 7 other modern warships, concentrating them at the newly fortified naval base of Port Arthur on the Yellow Sea.

Realizing China's relative weakness, Japan elected to conquer Korea and thereby deter further Western incursions into Eastern waters. The **Sino-Japanese War** began with the navies of both countries landing troops near Seoul in the summer of 1894. Admiral Sukenori Ito bombarded the Chinese bases at Port Arthur and Weihaiwei in August while the Japanese army drove north from Korean Pyongyang toward the Yalu River. The Chinese fleet of 2 battleships and 8 armored cruisers under Admiral Ting Ju-ch'ang escorted a convoy of reinforcements to the mouth of the Yalu, only to be intercepted there by Ito's 8 superior cruisers. In the **Battle of the Yalu River**, 17 September, Ito maneuvered in close line-ahead with concentrated fire to split the ragged Chinese formation and sink 5 cruisers; 2 others ran aground next day. Ting retreated with his remaining ships to Port Arthur, eluding Ito's blockade to escape to Weihaiwei in November. The Japanese army landed above Port Arthur and captured it, doing the same at Weihaiwei; there Ting committed suicide after his torpedo boats failed to break through Ito's blockade in February 1895. Japan's overland drive into Manchuria forced China to submit.

Led by Russia, the Western powers interceded in the peace settlement to prevent Japan from annexing any part of the East Asian mainland, namely Port Arthur, but Japan was allowed to annex islands—Formosa and the Pescadores. In 1896–98 Russia forced China to lease Port Arthur for a Russian naval base. When Russia began to move into Korea, Japan ordered modern battleships, cruisers, destroyers, and torpedo boats from Britain, Germany, France, and Italy for the navy.

A defeated China was powerless to resist European navies from seizing Chinese seaports between 1897 and 1900: Russia in Dairen near Port Arthur, Germany in Tsingtao, France in Kwangchow Bay, and Britain in Weihaiwei. The United States became a Western Pacific naval power by its acquisition of the Spanish Philippines. But instead of occupying Chinese territory, the United States protected its trade position by proclaiming the "Open Door" policy: China's trade should be open to all nations, none of which should seek to politically dismember the country. The other powers concurred.

The anti-Western **Boxer Rebellion** of fanatical nationalists erupted in 1899 when they besieged the foreign legations at Peking. A British-led naval force of over 30 warships from Britain, Germany, France, Russia, Japan, the United States, Italy, and Austria was repulsed in an assault on the Taku forts at the Peiho River. But the fleet bombarded them into submission early in 1900. That summer the Western and Japanese navies landed 18,000 troops which captured Tientsin, drove up the Peiho, and fought their way into Peking. With the Boxers crushed, Russia occupied Manchuria, further stimulating Japanese naval expansion. By 1900 East Asia had become a strategic arena in its own right, one closely linked to the naval arms race in Europe.

Naval Alliance Systems. The massive naval building programs of the other powers created financial strains on Britain's resources to maintain global stability. Between 1900 and 1907, therefore, Britain initiated treaties with kindred nations to protect its far-flung colonies and to assist it against the challenge of the German fleet. The 2 goals were combined from 1904 to 1906, when Britain recalled its overseas heavy fleet units to concentrate against the German High Seas Fleet in the North Sea.

The British had growing doubts about the efficacy of battleships operating in the North Sea in the face of greatly improved German submarines. When Admiral Fisher, architect of *Dreadnought,* became First Sea Lord in 1904, he promoted a hybrid vessel, the battle cruiser, to give the Royal Navy numerical superiority in capital ships over the Germans. It mounted the guns of a battle-ship, and its light armor gave it the speed of a cruiser in order to outmaneuver enemy battleships and lurking submarines. In addition, when coordinated by wireless communications from shore bases, battle cruisers could be deployed abroad to protect trade and colonies. Fisher also advanced submarines to repel invasions of Britain's shores. Although he retired in 1910, his successors, due to the soaring costs of "dreadnoughts," curtailed some battleship construction in favor of battle cruisers and submarines.

Germany began the century determined to build sufficient modern battle-ships, 38 in all, to deter Britain from dominating the North Sea—Tirpitz's risk theory. But *Dreadnought* made even Germany's newest battleships obsolete, forc-ing the Germans to cease construction for 2 years (1905–7) until they could de-sign and build their own dreadnoughts. The appearance of the British battle cruiser in 1908 created another challenge to which Germany was even slower to respond with battle cruisers of its own. The costs were staggering to the Ger-man economy, but Tirpitz now demanded 60 capital ships. Neither the army nor the liberal members of the Reichstag would support it, the army because it had to be enlarged to counter the French army. The army prevailed in 1912, by which time Britain had reconcentrated its main fleet units in home waters, wrecking the Tirpitz plan.

Domestic politics and economics figured subtly but importantly in the Eu-ropean naval arms race. The growing liberalism of the era posed an internal threat to the monarchies of the continent. The kings, aristocrats, generals, and admirals of Germany, Russia, Austria-Hungary, and Italy faced parliamentary opposition to high taxes for extravagant military and colonial programs that hurt the working classes, which needed funds for social reforms. Appeals by the rul-ing elites to nationalism and defense achieved parliamentary funding but mostly for armies at the expense of navies. The opposite was true in democratic Britain and the United States whose equally tax-conscious legislatures concentrated de-fense spending on their navies, neither country having need of a large army. Republican France pragmatically focused on its army to challenge Germany's.

Britain's diplomatic offensive of 1900–1907 created formal and informal al-liances with the other major naval powers both to isolate the German navy and to guard Britain's overseas possessions and trade. In descending order of naval strength, these powers were the United States for the Western Hemisphere, Japan for Asia, France for the western Mediterranean, and Russia for the Baltic and Black Seas.

The United States asserted naval hegemony in the Americas in 1900–1901, when Britain granted it exclusive rights to build and fortify the canal across

Panama. From 1904 to 1906 Britain closed its West Indies naval bases and turned over the bases at Halifax and Esquimalt to the dominion of Canada. Naval-minded President Theodore Roosevelt (1901–9) fashioned the third largest battleship fleet in the world. When Colombia balked at granting the U.S. canal rights in Panama in 1903, Roosevelt engineered a successful Panamanian revolution, supported by a U.S. gunboat, and proceeded with the canal's construction (completed in 1914).

Roosevelt in 1903 also responded to a German naval bombardment of fiscally insolvent Venezuela by establishing his "big stick" policy to police the Caribbean. As a corollary to the Monroe Doctrine the United States declared its right to intervene in Latin American countries to maintain economic order and prevent interventions by other powers. As a result, between 1905 and 1916 U.S. warships landed Marines and army forces in several Caribbean nations, including Mexico in 1914. In the process the Caribbean Sea became the strategic pivot of the U.S. Navy's operations in the Atlantic and Pacific.

Japan and Britain concluded an alliance in 1902 to deter Russian expansion in East Asia. By its terms Britain agreed to intervene in any Russo-Japanese conflict only if a third nation—Germany and/or France—joined Russia. Britain and Japan also allowed U.S. warships to use their Asiatic bases to intimidate the Russians. In addition, the United States joined Britain and Japan in establishing a permanent gunboat force to patrol the Yangtze River, protecting their merchants and shoring up China's Manchu government. In 1903, Russia threatened to intervene in Korea, whereupon 3 U.S. battleships dropped anchor at Chinese Chefoo as a warning.

Russo-Japanese tensions mounted as the Russians strengthened their naval bases at Vladivostok and Port Arthur, to which they dispatched a fleet by sea and prefabricated submarines over the Trans-Siberian railroad. Before a Russian army could follow, Japan initiated hostilities with a sneak attack on the Russian squadron at Port Arthur. On the night of 8–9 February 1904 10 Japanese destroyers swept into the roadstead, launching torpedoes which disabled 2 Russian battleships and damaged a cruiser. In the morning the 6 new battleships of the Japanese fleet under Admiral **Heihachiro Togo** bombarded the other Russian vessels. Simultaneously, a cruiser force escorted Japanese army transports to Inchon (Chemulpo), Korea, and destroyed a Russian cruiser and gunboat there. Next day, the 10th, Japan officially declared war.

Russo-Japanese War (1904–5). In spite of its supposed inferiority, Japan held the strategic advantage over Russia. From its nearby home ports the Japanese navy had only to control the Yellow Sea and support the army's offensives into Korea and Manchuria. In contrast, the Russian army and navy were spread out between the European Baltic and Black Sea regions and the Far East. Admiral Togo mined and blockaded the entrances to Port Arthur, enabling Japan's army to drive through Korea toward the Yalu River. Admiral S. O. Makarov took command of the Russian Pacific fleet and laid his own minefield against the blockaders. In April 1904, however, he perished when his flagship struck a Japanese mine and went down with all hands. Meanwhile, to relieve Port Arthur, Russia prepared its Baltic fleet for the long voyage from Europe.

In May 1904 the main Japanese army crossed the Yalu, and the navy landed a second army above Port Arthur, although Togo lost 2 of his 6 battleships to Russian mines. Admiral Wilhelm Vitgeft's Russian fleet failed to break Togo's blockade and reach Vladivostok in June but tried again on 10 August. Togo engaged it in the **Battle of the Yellow Sea.** Although Vitgeft's 6 battleships battled their way through Togo's fleet, Togo gave chase and caught up in late afternoon. The gunnery of Japan's 4 battleships and 10 cruisers killed Vitgeft and broke up the Russian formation. Most ships escaped back into Port Arthur, and several fled to neutral Chinese ports where they were interned under international law by U.S. warships. The 3 Russian cruisers based at Vladivostok headed south, only to be driven back, 1 of them sunk, by 6 of Togo's cruisers on 14 August.

The Japanese navy was free to support the army's descent on Port Arthur and prepare for the arrival of Russia's "Second Pacific Squadron." This motley collection of ageing and new but inferior vessels embarked on its 18,000-mile voyage from the Baltic to the Pacific in October 1904 under the command of Admiral Zinovi P. Rozshestvensky. After bombarding a helpless group of British North Sea fishing trawlers it mistook for Japanese torpedo boats, the main force lumbered down the European and West African coasts while 1 division detoured through the Mediterranean and Suez Canal. They rejoined at Madagascar in the Indian Ocean at the end of December. Earlier that month Japanese army artillery sank 2 anchored battleships at Port Arthur, and the beleaguered port surrendered on 2 January 1905, forcing Rozshestvensky to head for Vladivostok. In spite of numerous machinery breakdowns, low morale, and mutinous crews, the fleet left Madagascar in March. Joined by another squadron from the Baltic off French Indochina in early May, it headed north.

Togo meanwhile exercised his fleet of 4 modern battleships, 25 cruisers, 21 destroyers, and 60 torpedo boats in anticipation of intercepting the Russian fleet near Tsushima Island in the straits separating Korea and Japan. Rozshestvensky's 8 battleships, 12 cruisers, 9 destroyers, and assorted auxiliary ships entered the Korea Straits on 27 May 1905 and were taken under fire in early afternoon. The **Battle of Tsushima** began in parallel battle lines, but Japanese maneuvers and gunnery soon turned the Russian line, wounding Rozshestvensky and sinking or disabling several battleships by nightfall. Japanese destroyers and torpedo boats finished off most of them in the darkness. So thoroughly defeated were the Russians that their surviving ships surrendered the following morning. Togo's fleet had sunk 6 battleships, 7 cruisers, and 5 destroyers, capturing the rest, and at a cost of only 3 torpedo boats. The Russians lost some 5,000 men killed, the Japanese 600. Three Russian cruisers escaped to Manila, where they were interned by the Americans, and 1 reached Vladivostok.

Japan's destruction of Russia's fleets prompted political upheavals and naval mutinies in Russia, notably by the crew of Black Sea battleship *Potemkin,* which sailed her to Rumania and went into exile. The war had also exhausted Japan's economy. So both nations accepted President Roosevelt's offer to mediate a peace settlement at Portsmouth Navy Yard in New Hampshire in September 1905. Russia gave up Port Arthur to Japan and with the other powers accepted the Open Door in China, whose Manchu dynasty was replaced by a republican government in 1912.

A new balance of Pacific powers and naval arms race ensued between Japan and the United States. Roosevelt therefore divided the navy into the Atlantic and Pacific fleets in 1906 and 1907, at the end of which year he dispatched the 16 battleships from the Atlantic—his "Great White Fleet"—round the world via Japan as a training cruise and show of force. In 1910 the United States created a small Asiatic Fleet at Manila and began to develop Pearl Harbor, Hawaii, into a forward naval base. Japan ceased foreign purchases and began building all its own warships toward a strength of 70 percent that of the U.S. Navy. The Pacific had become an arena of naval tension virtually independent of Europe.

European Naval Strife (1905–14). Britain strengthened its strategic position vis-à-vis Germany not only by befriending the United States and Japan but also by courting France and Russia for their armies and regional navies. In 1904 Britain concluded the Entente Cordiale with France. It recognized British control of Egypt in the eastern Mediterranean and the extension of French North Africa to include Morocco in the western half. German protests (and warship appearances) in the middle sea were mediated by President Roosevelt, backed up by visiting U.S. battleship squadrons there in 1904–5. In 1907 Russia joined the Anglo-French pact to create the Triple Entente, thereby adding the Baltic and Black Sea Fleets to the encirclement of the German-Austro-Italian Triple Alliance.

As tensions mounted, Britain abandoned its 2-power naval standard in 1912. No longer concerned with the U.S. Navy, now expanding at a rate of 2 new battleships per year, Britain decided to build a battle fleet of 60 percent more dreadnoughts than Germany's. France and Russia also initiated new battleship construction programs to help Britain counter those of Germany, Austria-Hungary, and Italy. The possibility of a general war had led to inconclusive disarmament conferences at the Hague in Holland in 1899 and 1907. The naval aspect was addressed at London in 1909, where the powers issued the **Declaration of London** endorsing the principle of safe passage for neutral merchant ships in time of war. But, for various reasons, no nation ratified it. The United States displayed its interest in European affairs with battleship visits to British, French, German, Russian, and Mediterranean ports between 1910 and 1913. And Italy gradually strengthened its ties with France against Austria-Hungary, especially after the Austrian annexation of Ottoman Bosnia in the Balkans in 1908.

Ottoman Turkey had become so weak that its neighbors, including Greece, used their naval forces to attempt to dismember it. The **Italo-Turkish War** of 1911–12 erupted when the Italian navy bombarded and captured the port cities of Ottoman Libya, then took Rhodes and the Dodecanese Islands in the eastern Aegean. The British-led Ottoman navy could do nothing, and Turkey ceded these possessions to Italy. Two Balkan wars in 1912–13 cost Turkey more European territory and islands to the Greek navy and to Balkan neighbors, some of whom created the nation of Albania on the Adriatic Sea. This body of water was policed by the navies of Austria-Hungary and Italy, formal allies but actual rivals for local naval supremacy. Germany dispatched 2 warships to the region and began to replace the British officers in the Turkish navy with its own.

Suddenly, in June 1914, a Serbian terrorist assassinated the Austrian archduke in Bosnia, touching off the string of great power mobilizations that triggered World War I.

13

World War I

(1914–1918)

IVAN S. BLOCH, a Polish-Russian military analyst, predicted in 1899 that the new high technology weapons of the great powers would lead to stalemate in a major war. That is, if each side had them, neither one would prevail; opposing armies and navies would simply hammer away to no decision in a bloody war of attrition. Each new weapon introduced would be imitated and counter-weapons developed. Bloch's predictions came true during the Great War of 1914–18. On land, neither machine guns, modern artillery, poison gas, nor tanks significantly altered the static trench warfare of the western front. Similarly at sea, not "superdreadnoughts," battle cruisers, nor submarines proved decisive. The introduction of rudimentary airplanes and airships was piecemeal and for use in traditional tactical missions over land and sea—reconnaissance, commerce protection, light bombardment, and fighting other aircraft.

But material strategists clung to the prewar promise of their modern machine weapons as Europe and other parts of the world were swept up in this un-precedented industrialized total war. For the navies, only 1 major fleet engage-ment occurred, and the war at sea eventually focused on commerce—attacks by and against submarines (U-boats). As material strategy failed to achieve victory at sea, naval leaders turned to the historical strategies of the preindustrial era: blockade, amphibious operations, convoy. Respect for international law—the trading rights of the United States and other neutral nations—succumbed to the demands of total war. Whatever the navies did, however, World War I was fun-damentally a continental struggle involving massive armies and entire civilian populations.

The outbreak of war during the summer of 1914 brought 2 great power coali-tions into conflict. The Allies consisted principally of Britain, France, Russia, and Japan. The Central Powers were dominated by Germany but included Austria-Hungary and the weak Ottoman Empire. Italy elected to remain neutral because of its antagonism toward Austria-Hungary, against which it declared war in May

1915. Italy became a full-fledged Allied partner in August 1916 when it joined the fight against Germany. The neutral United States, fearing a German victory, in 1915 accelerated capital ship construction for defense against a possible German invasion. The United States finally joined the Allies early in 1917.

Naval Strategies. Britain sealifted its army to France at the outbreak of war to help France stop the German attack through neutral Belgium. As the western front stabilized into static trench warfare, Britain's prewar plans were put into effect by the naval high command—First Lord of the Admiralty **Winston Churchill** and First Sea Lord Admiral Sir John Fisher, recalled to duty out of retirement. They established an open blockade of the German North Sea coast from distant Scapa Flow in the Orkney Islands and Rosyth, Scotland. Instead of a close blockade with its danger of German mines and U-boats, the Royal Navy planned to lure the German High Seas Fleet into the North Sea. The Grand Fleet under Admiral Sir **John Jellicoe** would then sortie from Scapa Flow to engage and destroy its German counterpart. Jellicoe had 24 dreadnoughts and 6 battle cruisers (with 17 more capital ships building), dominated by the 5 superdreadnoughts of the *Queen Elizabeth* class: each 30,000 tons, oil-driven to 25 knots, 13-inch armor belt, and 8 15-inch guns in twin turrets with ranges to 35,000 yards (20 miles). Churchill and Fisher dispatched other forces abroad to protect merchant shipping, assisted by the Allied navies.

Germany was unprepared for Britain's naval strategy. Admiral Alfred von Tirpitz, expecting a close British blockade, had planned to lure the Grand Fleet into the confined waters around the Heligoland Bight area, where mines, U-boats, and the High Seas Fleet could inflict a decisive defeat. When Tirpitz realized the Grand Fleet would not come, he wanted to send out the High Seas Fleet to seek battle, but the Kaiser would not permit it. Germany's ships were every bit as good as Britain's, some even better, but they were outnumbered—15 dreadnoughts and 5 battle cruisers (with only 8 more capital ships on the way). Because German army and navy planning had never been coordinated, Tirpitz had no plans to utilize the captured Belgian naval bases at Antwerp, Ostend, and Zeebrugge. He had a squadron in Asian waters and 8 independent cruisers outside Europe, too few to jeopardize Allied shipping. Germany had only 25 U-boats for fleet reconnaissance and coast defense, not for *guerre de course*. Neutralized by British naval dispositions, the High Seas Fleet became a "fortress fleet," passively augmenting coastal defenses.

Both fleets employed their lighter warships for patrols and lightning raids in the North Sea during the early months of the war. On 28 August 1914 Admiral **David Beatty** with 5 battle cruisers, 8 cruisers, and several destroyers surprised a German force patrolling off **Heligoland Bight.** The British sank 3 light cruisers and a destroyer. In September and October, however, German submarines sank 2 British cruisers off Scotland and 3 old armored cruisers off the neutral Netherlands, and a German mine claimed a dreadnought off northern Ireland. German battle cruisers bombarded the eastern coast of England during the autumn. The British developed 3 seaplane-carrying ships, which on Christmas day lowered 7 seaplanes into the waters off Germany. They took off and bombed the Zeppelin-airship hangars near Cuxhaven—the first naval air raid in history. Britain's breaking of German naval codes enabled Admiral Beatty to surprise a German raider force under Admiral **Franz von Hipper** at **Dogger Bank** on 24 January 1915. Although German guns damaged Beatty's flagship, the British sank a German armored cruiser and battered a battle cruiser. The engagement brought an end to surface actions in the North Sea.

Overseas Operations. Allied naval forces captured German colonies in Africa and the Pacific, pursued the German China Squadron, and hunted down surface raiders. The most successful of these was light cruiser *Emden,* which sank over 100,000 tons of Allied merchant shipping (and a Russian light cruiser and French destroyer at Malayan Penang) before being sunk by Australian cruiser *Sydney* west of Panama in November 1914. Cruiser *Königsberg* sank a British cruiser at Zanzibar in October, only to be blockaded in German East Africa and sunk the following July by 2 British monitors. By then, the Indian Ocean was safe for escorted convoys transporting Indian, Australian, and New Zealand troops to the Middle East.

Japan's blockade of German Tsingtao forced the German China Squadron, training in the Caroline Islands of the central Pacific when war began, to operate in South American waters. Commanded by Admiral Count **Maxmilian von Spee,** the 2 heavy and 3 light cruisers encountered and sank 2 old British cruisers at dusk on 1 November 1914 off Coronel, Chile, forcing 2 light cruisers to flee. Spee then rounded Cape Horn to attack Britain's Falkland Islands in the South Atlantic.

The Admiralty rushed Admiral Sir **Doveton Sturdee** with 2 battle cruisers and 6 cruisers to defend the islands, arriving there on 7 December. Next morning Spee attacked the harbor, then turned away when he discovered the presence of the battle cruisers *Invincible* and *Inflexible.* They pursued and sank the 2 heavy cruisers, killing Spee. The British cruisers claimed 2 German light cruisers; the third was scuttled in coastal waters 3 months later. The **Battle of the Falkland Islands** ended the threat of German surface raiders. Meanwhile, the Japanese navy and landing forces captured Germany's Pacific island groups—the Marianas, Carolines, and Marshalls—as well as Tsingtao.

Baltic and Mediterranean Theaters. Churchill and Fisher hoped to exploit the Baltic or Black Sea regions in support of the Russian army for an active eastern front after the western front became stalemated. Fisher had long advocated a landing in the Baltic using the entire Grand Fleet. But the army lacked an amphibious doctrine, and despite the Russian navy's effective use of mines there the Admiralty considered sending the fleet into these confined waters too risky. It rejected Fisher's idea in January 1915. During 1915 in the Baltic, Anglo-Russian submarines under Lieutenant Commander **Max Horton** sank a German cruiser and several merchantmen. The Black Sea option was frustrated when a German battle cruiser and light cruiser eluded Allied naval forces in the Mediterranean to reach the Dardanelles in August 1914. They were turned over to the Ottoman navy, their admiral appointed to command it. Aggressive Austrian submarines drove the French fleet out of the Adriatic the following spring, and the Austrian fleet was otherwise blockaded by the French from Pylos.

In 1914 the German-led Ottoman fleet sealed off the Black Sea to Allied shipping, bombarded Russian ports, and supported a ground offensive toward the Suez Canal. The Allies rushed to its defense and that of the Middle East because its oil was preferred over coal in new warships and industry in general. Britain prevented the Turks from crossing the Suez Canal early in 1915 and annexed Cyprus, the French navy occupied Palestinian ports, and Anglo-Russian forces defended the Persian Gulf region. These events added to Churchill's determination to mount a major offensive into the Black Sea via the Aegean.

Gallipoli. Against Fisher's objections, Churchill convinced Allied leaders to use the Anglo-French Mediterranean fleets to drive through the Dardanelles, Sea of Marmara, and Bosphorus; capture Constantinople; and link up with the Russians on the eastern front. The 5-battleship Russian Black Sea Fleet blockaded and mined the Bosphorus and bombarded the northern Turkish coast. Otherwise, it was too occupied supporting the army to cooperate in the Anglo-French operation. In November 1914 British and French warships shelled Turkish artillery positions flanking the Dardanelles—the tip of the Gallipoli peninsula on the western side and the Anatolian mainland on the eastern side. Churchill believed that naval bombardments and small landing parties alone could accomplish the task. This would avoid a major amphibious campaign, for which neither the Allied armies or navies were prepared. He minimized the threat to the battleships of underwater weapons, namely, extensive minefields the Germans laid in late 1914 and early 1915 in the Dardanelles and the Chanak Narrows connecting the strait and Sea of Marmara.

The Gallipoli campaign began in mid-February 1915. Based at the island of

Lemnos, the Anglo-French fleet under Admiral John de Robeck commenced bombarding the Turkish guns on both sides of the Dardanelles. It was gradually reinforced to a strength of 13 British and 4 French battleships led by *Queen Elizabeth,* along with a battle cruiser and several cruisers, destroyers, and crude, makeshift minesweepers. On 18 March the battleships silenced the Ottoman guns and drove toward the Chanak Narrows—and minefields. Three predreadnoughts struck mines and sank, and the battle cruiser was damaged by a mine, forcing de Robeck to call off the attempt.

Churchill decided to mount an amphibious assault on the Gallipoli peninsula and began assembling 80,000 British, Australian, New Zealand, Indian, and French troops for the operation. Although an astute student of history, Churchill displayed remarkable ignorance of the basic tenets of Britain's combined army-navy landing operations in the past:

1. *Unity of command.* No one commander, army or navy, in London or at the Dardanelles, was given supreme authority, leading to uneven leadership and confusion in planning and execution.

2. *Control of local waters.* Minesweepers converted from fishing trawlers failed to sweep the waters of the assault area, where German and Austrian U-boats and Turkish destroyers also constituted a threat.

3. *Element of surprise.* It was lost when the unsuccessful bombardment in March alerted the German and Ottoman generals to concentrate 30,000 troops at Gallipoli, and 2 subsequent Allied feints and a diversionary landing farther up the western side of the peninsula failed to fool the defenders.

4. *Rehearsal.* Complex amphibious operations require a run-through, but these were canceled because of delays caused by having to rearrange equipment and supplies at Alexandria in ships improperly loaded in Britain.

5. *Beach reconnaissance.* Little attention was given to reconnoitering local sea currents and the landing beaches by small vessels and aircraft.

6. *Shore bombardment.* Naval gunners lacked training and experience for close-in pinpoint fire support against beach defenses, and thus they delivered an ineffective barrage.

7. *Specialized landing craft.* Though Admiral Fisher had produced motorized armored landing barges for his stillborn Baltic operation, none were available at Gallipoli, where 200 large and hundreds of makeshift assault craft were pressed into service.

8. *Ship-to-shore movement.* Successive waves of assault craft had to be well timed and coordinated for efficient establishment, supply, and reinforcement of the beachhead, none of which occurred.

9. *Aggressive exploitation of the beachhead.* The assault troops failed to probe enemy positions quickly and drive inland to the high ground before the enemy concentrated there.

10. *Commitment of floating reserves.* Once the beachhead was established, fresh reinforcements waiting offshore were not committed to consolidate a defense perimeter around the beach and then prepare for the breakout into the interior.

The Allied assault took place on 25 April 1915 under cover of ineffective naval gunfire. The shoddy assault left the initial troops pinned down or slaughtered outright along the water's edge by enemy fire. Without adequate supply and reinforcements, Allied troops failed to make any progress against the Turks, who rushed to the high ground which they firmly held by the end of the day. Nothing changed over succeeding days, except for mounting Allied casualties and counterattacks at sea by the Central Powers. On 13 May a Turkish torpedo boat sank a predreadnought off the landing beach. On the 25th German sub *U-21* sank another off the diversionary landing area and yet a third near the main beach on the 27th. It then joined other Austrian and German submarines for a general attack on Allied shipping in the Mediterranean. Churchill demanded more warships for the operation, whereupon Fisher resigned in protest as First Sea Lord.

The Gallipoli stalemate did not change. British submarines penetrated the Sea of Marmara to sink 2 Turkish battleships and several smaller vessels during the summer; 1 was a freighter, finished off by a torpedo dropped from a British seaplane. The Allies landed Australian and New Zealand troops on Gallipoli's western coast in August in an effort to break the stalemate, to no avail. Upon Italy's entry into the war, Austrian saboteurs destroyed an Italian predreadnought at Brindisi in September 1915. Bulgaria joined the Central Powers in October and overran Serbia and Montenegro, forcing the evacuation of their armies by the French and Italian navies. Similarly, the Allies ordered the evacuation of Gallipoli in November, whereupon Churchill resigned as scapegoat for the debacle. So masterful was the amphibious-operation-in-reverse that it was completed the following January before the Turks realized what was happening.

Commerce Warfare (1915–16). Britain's blockade of Germany included the time-tested principle of stopping, searching, and seizing neutral merchantmen — the old Rule of 1756, now enforced by Orders-in-Council. This meant bending the spirit of the 1909 Declaration of London, much to the displeasure of the United States, major neutral shipper to both sides. American merchants traded with Germany through the neutral Netherlands, leading the Royal Navy to lay mines in the Straits of Dover and to impound Holland-bound neutral vessels.

But Britain could do little to prevent neutral Sweden, Norway, and Denmark from trading with Germany via the Baltic.

Germany implemented a counterblockade of the British Isles and in February 1915 declared the surrounding waters to be a war zone, warning Americans about the danger of traveling through it aboard British passenger liners. With their surface raiders neutralized, the Germans turned to the U-boat for this *guerre de course*. In May 1915, however, a sub sank liner *Lusitania* in the war zone, taking many American as well as British lives. The feat was repeated against *Arabic* in August. Both sinkings brought loud diplomatic protests from U.S. President Woodrow Wilson against such inhumane attacks on civilians. In mid-September, the Germans, unwilling to antagonize the United States, suspended all U-boat operations in British waters. The subs were also exposed to British air and naval patrols when—as required by international law—they surfaced to search neutral merchantmen and, after allowing the crews to escape on lifeboats, sank those carrying contraband.

The Mediterranean offered safer hunting grounds. Allied antisubmarine defenses were so weak that German and Austrian U-boats could search neutral vessels and transit the Strait of Gibraltar and the Adriatic Straits of Otranto with relative impunity. Overall, throughout 1915 Central Powers submarines sank 748,000 tons of merchant shipping (the average "target" displaced 3,000 tons), mines claimed 77,000 and surface raiders 29,000 tons, all at a cost of only 20 subs. During the first half of 1916 half a million Allied tons went down against 34 U-boats lost.

The Mediterranean was the scene of most sinkings; in the autumn of 1915 a mere 6 subs claimed 92 cargo ships. The French and Italians failed to cooperate against the underwater raiders, using only ineffective defensive nets and cruiser patrols at the Straits of Otranto. The British merely dispatched older battleships to the Mediterranean. Such big warships were not only useless against subs or mines but also had to remain in port lest the subs sink them. Indeed, between mid-1915 and mid-1917 no fewer than 9 Allied predreadnoughts (British, French, Italian, Russian) were sunk by subs, mines, or sabotage in or near Mediterranean ports (one off Lisbon).

The British and German navies both refused to weaken their main battleship fleets in the North Sea to participate in the war over commerce. Most admirals were material strategists weaned on their high technology behemoths as well as historical Mahanians committed to the decisive fleet engagement. To them, commerce warfare was an indecisive, unglamorous sideshow. The offensive-minded British eschewed defensive convoys in favor of sporadic hunt-and-kill patrols using destroyers armed with depth charges, but most failed to locate

Battleships and battle cruisers of the German High Seas Fleet execute a perfect 180-degree turn in the face of the British Grand Fleet (near horizon) at the Battle of Jutland, 31 May 1916. British admiral Sir John Jellicoe has succeeded in "capping the T" for concentrated broadside fire at the head of the German battle line. But Admiral Reinhard Scheer's adroit maneuvering finally enabled his fleet to escape to safety during the night. From a painting by Montagu Dawson. (National Geographic Image Collection)

U-boats. Part of the problem was underwater detection using primitive hydrophones. Britain armed its merchant ships, had them zigzag to throw off the aim of submerged subs, and used heavily gunned decoy merchant "Q-ships" to trap unsuspecting U-boats on the surface. Small inshore craft and shore-based flying boats patrolled the coasts. But none of these countermeasures proved decisive, and merchant ship losses mounted.

Battle of Jutland

The Battle of Jutland (or Skaggerak) was the only major fleet engagement of World War I. It pitted the British Grand Fleet of Admiral Sir John Jellicoe against the German High Seas Fleet under Vice Adm. Reinhard Scheer in the North Sea west of the Jutland peninsula of Denmark. Scheer sortied from his bases on the German coast the night of 30–31 May 1916 with the intention of attacking British shipping to Norway in the Skaggerak. Jellicoe, alerted to Scheer's plan, had weighed anchor only hours before. Their respective battle cruiser forces steamed ahead of their battleships, which trailed behind just over the horizon, hoping to lure each other within gun range of the battleships. The British also had 2 seaplane carriers, but 1 had failed to receive the order to sail, and the other sent 1 plane aloft with negligible results.

The opposing battle cruiser forces made contact and exchanged fire midafternoon of 31 May. Vice Adm. Franz von Hipper steamed northwest with his 5 battle cruisers, 5 light cruisers, and 30 destroyers, then turned around to run on a parallel southeast tack with Vice Adm. David Beatty's 6 battle cruisers, 4 new dreadnoughts, 14 light cruisers, and 27 destroyers. The distance between the 2 lines narrowed from 16,500 to 13,000 yards as the leading battle cruisers exchanged salvos. Superior German gunnery scored several hits, and the flash of their exploding shells reached the magazines of *Indefatigable* and *Queen Mary*, igniting their ammunition, causing them to explode and sink. Each side also lost 2 destroyers. At about 4:45 P.M. Beatty sighted Scheer's battleships approaching from the south and turned about to avoid being trapped and to lure the German fleet into gun range of Jellicoe's main body, approaching from the north.

Jellicoe entered the fight about 6:00 P.M., absorbing Beatty's force into his own formation of 24 dreadnoughts, 3 battle cruisers, 8 armored cruisers, 12 light cruisers, 51 destroyers, and 1 minelayer. By the same token, Scheer joined Hipper with the main body of 16 dreadnoughts, 6 predreadnoughts, 6 light cruisers, and 31 destroyers. Jellicoe's fire seriously damaged 3 light cruisers as

The German high command saw in its Mediterranean U-boat successes the efficacy of unrestricted submarine warfare. In February 1916 it therefore resumed U-boat attacks in the war zone around Britain, only to have a sub sink cross-Channel liner *Sussex* in March. The resulting loss of American and British passengers brought another stern protest from President Wilson. The German Kaiser fired Admiral Tirpitz and yielded to Wilson's demands again to impose restrictions on Atlantic U-boats. Wilson had unwittingly bought time for the Allies,

he capped the German "T"—broadside salvos concentrated against the approaching head of the German line. He then swung eastward to silhouette Scheer's ships against the setting sun and to cut off Scheer's possible retreat back to the German coast. The devastating gunnery exchange at 12,000 yards in this "Windy Corner" caused British battle cruiser *Invincible* to explode and German battle cruiser *Lützow* to limp away and eventually sink. Several other vessels were also put out of action.

Scheer then executed a 180-degree battle turn to the southeast, surprising the British who did not believe such a maneuver possible. Had melee tactics existed, British commanders might have pursued Scheer vigorously on their own initiative, but Jellicoe adhered to his rigid formal line-ahead—tactics cemented before the war. Jellicoe kept moving eastward to cut off Scheer, who then reversed course and tried to break through Jellicoe's line, only to find his "T" still capped by Jellicoe's murderous broadsides. A determined German destroyer attack at 7:15 caused Jellicoe's cruisers to turn away from the dreaded torpedoes, while Scheer executed another 180-degree turn to the south. By sunset at 8:19 both fleets were running south on parallel tracks, with Jellicoe's fleet situated between Scheer and Germany. British radio listeners intercepted a message from Scheer to the German Admiralty asking its approval for him to break through the rear of Jellicoe's line during the night, but they failed to inform Jellicoe. Scheer began his maneuver at 11:00 P.M. and soon after midnight on 1 June made good his escape.

By dawn, Scheer's fleet was back in German waters, leaving Jellicoe no choice but to return to base. The British had lost 3 battle cruisers, 3 cruisers, 8 destroyers, 6,090 men killed; the Germans 1 predreadnought, 1 battle cruiser, 4 cruisers, 5 destroyers, and 2,550 killed. Not one dreadnought was sunk in either fleet, nor had torpedoes proved decisive. The Germans had outshone the British, yet the battle was a tactical draw and a strategic British victory inasmuch as the Grand Fleet continued to dominate the North Sea. The generally accepted superiority of material strategy embodied in the dreadnought was disproved, and the 2 fleets never met again.

now hard-pressed to supply their armies on all fronts. But the Germans also extended submarine operations as far as the U.S. East Coast, sinking over 2 million tons of Allied shipping—1,152 vessels—between May 1916 and January 1917.

The North Sea (1916). By 1916 both the British and German fleet commanders hoped to break the stalemate on the western front by winning control of the North Sea. Admiral Jellicoe had standing orders not to expose his battleships to German torpedoes and mines, one of which—laid by an auxiliary

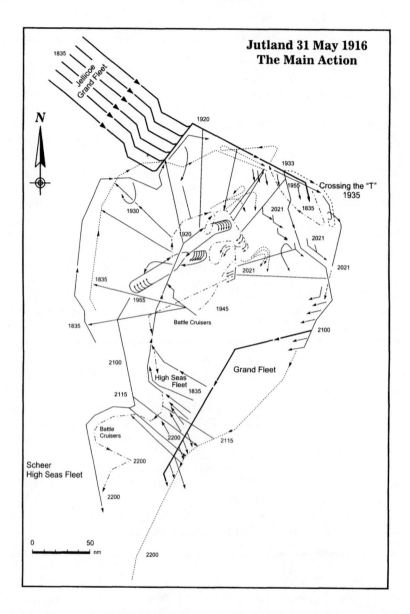

**Jutland 31 May 1916
The Main Action**

1835

Jellicoe
Grand Fleet

N

1920

1933

1955

Crossing the "T"
1935

1930

1920

2021

1835

2021

1835

2021

1955

2021

2021

1945

1835

Battle Cruisers

1835

2100

2100

Grand Fleet

High Seas
Fleet
1835

2115

Battle
Cruisers

2200

2115

Scheer
High Seas Fleet

2200

2200

0   50
╰─────╯ nm

2200

cruiser—sank a predreadnought west of Scapa Flow in January 1916. But he hoped to lure the German High Seas Fleet into battle using cruiser bombardments as bait. In March they struck the Sylt Island radio station and in May the Zeppelin sheds at Tondern, from which the high-altitude dirigibles flew bombing missions over London. Both cruiser raids failed to draw out the German fleet. However, its new commander, Admiral **Reinhard Scheer,** used his battle cruisers to shell the British coast at Lowestoft in April, hoping to lure out Jellicoe, but without success. When, however, at the end of May, the High Seas Fleet sortied to attack British merchant shipping to Norway, Jellicoe put to sea as well. The 2 fleets then clashed in the titanic though indecisive **Battle of Jutland** (see essay).

Remarkably, given the fact that the much-vaunted dreadnoughts had failed to alter the course of the war, the opposing navies continued to build new battleships and battle cruisers. Scheer managed to bombard the British coast at Sunderland in August 1916 but retired upon Jellicoe's approach. The British then began the transfer of the Grand Fleet from Scapa Flow to Rosyth and the Firth of Forth to improve the prospects of intercepting Scheer. But the German high command never again sought battle. Instead, it sent heavy fleet units through the Kiel Canal into the Baltic to blockade the Russian fleet at Kronstadt and close the Baltic to Allied shipping. Britain thus shifted its Russian supply routes away from the Baltic to Kola and Archangel via the Arctic Ocean and mined the North Sea to thwart U-boat movements.

Commerce Warfare (1916–18). Admiral Jellicoe, finally convinced that the submarine had become the final arbiter in the war, was elevated to First Sea Lord to deal with the menace; he was succeeded in the Grand Fleet by Beatty. Jellicoe's antisubmarine reforms late in the year had little effect. The Germans simultaneously stepped up U-boat operations and sank a monthly average of 94,000 tons of merchant shipping the last third of 1916. Admiral Scheer and the German army argued strongly for the resumption of unrestricted submarine warfare, even at the risk of bringing the United States into the war. Scheer reasoned that the United States would require at least a full year to raise and transport an army to Europe, during which time the U-boats would strangle Britain into submission. The Kaiser accepted his argument, and Germany unleashed its subs against all Allied and neutral shipping on 1 February 1917.

Germany's unrestricted U-boat campaign was wildly successful. The 125 or so subs that were always available throughout 1917 ranged the Atlantic, augmented by 3 surface raiders as well as destroyers operating out of German ports and Belgian Zeebrugge. In April alone, Central Powers naval forces sank almost 870,000 tons of Allied and neutral shipping. But the conservative German admirals refused to coordinate North Sea and Flanders U-boat operations from shore, although they did allow many of the best junior officers to transfer from High Seas Fleet vessels to the subs. Morale in the battleships plummeted, also due to mistreatment of the crews by aristocratic officers, resulting in several mutinies in the fleet during the summer.

The United States, after losing many merchantmen to U-boats and determined to save the democratic Allies, declared war on Germany in April 1917. The previous summer the United States had authorized construction of an immense battleship fleet on a 2-power standard—to deter and possibly fight both Germany and Japan, especially if Britain was defeated. Early in 1917 the United States purchased the Danish Virgin Islands to complete the defenses of the Panama Canal, through which its major warships transitted from the Pacific to the Chesapeake Bay. With Japan now an ally, the fleet's presence was no longer required on the West Coast. On the advice of Admiral **William S. Sims,** senior American naval officer in Europe, President Wilson suspended battleship construction in favor of destroyers and other antisubmarine vessels for the duration.

Simultaneously, the British decided to adopt convoy as the solution to the U-boat menace. Following successful local convoys to France, Holland, and Norway since mid-1916, 2 experimental convoys from Gibraltar and the Chesapeake Bay in May 1917 reached Britain without losses (except for 1 straggler). Against conservative opposition, and strongly supported by Admiral Sims, the Royal Navy made the convoys permanent and integrated the U.S. Navy into a vigorous new convoy system. Except for 1 battleship squadron sent to the Grand Fleet, the U.S. Atlantic Fleet remained in the Chesapeake, releasing many destroyers and subchasers to be convoy escorts. They were equipped with improved "asdic" underwater detection devices and were covered near the coasts by patrols of shore-based naval aircraft. The British reformed their commerce protection operations in the Mediterranean, turning over most convoy escort duties to Japanese destroyer squadrons based at Malta.

The convoys always got through. With U-boat captains deterred from attacking them for fear of the escorts, Allied merchant ship losses declined from 600,000 tons in May 1916 to fewer than 175,000 tons in September, at which time Germany had its greatest number of U-boats at sea, 55. The Germans then shifted their subs and mine-laying activities from the Western Approaches and open sea to the English Channel and Irish Sea, only to be countered there by more and improved Allied minesweepers, patrol boats, and aircraft. The first 12 months of Germany's unrestricted submarine campaign—February 1917 to January 1918—saw 6 million tons (over 2,500 vessels) of Allied and neutral shipping sunk, and the Germans replaced their own sunken subs, about 10 per month, with new construction. But they could not replace the experienced captains and crews lost, nor could their kills keep pace with the vast construction of new Allied merchant vessels and escort ships. The one potential target that U-boats carefully avoided were American and Canadian convoys of troop transports escorted across the Atlantic by capital ships.

The German gamble to blockade and defeat Britain by unrestricted submarine warfare failed. Worse, the 1-million-man American army that reached England and France safely during 1918 would provide the margin of Allied victory
on the continent. In the North Sea, High Seas Fleet units sank 2 Allied convoys during the fall of 1917. But Admiral Beatty made the momentous decision
the following January to devote the Grand Fleet to antisubmarine operations,
a move the Germans would not make for their fleet until the summer when Admiral Scheer succeeded to supreme naval command. By then it was too late.

Major command shakeups improved Britain's naval leadership, notably the replacement of Jellicoe as First Sea Lord by Admiral Sir Rosslyn Wemyss. By 1918,
each transatlantic convoy averaged 15 to 25 merchantmen and 6 to 8 escorts. In
March the U.S. Navy inspired the laying of a 240-mile-long antisubmarine mine
barrage—over 70,000 mines—across the North Sea from the Orkney Islands to
Norway. In April Beatty completed the move of his 34 battleships and 9 battle
cruisers from Scapa Flow to Rosyth to tighten the blockade of Germany. To stop
German U-boats and destroyers from transitting the Strait of Dover into the
Channel, Admiral Sir Roger Keyes illuminated the strait with searchlights at
night, increased patrols and minefields, and in April tried to close the U-boat
bases at Ostend and Zeebrugge with sunken blockships, without success. In the
Mediterranean the Allies laid a mine barrage across the Strait of Otranto. When
4 Austrian dreadnoughts tried to break through it in June, 1 hit a mine and sank,
the rest being driven back by Italian torpedo boats.

Naval Aviation. The initial and most general use of flying machines by navies
was for scouting enemy movements at sea, on land, and underwater. The earliest naval seaplanes—small single-engine aircraft fitted with floats for launching
from the water—were first used in combat by the Greeks during the Balkan wars
(1913) and the U.S. Navy during its occupation of Mexican Veracruz (1914). The
warring powers followed suit but developed larger multiengine flying boats—
wings added to a small hull—for longer-distance flights, augmented by land-
based patrol planes. Britain, France, and Russia converted merchant ships into
seaplane carriers which lowered their aircraft into the water, from which they
were recovered by hoist. As with army landplanes, naval aircraft gradually took
on attack functions, carrying guns, bombs, mines, and torpedoes. In September
1916 2 Austrian seaplanes sank a French submarine with bombs, and 1 year later
an aircraft-laid German mine sank a Russian destroyer in the Baltic.

British and German naval aircraft and airships vigorously contested the skies
over the North Sea and coastlines. German rigid dirigibles and British navy
planes had only marginal success scouting for their respective battle fleets. But
they had nuisance value as bombers—Zeppelins against London, British sea-

planes raiding Zeppelin sheds. In 1914 the Royal Naval Air Service reluctantly accepted the role of defending the homeland against the high flying Zeps until the army's Royal Flying Corps assumed the task in 1916. However, British naval planes flew long-distance bombing missions against German industrial targets and submarine bases until they were shifted to supporting the army on the western front in early 1917. Thereafter, the U.S. Navy greatly augmented British and Italian aerial antisubmarine and antishipping operations.

So heavily intertwined did British army and naval aircraft missions become that in April 1918 both air arms were merged into a single service, the Royal Air Force (RAF). The Royal Navy concurrently developed 2 aircraft carriers capable of launching and recovering landplanes on their flight decks. Seven such planes launched from carrier *Furious* successfully bombed the Tondern airship base in July 1918, destroying 2 dirigibles. By then the Grand Fleet had over 100 aircraft for scouting and fighter defense and was developing torpedo planes for possible use against the German High Seas Fleet.

The major success of naval aircraft was in the Allied anti–U-boat campaign. During 1918 hundreds of British, American, Italian, and French flying boats and seaplanes patrolled the coastal waters of the British Isles, the Mediterranean, and North America. Rarely were they able to attack and sink a submarine, but their mere presence forced U-boats to remain submerged to avoid detection and thus unable to attack shipping. From a virtual toy at the outbreak of war the naval airplane rapidly evolved into a vital tactical component with immense promise for future development.

Allied Victory. The war took on strong moral tones that affected both sides and their navies in 1917–18. The Russian Revolution in March 1917 replaced the czar with a tenuous democratic regime, an event that helped inspire Woodrow Wilson to lead the United States into the war in April. During the summer and fall, however, a German ground offensive to the Gulf of Finland took Riga, amphibious forces captured several Baltic islands, and units of the High Seas Fleet blockaded Kronstadt. In November, the Russian Bolsheviks, assisted by frustrated sailors of the Baltic Fleet, overthrew the democratic regime, established a communist government, and in December concluded an armistice with Germany. Sailors of the Austro-Hungarian and German fleets, similarly restive under their aristocratic officers, staged unsuccessful mutinies between the autumn of 1917 and spring of 1918. Finland revolted from Russia late in 1917, only to be put down by Germany the following April, partly by landings. With Russia out of the war, the remaining Allied powers could do nothing in the Baltic and Black Seas.

The flood of sealifted U.S. troops into France began in April 1918, just in time to offset the collapse of Russia and enable the Allied armies to drive back the

Germans on the western front during the summer. Although the Northern Mine Barrage sank only a half-dozen U-boats, the North Sea was effectively closed to German warships. In September the U-boats quit the Channel after Allied countermeasures sank over half of the 43 subs based in Flanders. The Germans abandoned these bases during the fall under bombings by Allied naval aircraft.

Admiral Scheer became supreme German naval commander in August and tried to redivert naval resources to his subs, but the convoy had already triumphed in both the Mediterranean and the open Atlantic. In October, revolutionary movements destroyed the Austro-Hungarian Empire and made peace, enabling Allied warships to occupy all seaports in the Adriatic. With the Kaiser's army in full retreat, Germany faced collapse. On 21 October Scheer yielded to President Wilson's ultimatum to cease all U-boat operations, after they had sunk over 1,000 merchantmen (some 2,650,000 tons) since January.

Scheer and the new High Seas Fleet commander, Hipper, ordered a fleet sortie for 1 final glorious battle against the British Grand Fleet. But a general mutiny by the German sailors against this mad scheme on 29 October forced its cancellation. The mutineers then joined other revolutionaries to overthrow the Kaiser and institute a democratic government on 9 November. Two days later Germany agreed to an armistice, ending the war. By its terms the armistice was little more than complete German surrender. It included the immediate internment at Scapa Flow of the newest High Seas Fleet vessels, including 11 battleships, 5 battle cruisers, and all surviving U-boats. Before these trophies could be distributed to the victors, however, in June 1919 the skeleton German crews opened the sea cocks of each vessel, allowing them to sink at their anchorage.

In material terms the dreadnoughts had fulfilled Bloch's prophecy that advanced machine weapons canceled out any advantages, resulting in the stalemate of the battleship fleets. The Allied naval blockade had hemmed in the German fleet and seriously affected Germany's war economy. The advent of the U-boat as commerce raider had nearly succeeded in establishing a counterblockade of Britain, sinking over 7.6 million tons of British and more than 3 million tons of other Allied and neutral shipping. But the adoption of the historical stratagem of convoy had finally checked this revolutionary weapon, assisted importantly by the equally revolutionary patrol seaplane. The failure of the Allied Gallipoli campaign thoroughly discredited major amphibious operations for the rest of the war and for years to come.

The conservatism of most admirals had been the reason for many naval failures until the Allied naval leaders adopted the changes necessary for final victory. The key naval success, however, was the sealift and supply of the Allied armies which proved ultimately to be the decisive factor in this fundamentally continental war.

14

Naval Arms Control
(1919–1939)

No NATION WANTED ANOTHER World War, but mutual distrust prevented any from eliminating their navies. The Allied powers only agreed that the new German Weimar Republic be allowed a token navy of 6 10,000-ton battleships plus escorts and no submarines. Most nations joined the League of Nations to preserve global peace but would not subordinate their navies to League control. The United States refused to join; Soviet Russia and Germany were not invited. Britain retained the largest postwar navy but was challenged by Japan and the United States, which resumed their prewar naval building race. During the 1920s and 1930s, therefore, the naval powers agreed at several international conferences to control the size of navies and thus prevent war. But the rise of fascism and resurgent militarism overturned these compromises and brought on World War II.

All nations downsized their navies in the 1920s to concentrate on economic recovery. Their admirals could do little more than improve the tactics and weaponry of the wartime experience and police politically troubled regional waters. The major lesson *not* learned by any navy was the failure of material strategy, meaning the modern battleship, to have played a decisive role in World War I. Consequently, this capital ship remained the index of naval power between the world wars.

The submarine and airplane had great potential for dominating naval warfare but remained in the shadow of the big gun battleship. Incredibly, most navies rejected the submarine's wartime role as a deadly commerce raider in favor of its supporting the surface fleet. Advocates of land-based bombing planes used material arguments to predict that their "strategic bombers" would make traditional armies and navies ineffective if not obsolete by striking military, industrial, and civilian targets. The admirals responded by adding antiaircraft guns to their ships and constructing aircraft carriers, but only for reconnaissance and defending the battle line (see essay).

The basic design of aircraft carriers did not change throughout the 20th century: flight deck, with hangar deck beneath it, both connected by aircraft elevators. Flight operations were directed from the above station on the "island" superstructure. Navigational data was posted for pilots before each launch. Point Option was the geographical position of the carrier at time of launch. Folding wings maximized the number of planes in an air group/wing: 90 on this American *Essex*-class fast carrier of World War II. Having attacked Japanese airfields on Formosa (Taiwan) the morning of 12 October 1944, these planes landed and parked near the bow. Here they are "respotted" (towed aft to be launched again): SB2C Helldiver dive bombers (wings folded vertically) and TBF/TBM Avenger torpedo-bombers and F6F Hellcat fighters (wings folded along the fuselage like a bird's). (U.S. Navy)

The Aircraft Carrier

Invented by the British navy during World War I, the aircraft carrier remained a basically experimental vessel during the 1920s. It consisted of a long flat flight deck (hence the carrier's nickname, "flattop") superimposed on girders above the hangar deck and hull. Aircraft were shuttled between hangar and flight decks by large elevators; the planes were maintained, repaired, and usually stowed in the hangar area. Smaller elevators hoisted bombs and ammunition from lower deck magazines to the hangar and flight decks.

The flight deck was made of wood so that enemy bombs might penetrate it and not explode until striking the armored hangar deck, thereby preserving the easily repaired flight deck for air operations. The British began armoring the flight deck in the late 1930s to absorb bomb hits because their carriers operated in close proximity to enemy bomber fields in Europe. The Americans kept the wooden flight deck because their carriers operated in the open Pacific, not armoring them until after World War II. Flight operations were directed on most carriers from spaces located on the "island" superstructure affixed to the smoke stack projecting above the flight deck on the starboard side.

Britain's initial carriers proved clumsy in contrast to the new "fast" 30-knot carriers which the American and Japanese navies converted from battle cruiser and battleship hulls under the terms of the Washington treaties of 1922. By the time these became operational at the end of the decade, 3 types of single-engine carrier aircraft had been developed—the fighter for aerial defense of the fleet and of the other planes; the dual-mission scout-bomber for reconnaissance and for horizontal and dive bombing of enemy ships and ground targets; and the antiship torpedo plane.

The primary mission of carriers during the 1920s and 1930s was as "eyes of the fleet"—scouting for the battle line. The officers and aviators who specialized in carrier duty, however, soon developed an independent attack function for carriers, with bombing and torpedo planes outnumbering the fighters.

Russian Civil War (1918–21). Britain, France, the United States, Italy, and Japan agreed that the communist regime in Russia posed a threat to world stability. Thus, in 1919, they supported the counterrevolutionary "White" Russians under Admiral Alexander V. Kolchak, former commander of the Black Sea Fleet, fighting to overthrow the "Reds." In a complicated undeclared naval war in the Baltic the British navy under Admiral Walter H. Cowan supported the warships of the newly created nations of Poland, Latvia, Estonia, and Lithuania in de-

Each carrier mounted its own antiaircraft guns. During World War II, the fighters and torpedo planes doubled their attack functions as fighter-bombers and torpedo-bombers. Each plane type belonged to its own squadron, the 3 or 4 squadrons to a carrier air group (later air wing), which numbered between 50 and 90 planes. U.S. and Japanese World War II carriers each displaced about 30,000 tons, Britain's slightly less.

The British carrier air attack on the Italian fleet at Taranto in 1940 and Japan's sinking of the U.S. battle line at Pearl Harbor in 1941 conclusively demonstrated the striking power of carriers. Subsequent naval battles forced the 3 major navies to accept the carrier as the new arbiter of naval power as capital ship. Several carriers were concentrated at the center of a circular cruising formation of battleships, cruisers, and destroyers providing antiair and antisub protection. In addition to waging naval battles in which the opposing carrier forces were separated by hundreds of miles, carrier planes bombed and strafed ahead of amphibious assault troops, escorted convoys, and attacked enemy merchant shipping and inland targets. All 3 navies augmented their heavy attack carriers with smaller light and escort carriers, some converted from cruiser and merchant hulls. The primary function of the escort carrier was protecting merchant shipping, especially against submarines.

The unique tactical feature of the World War II carrier was its mobility and range, with its planes able to fly up to 500 miles on a round-trip mission. Naval aviation also included the single-engine float plane catapulted from battleships and cruisers to spot the fire of its own ship's guns; the multiengine amphibian and land-based patrol bomber; and the nonrigid lighter-than-air patrol blimp, developed for antisub work after the interwar demise of U.S. Navy rigid airships because of several crashes. The same roles and missions of carriers and their planes continued after World War II, except that jet planes replaced most piston-engine propeller aircraft. The heavier weight of such planes required larger carriers. After 1960 the largest carriers were powered by atomic energy instead of oil and eventually displaced over 80,000 tons.

feating communist naval units along the coast, in the Gulf of Finland, and on Lake Peipus. Cowan's torpedo boats sank a Red cruiser and, covered by carrier bombing planes, sank 2 battleships off Kronstadt at a cost of 3 boats. Anglo-American gunboats based at Archangel and Murmansk in northern Russia joined the Finns in assisting White forces on the Dvina River and Lake Onega. Allied naval and ground forces, mostly Japanese, occupied Vladivostok in the Russian Far East until the Reds defeated the Whites on land and executed Kolchak early in 1920. The Allies withdrew, enabling the victorious Red regime to make peace with its neighbors.

The crews of the "Socialist Worker–Peasant Red Fleet"—commanded by fellow "comrades" without formal naval officer ranks they considered elitist—had fought ably but fruitlessly against the seasoned Allied navies. However, the crews of the "Soviet Activated Squadron" (Baltic Fleet) at Kronstadt so chafed under their rigid communist masters that they mutinied in 1921. Red leaders V. I. Lenin and Joseph Stalin brutally crushed them and thereafter regarded the navy as politically suspect, partly because it had to employ former czarist officers for their experience. The communist regime downgraded and redesignated the navy as the "Naval Forces of the Red Army" but eventually restored traditional naval ranks.

The new Soviet Union (USSR), politically isolated by the international community, used light surface forces in its Baltic, Northern, Black, and Pacific Fleets to augment the army's coastal defenses. Alone among the powers, it developed submarines specifically for commerce warfare. In the late 1930s Stalin purged his former czarist officers and flirted with creating a surface fleet of coastal battleships for deterrence value, but World War II prevented development.

Balkan–Middle Eastern Interventions (1918–25). Anglo-American naval support of the White Russians in the Black Sea region coincided with the dismemberment of the defeated Austro-Hungarian and Ottoman Turkish empires, from which new states were created. Italy's annexation of territory at the head of the Adriatic Sea so threatened the new Balkan nation of Yugoslavia that British and other warships patrolled the Adriatic and Danube River until stability was achieved by 1925. Middle Eastern lands taken from the Ottomans were mandated to Allied control by the League of Nations: Palestine, Transjordan, and Iraq to Britain; Syria and Lebanon to France. Anglo-French naval and ground forces policed and pacified the region both to restore order and to ensure their uninterrupted access to Middle Eastern oil.

A Muslim Turkish nationalist movement led by Mustapha Kemal prevented the dismemberment of Turkey proper (Anatolia) by the West and expelled religious and ethnic minorities. The resulting bloodshed prompted Anglo-Greek, French, and Italian landings on the Turkish coasts for a ground offensive in 1919. A squadron of U.S. battleships also arrived to protect American trade. Early in 1920 the European powers occupied Constantinople, and in June a British force built around battleships and carriers occupied the eastern shore of the Sea of Marmara to help drive back Kemal's army. The U.S. naval commander on the scene, Admiral Mark L. Bristol, used his squadron rigorously to enforce the neutrality of Turkish waters, hindering European naval movements. When Kemal finally won, the powers concluded peace in 1923, creating the Republic of Turkey and neutralizing the Dardanelles and Bosphorus. The Western navies then withdrew from the Black Sea.

The Mediterranean remained the focus of British imperial strategy. Using its base network of Gibraltar, Malta, and Alexandria, the Royal Navy shifted forces between the Atlantic and Indian Oceans. British warships patrolled the Persian Gulf, helped pacify Afghanistan in 1919 and Iraq in 1920, and achieved a standoff with Russia in the Caspian Sea, until both powers withdrew from Persia (Iran) in 1921. Because of severe budgetary constraints (the so-called Geddes axe, named for the First Lord of the Admiralty), Britain could strengthen Singapore only enough to hold out in event of war with Japan until fleet units could be sent from the Mediterranean. But India and Britain's Pacific dominions of Australia, New Zealand, and Canada demanded that the mother country replace the Anglo-Japanese alliance of 1902 with a more realistic arrangement to guarantee peace in Asia.

Washington Naval Conference. Britain, the United States, and Japan wished to end the expensive postwar naval arms race. Powerful Japan had wrested wartime concessions from China and obtained a League of Nations mandate to occupy Germany's Pacific islands—the Carolines, Marshalls, and Marianas. A wary United States, anxious to deter the Japanese and restore the Open Door policy in China, transferred its main battleship strength from the American East Coast to California. With tensions mounting, all the naval powers welcomed an American invitation to meet in Washington to resolve their differences in the Pacific and defuse the arms race.

Under the guiding hand of American Secretary of State Charles Evans Hughes, over the winter of 1921–22 Britain, the United States, Japan, France, and Italy worked out the terms of this conference to "limit naval armaments." Popularly known as a disarmament conference, it implied that the powers would actually eliminate their navies, which none were willing to do. Instead, the control of weaponry through compromise was feasible, as long as all the signatories agreed to abide by the treaties. The powers therefore signed several realistic agreements which established ratios of capital ship strength and recognized spheres of political influence in the Pacific. No administrative vehicle for the inspection of naval arsenals was established to enforce these agreements, but because the signatories genuinely desired peace, they obeyed the treaties.

The 4 major Pacific powers froze the status quo of their respective zones of political control and agreed not to build new fortifications in their colonial or mandated possessions: Britain in the Indian Ocean and South Pacific; the United States in the Hawaiian, Philippine, and Aleutian island groups and Guam and

Wake; Japan in the Central Pacific islands and Formosa (Taiwan); and France in Indochina. The only exceptions which allowed naval base improvements were British Singapore and American Pearl Harbor. The 4 naval powers were joined by 5 other nations in endorsing the Open Door policy in China, although the British, American, and Japanese navies were permitted to maintain their regular gunboat patrols protecting merchants on the Yangtze River. The agreement preserved China's sovereignty, although the country was soon wracked by internal strife between the Nationalist regime and communist revolutionaries.

The hallmark of the Washington Conference was the 5-power pact, which fixed the size of each navy. Virtually all capital ship construction—battleships and battle cruisers—was to cease, except for a few replacement vessels then nearing completion. This "building holiday" was fixed to last 10 years. The powers agreed on a ceiling of capital ship strength arranged in a ratio of 5:5:3:1.75:1.75, that is, 525,000 tons each for Britain and the United States; 315,000 tons for Japan; and 175,000 tons each for France and Italy. The maximum sizes of capital ships and their main gun calibers were set at 35,000 tons and 16 inches, respectively. The same ratio was established for aircraft carriers, but in smaller numbers: the United States and Britain 135,000 tons each; Japan, 81,000 tons; France and Italy, 60,000 tons each. Maximum carrier size was set at 27,000 tons except for some larger capital ships designated to be converted into carriers.

With the capital ship as yardstick of naval power, only a few restrictions were placed on lesser ships of war. The powers agreed on maximum sizes of cruisers and their main batteries at 10,000 tons and 8 inches, respectively. All the signatories concurred that submarines should be limited as commerce raiders, but France was unwilling to accept any restrictions on submarine strength because of their cheaper cost than battleships. So no limits were placed on subs, nor on the multipurpose destroyers, nor on the number or sizes of aircraft which operated off carriers. Neither Weimar Germany nor Soviet Russia were parties to the Washington treaties.

The 5 naval powers agreed to renegotiate the treaties before they expired in 10 years. All of them strictly abided by the agreements during the interim. Britain, the United States, and Japan met at Geneva in 1927 in a futile attempt to limit the number of cruisers, destroyers, and submarines. France and Italy, having no real interest in the Pacific, did not play a major role when the powers reconvened at the **London Naval Conference** in 1930. They renewed the Washington tonnage ratios and established another for cruisers—10:10:7, with Japan last. British and American delegates tried to abolish submarines altogether, but Japan, France, and Italy refused, having already built a great many. A 6-year time limit was placed on this agreement, with a 2-year advance notice to be given by any nation not planning to renew it. Japan did so on the last day of 1934, and one year later, at a second London meeting, it demanded parity with Britain and the United States in all classes of warships. When the 2 English-speaking nations refused, the Japanese withdrew and allowed the naval treaties to expire at the end of 1936.

The Washington and London conferences accomplished the first successful arms control agreements. Because the signatories wanted the warship ratios to succeed, they did and over a prescribed period of time. The unresolved matter which troubled them all was the possibility of unrestricted submarine warfare against merchant shipping as practiced by Germany in World War I. Because most nations' submarines now targeted enemy warships, in 1936 the 5 naval powers agreed upon a special protocol at London which prohibited submarine attacks on unarmed shipping in wartime. Within weeks it was also ratified by Germany and Russia. As before, enforcement of such an international law depended upon the willingness of the signatories to abide by it.

Naval Rivalries (1922–39). Though navies were reduced to meet treaty requirements, they developed doctrines for possible future wars and policed their respective spheres of influence. The 1920s were relatively tranquil except in China, where civil war so endangered foreign nationals that to protect them in 1927 no fewer than 21 cruisers and lesser warships from 7 navies supported the landing of 40,000 British and Indian troops at Shanghai. The coming of global Depression in 1929–30, however, helped trigger truculent militarism, notably in Japan by its army and in Germany, where the Nazi dictator Adolf Hitler rose to power in 1933. The naval treaties expired and rearmament began, with the League of Nations powerless to block the road to war.

Britain. The granting of parity with the U.S. Navy at the Washington Conference ended the Royal Navy's centuries-old preeminence (since the 1670s). Though the navy received more funding than the army and RAF during the interwar years, the government chose not to build up to the strength allowed by the treaties. The fleet declined from 61 battleships and 9 battle cruisers in 1918 to 12 and 3, respectively, in 1939. The loss of the navy's Fleet Air Arm to the RAF in 1918 led to a system of dual control by the 2 services of the half-dozen carriers and their downright inferior aircraft. But the conservative admirals planned to wage a decisive Jutland-style gunnery duel, minimizing the vulnerability of their battleships to air attack. Again, cruisers trained to hunt down surface raiders; convoy escorts guarded against submarines; and amphibious operations were virtually ignored.

The high cost of empire led Britain to grant its major colonies semi-independent Commonwealth status in 1931 and a larger role in their own defense.

Hitler's rearmament program prompted Britain to adopt diplomacy in a vain attempt to restrict his new navy: the **Anglo-German Naval Treaty** of 1935 allowed Germany a fleet 35 percent the size of Britain's, and parity in—of all things—U-boats! The threat of fascist Italy led the British to depend on France to protect the western Mediterranean, and Japan's truculence meant that American help would be necessary to protect Commonwealth nations in the Far East.

As Britain began to rearm in the late 1930s, the RAF returned the Fleet Air Arm to the navy in 1937, and armored deck carriers of the *Illustrious* class were laid down. So were new battleships of the *King George V* class, mounting 14-inch guns. Falling behind its potential foes, Britain in 1938 shifted major funding from the navy to the RAF for the aerial defense of the homeland.

France. The French navy, traditionally subordinate to the army, briefly lost control of its fledgling air arm to the Air Ministry from 1928 to 1932. The admirals spent the 1920s debating the relative merits of the battleship, of which France had 20 in 1918, and the cruiser, torpedo boat, and submarine all still championed by the *jeune école*. The major naval theorist, Admiral Raoul Castex, argued that in a war France should abandon its overseas possessions (North Africa, Syria-Lebanon, Indochina, Madagascar) in order to fight Italy in the Mediterranean. In such a conflict Castex advocated whittling down the enemy fleet in order to control the middle sea. His conservative superiors ignored him and began building new capital ships, all the while planning to defend the empire. By 1939 France had only 5 battleships, 1 battle cruiser, and 1 carrier, but 76 submarines, 22 more than Britain.

Italy. Benito Mussolini became fascist dictator of Italy in 1922 and embarked upon a program of imperial expansion in the eastern Mediterranean and East Africa. The navy's 14 wartime battleships were less important than the destroyers, torpedo boats, and submarines with which he asserted control over the Adriatic Sea and eastern Aegean. Mussolini had little use for naval aircraft, preferring to make all Italy a giant aircraft carrier for the separate air force of strategic bombers advocated by General Giulio Douhet. In 1935–36 Italy invaded and conquered East African Abyssinia (Ethiopia) with impunity; Britain and France were too preoccupied with Nazi Germany to risk war with Italy over Abyssinia. By 1939 Mussolini's rearmament program had forged a respectable navy of 4 modern battleships, 21 cruisers (to France's 18), 48 destroyers (to France's 58), 69 torpedo boats (to France's 13), and 104 submarines, the most of any navy.

Germany. The minuscule navy of the Weimar Republic violated the postwar Treaty of Versailles by surreptitiously developing U-boats, aircraft, and a naval war college course. Admiral Hugo Wegener, rejecting a blue water fleet on the Tirpitz model, advocated a *guerre de course* navy of surface ships and torpedo craft. This was adopted when Admiral **Erich Raeder** assumed command of the navy in 1928, initiating construction of 3 11,000-ton "pocket battleships" with 11-inch guns, plus cruisers and torpedo boats. When Hitler took power in 1933 he added more U-boats to Raeder's commerce raiding navy and followed Mussolini in creating a separate air force, the Luftwaffe, at the expense of naval aviation. To counter France's battleships he laid down 2 42,000-ton *Bismarck*-class battleships with 15-inch guns, and he arranged the Anglo-German naval treaty.

Like continental France and Russia, which Hitler regarded as his major potential enemies, and Mussolini's Italy, he devoted most of Germany's military resources to the army. Even should he fight Britain, Hitler planned to use his *guerre de course* surface ships and subs to blockade the British Isles. The 2 battleships, 3 pocket battleships, 2 battle cruisers, 6 cruisers, 17 destroyers, and 57 U-boats that Germany had by 1939 were to wage "tonnage warfare" against merchant shipping. Commodore **Karl Doenitz** developed "wolf pack" tactics whereby teams of subs would be coordinated by radio. To maximize the amount of tonnage his navy could sink, Hitler in 1938–39 developed the Z-Plan for more battleships, cruisers, destroyers, and even carriers to raid enemy shipping in small task forces. He also authorized 200 more U-boats. Hitler assured Raeder he would avoid war until this construction was completed in 1944.

Between 1935 and 1939 Nazi Germany forged alliances with Italy and Japan against France, Russia, Britain, and Turkey, which began refortifying the Dardanelles in 1936. Using diplomatic maneuvers and shows of force Hitler annexed all or parts of neighboring countries and joined Mussolini in giving military aid to fascist General Francisco Franco seeking to overthrow the Spanish government. The Soviet Union responded by sending volunteers to support Spain's procommunist regime.

During the **Spanish Civil War** (1936–39) the Republican government used its navy to blockade Franco's Nationalist fascists in Morocco. But Franco successfully appealed to sympathizers within the Spanish navy to help him land in Spain and blockade Republican ports. In 1937–38 Britain, France, Germany, and Italy established a joint naval patrol to prevent foreign intervention, a fiction revealed when German pocket battleships and Italian subs attacked Republican shipping and ports. Anglo-French antisubmarine measures proved effective, but they were too late to prevent Franco's victory early in 1939. German armed forces had gained invaluable combat experience for the general war that was fast approaching.

United States. Although the United States emerged from the Washington Conference with a navy theoretically equal to Britain's, like Britain it did not build up to the maximum strength allowed by the treaty. This was because most

Americans, their Congress, and the army all opposed the navy's desire to deter Japan by actively policing the Pacific and protecting China. Isolationistic Americans wanted only to defend the Western Hemisphere, and the fleet was pared down from its wartime strength of 39 battleships to 18. In 1922 the 12 newest battleships and their escorts were designated the U.S. Fleet and concentrated in California to keep watch on Japan; the 6 older battleships remained on the East Coast.

The Caribbean Sea and Panama Canal remained the navy's strategic pivot but a politically unstable region patrolled by the "special service squadron" of old cruisers and gunboats based in Panama. It made shows of force and intervened with U.S. Marines to restore order in Nicaragua, Haiti, Cuba, and elsewhere. President Franklin D. Roosevelt terminated the interventions in 1933, whereupon local dictators took power, but at least they could be counted on to ally with the United States in a major war.

American naval leaders and planners assumed the United States would eventually fight Japan and developed fleet doctrine accordingly. Under War Plan Orange, evolving since 1906, the battle fleet would steam across the Pacific to relieve the Philippines after Japan initiated war. It would engage and defeat the Japanese fleet in a Jutland-style battle somewhere in the western Pacific, then blockade Japan.

During the 1920s and 1930s the fleet conducted annual war games between California and Hawaii. In 1929 its new fast 30-knot carriers *Lexington* and *Saratoga* first demonstrated the offensive possibilities of naval air power by using fighters, dive bombers, and torpedo planes in a mock sneak attack on the Panama Canal. Under the guiding hands of Admirals William A. Moffett and Joseph Mason Reeves, the U.S. Navy fought off the strategic bombing crusade of General "Billy" Mitchell, who advocated an independent air force, and soon took the lead in the world's carrier aviation. Because advanced bases would have to be captured in the Japanese Marshall, Caroline, and Mariana Islands, the U.S. Marine Corps took up the development of amphibious tactics with the creation of the Fleet Marine Force in 1933.

Isolationist sentiment and the Depression prevented the United States from significantly strengthening its navy until 1938 and then only slowly. Fleet maneuvers began to include amphibious forces using attack transports, specialized landing craft, and air support. The navy continued to produce submarines for scouting and attacking enemy warships. In 1939 the first at-sea refueling of ships took place, a logistical necessity for operations across the vast distances of the Pacific. By that year, the U.S. Navy had 15 battleships, 5 aircraft carriers, 32 cruisers, 209 destroyers (the most of any navy), and 87 submarines (second only to

Italy). With Britain dominant in the Atlantic, thus shielding the U.S. East Coast, the American navy focused on Japan as its primary potential foe.

Japan. Navy minister Admiral Tomosaburo Kato directed the postwar enlargement of the 13-battleship, 7-battle-cruiser Imperial Japanese Navy, but he also headed Japan's delegation to the Washington Conference which acceded to its terms. Kato, prime minister from 1922 to 1923, and his successors built up the fleet to maximum treaty strength as a deterrent force and abided by the 5:5:3 ratio in the interest of peace. Ever since 1906 Japan's admirals had viewed the U.S. Navy as the major potential enemy and had followed the strategic doctrine of Admiral Saneyuki Akiyama: when the American fleet entered the western Pacific, it would be whittled down in day and night attacks by swift cruisers, submarines, and destroyers using superior torpedoes. To these forces were added aircraft carriers and land-based bombers during the 1920s and 1930s. With the U.S. Fleet thus scaled down, the Japanese fleet planned to engage and defeat it in the manner of the Battle of Tsushima, hopefully at night with specially devised tactics.

But the army, senior military service in Japan, regarded Soviet Russia as the main enemy, especially when in the 1920s Russia annexed Mongolia, undermined Chinese authority in Manchuria, and appeared to be seeking hegemony over continental East Asia. Reactionary army officers therefore forced Japan to invade and conquer Manchuria in 1931 and the navy to land troops under cover of carrier planes at Shanghai in 1932. An Anglo-American naval demonstration forced the Japanese to evacuate the devastated city, but Japan's generals gradually forced their government to adopt an anti-Russian stance and to withdraw from the naval treaties in 1936. As 1937 began, Japan resumed massive naval construction, highlighted by the world's largest battleships and naval guns, the 72,000-ton *Yamato* class with 18.1-inch main batteries, as well as new aircraft carriers. The army's militarism sharply divided the navy's officer corps between the "treaty faction" dominated by Admiral **Isoroku Yamamoto,** which wanted peace, and the "fleet faction," which joined the army in advocating war.

The militants prevailed, and in 1936 Japan signed the anti–Comintern Pact with Nazi Germany against the Soviet Union. In 1937 Japan invaded China proper as the first step toward thwarting Soviet ambitions in East Asia. Japanese strategy was therefore fundamentally continental. The army—transported, supported, and supplied by the navy—undertook the creation of the "Greater East Asia Co-Prosperity Sphere"—the conquest of China as a springboard for an attack on Russia's Far Eastern provinces. The navy had little choice but to follow the army's dictates. Each service retained its own air arm, no interest having developed for a separate air force. Japan's carrier planes proved highly effective in China, which included sinking U.S. patrol gunboat *Panay* in the Yangtze River in December 1937. In 1938 the navy mounted an amphibious assault which captured Canton on the Chinese coast. But the war then bogged down at the foothills of the Himalaya Mountains, and Soviet forces severely punished the Japanese army in border clashes on the Manchurian frontier.

By 1939 Japan's Combined Fleet had 9 battleships, 5 carriers, 39 cruisers, 84 destroyers, 38 torpedo boats, and 58 submarines, all geared toward fighting the U.S. Fleet in a big battle within cruising range of Japanese bases in the homeland. The navy gave no attention to a wide-ranging naval war in the Pacific and did not even experiment with at-sea refueling until 1941. Neither did it address the need to defend its own merchant ships or to attack those of its enemies. Yamamoto's appointment to command the fleet in 1939 did not prevent the navy from following the fleet faction in accepting the army's aggressive posture, and he reluctantly prepared to fight the United States.

Japanese aggression had global repercussions. Not only was Russia forced to commit major ground forces to its Pacific provinces, but the European colonial powers beefed up their naval forces in Asian waters. In 1938 Britain completed new naval base facilities at Singapore, thereby strengthening its naval communications between Ceylon and Hong Kong. The Netherlands dispatched 3 light cruisers plus destroyers, mine vessels, and submarines to Batavia for the defense of the Dutch East Indies. France was helpless in 1939 to prevent the Japanese from capturing Hainan Island in the Gulf of Tonkin, commanding the approaches to Haiphong harbor in French Indochina. The U.S. Asiatic Fleet in the Philippines was woefully weak, as were the defenses of its main base at Manila.

If the Western democracies and the Soviet Union had any doubts about Japanese militancy, they were dashed in mid-1940 when Japan formally allied with Hitler's Germany and Mussolini's Italy to create the tripartite Axis.

15

World War II in the Atlantic

(1939–1945)

WORLD WAR II BEGAN IN September 1939 when Nazi Germany and Soviet Russia conquered and divided up Poland, leading Britain and France to declare war on Germany. The European fighting resembled World War I in its essential features: a continental struggle between Allied and Axis armies, and a maritime battle of Allied naval forces defending their merchant shipping against German commerce raiders, principally U-boats. Aircraft and other weapons had greater mobility, range, and destructive power but remained wedded to historic strategic practices such as convoy and amphibious operations. As in 1914 other nations declared their neutrality under international law but were eventually drawn into the fighting. Winston Churchill even returned to his 1914 post as Britain's First Lord of the Admiralty.

Anglo-German War (1939–40). The British Home Fleet transported the army to the French coast, then concentrated at Scapa Flow to mine the German coast and Straits of Dover and to counter German minelaying ships and subs, assisted by land-based bombers of the RAF's Coastal Command. Hitler warned the captains of his 39 U-boats and 2 pocket battleships already at sea to avoid sinking unarmed merchant ships. But a U-boat mistakenly sank a merchantman the first day of the war, leading Britain to institute limited convoys in the North Sea.

German raiders attacked with great zeal. One sub sank the carrier *Courageous* in the Irish Sea in September 1939, and in October *U-47* penetrated Scapa Flow to sink the battleship *Royal Oak*. Pocket battleship *Graf Spee* plundered shipping in the South Atlantic until 3 cruisers under Commodore Henry Harwood engaged and damaged it off Uruguay's **River Plate** on 13 December. Forced to put into neutral Montevideo for repairs, the outgunned *Graf Spee* was soon blockaded by more British warships closing in. Her captain elected to scuttle her offshore and commit suicide. Admiral **Karl Doenitz,** German U-boat chief, initiated "wolf pack" group tactics, coordinated by radio from Germany. For the first 7 months of the war, the Germans lost 18 U-boats to the British but sank 222 merchantmen; surface raiders, mines, and aircraft claimed another 181.

The United States modified its neutrality laws to sell aircraft and munitions to the Allies late in 1939. An alarmed Hitler gradually lifted the restrictions on his commerce raiders, especially since Britain broke the rules: in February 1940 British destroyer *Cossack* violated neutral Norwegian waters to liberate 300 British prisoners from German supply ship *Altmark*. But Norway's vital resources caused both sides to violate Norwegian neutrality, thereby widening the war.

The Blitz (1940). On 9 April 1940, Hitler unleashed his *blitzkrieg*, lightning war, against Denmark and Norway. The land-based Luftwaffe augmented the surface navy and U-boats by attacking British fleet units with Stuka dive bombers trained in attacking ships. Denmark fell in a day, but Germany's amphibious landings at several Norwegian ports brought an immediate British response in the hard-fought **Norwegian campaign.**

Battle cruiser *Renown* drove away battle cruisers *Scharnhorst* and *Gneisenau*, and Norwegian coastal defenses sank a heavy cruiser in Oslo fjord. A successful British surface attack culminated in battleship *Warspite* and 9 destroyers sinking 8 German destroyers in Narvik fjord on 13 April. But the Luftwaffe forced the British to evacuate some of their troops and to occupy Iceland on 10 May for its air and naval bases. That same day Hitler's armies swept into the Low Countries and then France, obliging the Allies to abandon Norway in early June. *Scharnhorst, Gneisenau,* a cruiser, and 4 destroyers attacked the evacuation force, sinking the carrier *Glorious,* 2 destroyers, and 2 transports.

So successful was the German blitz into France that it pinned the British army against the sea at **Dunkirk.** Between 28 May and 4 June 861 British, French, and private vessels evacuated over 338,000 Allied troops from Dunkirk, covered by RAF fighters. German planes, U-boats, and torpedo boats sank 6 British and 3 French destroyers and 234 assorted craft. On 10 June Italy invaded France from the south. Its bombers forced Allied Mediterranean fleet units to retire out of range to Alexandria and Gibraltar. Allied warships evacuated another 192,000 Allied troops from the French Atlantic coast to England. But on 22 June France surrendered, giving Hitler naval bases on the French coast.

Churchill, now prime minister, redeployed several Home Fleet ships to Gibraltar to comprise Force H under Admiral Sir **James Somerville.** From there it could shift between the Atlantic and western Mediterranean to fight not only Germany and Italy but the French Mediterranean Fleet controlled by the Vichy French collaborationist government. Admiral Sir **Andrew Cunningham**'s Mediterranean Fleet kept several French warships in exile at Alexandria, but the main French fleet at Mers-el-Kebir in Algeria refused a British ultimatum to be handed over. Churchill ordered Force H to attack it in port. On 3 July Somerville's 2 battleships, battle cruiser, and carrier sank a French battleship and disabled a battle cruiser, but another battle cruiser and 6 destroyers escaped to Toulon. On the 9th Cunningham's fleet, covering a convoy, drove back an Italian naval force off Punto Stilo on the Calabrian coast of Italy.

Hitler contemplated a cross-Channel invasion of England (Operation Sea Lion) in mid-July 1940 but realized he lacked the amphibious capability. Instead, he spent the summer sending the Luftwaffe against the RAF in the futile Battle of Britain, while Doenitz coordinated U-boat wolf packs operating out of French and Norwegian ports. They sank an average of 450,000 tons of shipping per month, mostly unescorted vessels.

The fall of France and Britain's desperate defense galvanized the United States. In July 1940 the United States authorized construction of a 2-ocean navy capable of fighting both Germany and Japan, and in September President Franklin D. Roosevelt transferred 50 World War I–vintage destroyers to the British for convoy escort duty. In return, Britain leased naval and air installations in Bermuda, Newfoundland, and the Caribbean to the United States. The U.S. Navy strengthened its own warship and aircraft patrols which reported German U-boat movements to the British.

The Mediterranean (1940–41). In the autumn of 1940 Cunningham's fleet occupied Crete and helped the British 8th Army repulse Mussolini's invasion of Egypt. When new construction increased the Italian fleet at **Taranto** to 6 battleships, Cunningham sent 21 Swordfish torpedo planes from carrier *Illustrious* to attack them during the night of 11–12 November. Launched 170 miles out, the Swordfish braved heavy antiaircraft fire to sink brand new *Littorio* with 3 torpedoes, the older *Conte di Cavour* with 1, and disable a third. Two carrier aircraft were lost. The 3 surviving battleships abandoned Taranto. British gunships bombarded the Italian army in Albania as it retreated from an ill-fated invasion of Greece.

To retrieve Mussolini's fortunes Hitler sent Field Marshal Erwin Rommel to Libya with a new "Africa Corps" and redeployed his antiship Stuka dive bombers to Sicily in January 1941. On the 10th and 11th they attacked Force H off Sicily, sinking a cruiser and hitting *Illustrious,* forcing her to withdraw from the middle sea for extensive repairs. On 9 February Force H bombarded Genoa as carrier planes from *Ark Royal* aerially mined La Spezia, the Italian fleet's anchorage near Genoa.

In spite of increasing Luftwaffe raids on Malta, defended by the RAF, the British moved troops into Greece in March 1941, covered by Cunningham's fleet, augmented by carrier *Formidable.* Two-man Italian torpedo boats crippled a British cruiser at Suda Bay, Crete, on the 25th, followed by an Italian fleet sortie into the waters south of Crete to intercept British convoys. Alerted by aerial reconnaissance, Cunningham sortied from Alexandria. The 2 fleets clashed south of Crete on 28 March, but Admiral Angelo Iachino retired in the presence of *Formidable*'s aircraft. Joined by RAF planes from Crete and mainland Greece, Cunningham pursued Iachino in the running Battle of **Cape Matapan.** When aerial torpedo hits slowed down battleship *Vittorio Veneto* and a cruiser, Iachino rushed forward 2 other cruisers, both sunk by Cunningham's 3 battleships.

Axis spring offensives forced Cunningham to evacuate the army from Greece and Crete. With the Suez Canal imperiled by aerial mines, the British diverted troop convoys around South Africa to secure East Africa and the Middle East via the Red Sea. The Mediterranean fighting seesawed the rest of 1941 as planes and ships traded blows at sea and against naval and air bases. A special British anti-convoy force of light cruisers and destroyers, aided by codebreakers, decimated Axis convoys. In November, *U-81* sank carrier *Ark Royal, U-331* battleship *Barham.* In December an Italian submarine delivered frogmen (teams of underwater demolition swimmers) to Alexandria, where they attached explosives to the hulls of *Valiant* and *Queen Elizabeth.* Both battleships were totally disabled by the blasts. By Christmastime the Mediterranean front was virtually stalemated.

Battle of the Atlantic (1940–43). In August 1940 Hitler declared a block-ade of all shipping—enemy and neutral—in British waters. Italian submarines joined Doenitz's wolf packs and 7 disguised German auxiliary cruisers in the At-lantic. Churchill, to protect the southern route, sent a heavy surface force and Anglo–Free French amphibious troops to seize the Vichy French base at Dakar, French West Africa. Although the landing was repulsed in late September, British South Atlantic sea lanes were covered by ships and planes from West African Freetown, South African Simonstown, and the Falkland Islands.

Pocket battleship *Admiral Scheer,* battle cruisers *Scharnhorst* and *Gneisenau,* and heavy cruiser *Admiral Hipper* then plundered North Atlantic shipping, joined by wolf packs. On 17–20 October, 9 U-boats sank 32 ships (155,000 tons) in 2 Chan-nel convoys. On 8–11 February 1941, a U-boat, 5 long-range bombers, and *Hipper* decimated 2 convoys off Portugal's Cape St. Vincent. Both battles typified Doenitz's **tonnage war:** he concentrated his boats where they could sink the most ships, regardless of the relative military value of the cargo. U-boat skippers chafed under his tight control from headquarters by radio and preferred un-escorted targets to the more hazardous escorted convoys which sank 23 U-boats during 1940. On the other hand, the subs accounted for most of the 4 million tons of Allied shipping sunk that year.

Gradually improving antisubmarine countermeasures enabled the British to extend their defensive convoys ever further westward. By April 1941 Britain-based escort ships were relieving escorts bringing in convoys from Iceland at the Mid-Ocean Meeting Point, 18 degrees west longitude. This point was extended to 35 degrees in June, where convoys arrived under escort from Newfoundland. The tools of escorts included asdic (or sonar) echo-acoustical underwater detection gear, radar sets for locating surfaced subs, and high-frequency radio direction finders to pinpoint U-boat radio transmissions. British codebreakers enabled convoys to be routed around wolf packs until so many packs existed that not all could be avoided.

The role of land-based and amphibian patrol-bombers increased from bases in Britain, Canada, and Iceland, but none could reach an area of the mid-Atlantic south of Greenland known as the "black pit" for the many sinkings there. RAF Coastal Command bombers finally chased *Scharnhorst* and *Gneisenau* back to Brest in March 1941, where planes severely damaged them. On 21 May patrol planes sighted battleship *Bismarck* and heavy cruiser *Prinz Eugen* leaving Norwegian waters to attack convoys in the North Atlantic.

British Home Fleet units put to sea and tracked the Germans' sweep around Iceland. On the morning of the 24th battle cruiser *Hood* and battleship *Prince of Wales* engaged them. But the German ships exploded the *Hood* in the same way that *Hood*'s predecessors had been sunk at Jutland in 1916; all but 3 of her 1,500-man crew perished. The *Prince of Wales* took 7 hits and withdrew but not before hitting *Bismarck,* causing a fuel leak. The German admiral decided to return to base and released *Prinz Eugen* to operate independently (it reached Brest). During the night, Swordfish from carrier *Victorious* attacked *Bismarck* unsuccessfully, but Somerville rushed up from Gibraltar with Force H. On the evening of the 26th Swordfish from *Ark Royal* torpedoed *Bismarck* in the rudder, rendering her uncontrollable. The following morning, southwest of Ireland, battleships *King George V* and *Rodney* overpowered *Bismarck* with their guns, a cruiser torpedoed her, and the crew opened her scuttles. She went down with 2,300 men, a loss that greatly discredited German surface raiders.

The *Bismarck* episode prompted President Roosevelt to increase U.S. participation in the Battle of the Atlantic, resulting in an **undeclared German-American naval war** as shooting incidents occurred. On 22 June Hitler launched his blitz into Russia. His surface ships and bombers destroyed the Russian Baltic Fleet, and other German naval units pushed into the Black Sea. U.S. Marines took over the defense of Iceland in July, and convoys began to make the dangerous Arctic run past occupied Norway to Murmansk to supply the Russian army desperately defending Moscow and Leningrad (St. Petersburg).

The rest of 1941 the RAF used bombs to sink 75,000 tons of German merchant shipping from Norway to France, aerial mines for another 137,000 tons. An Iceland-based Hudson bomber damaged *U-570* so severely that it surrendered and was taken in tow by a British destroyer. The British added catapults to 35 cargo ships for launching Sea Hurricane fighters against attacking German bombers; the RAF pilot was recovered by "ditching" near the convoy and being picked up. By September U.S. destroyers were escorting convoys to midocean; 1 was sunk by a U-boat in October.

With Japan's attack on Pearl Harbor in December the United States officially entered the war just as the Battle of the Atlantic reached a critical stage. Britain's first escort carrier, U.S.-built *Audacity,* entered the fray as part of a convoy escort which sank 5 of 12 U-boats off the Portuguese coast in a 9-day battle. Most of the convoy survived but not *Audacity.* Doenitz's U-boats accounted for over half of the 4 million tons of Allied shipping sunk in 1941, the rest destroyed by warships, planes, and mines. But the Allies sank 40 Axis subs and 3 auxiliary cruisers during the last 7 months of 1941.

Doenitz shifted most of his 91 subs to U.S. East Coast shipping, unescorted because the crucial transatlantic convoys absorbed American escort ships. As a result, in the first 6 months of 1942 U-boats sank 585 merchantmen (over 3 million tons); aircraft, surface ships, and mines destroyed another 400 (1 million tons). But Germany lost 21 more subs, Italy 7. As new Allied escorts began to accompany U.S. coastal convoys, augmented by shore-based patrol planes and blimps, Doenitz shifted his boats to the safer Caribbean in the late spring. But U.S. and Brazilian convoys led him to recall them to the mid-Atlantic during the summer.

In July 1942 Raeder dispatched *Tirpitz* and other ships to attack heavily escorted convoy PQ 17—code designation for the Murmansk run. The British Home Fleet sortied for action, ordering the convoy to disperse, unaware the Germans had returned to base. U-boats and Luftwaffe spent a week sinking 23 of 35 dispersed ships. In September subs and planes sank 13 of 41 merchantmen of convoy PQ 18 in the North Sea, although planes from escort carrier *Avenger* and 20 other ships sank 3 subs and shot down 22 planes. The Allies suspended their Murmansk convoys to concentrate on the deadly transatlantic runs but resumed them in December. On the 31st, in the Barents Sea north of Norway, 2 British cruisers and 8 destroyers saved their convoy by driving off a German surface force. An irate Hitler forced Raeder to resign and replaced him with Doenitz as navy chief.

With U-boat strength at 240 by March 1943, Doenitz concentrated 3 wolf packs totaling 40 boats to attack 2 New York-to-Britain convoys, HX 229 and SC 122, in the "black pit." Over 6 days they sank 21 ships of the 92-ship convoys, whose 13 escorts—which did not include a carrier—managed to sink only a single sub. The running fight was fought beyond the range of aircraft from Newfoundland, Iceland, and northern Ireland.

Allied material strength and tactical innovations began to turn the tide: mass-produced American Liberty and Victory merchant ships, escort carriers, destroyers, frigates, carrier planes, and multiengine bombers. Both the U.S. and British navies had to battle their respective land-based air services—the RAF and U.S. Air Army Forces (AAF)—to divert many new long-range strategic bombers, especially B-24 (PB4Y) Liberators, to naval control. These began to reach out from North Atlantic airfields to cover the "black pit" and to bomb U-boat pens along the Bay of Biscay in France. In March the British and Canadian navies took over all convoy escort, releasing the U.S. Navy to form **hunter-killer groups** for independent operations in the "black pit." Admiral Sir **Max Horton** directed similar British groups in the Western Approaches. At the center of each group was an escort carrier equipped with fighters and torpedo-bombers.

U-boats could not maneuver freely and safely in the presence of aircraft. Liverpool-to-Halifax convoy ONS 5, covered by 19 escort ships and Liberator bombers, lost 12 ships during 4–6 May 1943, but the escort sank 6 and damaged 5 other subs. The surviving U-boats intercepted 2 convoys out of Halifax on 9–13 May, but the escorting carrier and destroyers traded 5 cargo ships for 5 U-boats. No fewer than 41 U-boats were sunk during May, 11 to escorting planes, bringing Doenitz's losses over the preceding year to 165 boats, plus 29 Italian subs. He terminated the U-boat offensive to consider his options. The course of the Battle of the Atlantic had turned against the Axis.

Allied Strategy. In 1942 Churchill, Roosevelt, and their military leaders agreed that the Soviet army would be the main force for defeating Hitler's armies on the continent, while Britain and the United States battled Germany for control of the seas around—and the skies over—Europe: the strategy of concentration. The embattled Murmansk convoys provided one-fourth of Anglo-American military aid to Russia; another fourth passed by sea around Africa through the Persian Gulf and Iran; and one-half of it crossed the North Pacific from U.S. West Coast ports to the Russian Far East—relatively unmolested by Japan, which had signed a nonaggression pact with the Soviet Union in April 1941. Premier Stalin demanded that his allies land an army on the coast of France to create a second front and force Hitler to divert ground forces from the eastern front, relieving pressure on the Red Army.

The Anglo-American leaders agreed with Stalin, but Churchill convinced Roosevelt that no cross-Channel attack against Hitler's "Fortress Europe" was possible until (1) the U-boat was neutralized to ensure safe transatlantic supply lines; (2) Rommel was beaten in North Africa and Italy defeated to open Mediterranean sea lanes to Suez and the oil-rich Middle East; and (3) Hitler's armies were thrown on the defensive by the Red Army. In addition, amphibious

Admiral Ernest J. King

Admiral Ernest Joseph King (1878–1956) masterminded American naval strategy in both the Atlantic and Pacific theaters of World War II. His keen intellect and strong will served him well in a uniquely diversified career. A 1901 graduate of the U.S. Naval Academy, he saw duty in destroyers and battleships, during World War I as assistant chief of staff to Atlantic Fleet commander Admiral Henry T. Mayo. As captain in the 1920s, he shifted to submarine duty but then underwent flight training at the age of 48—no small feat—to become a naval aviator. In the 1930s King successively commanded carrier *Lexington,* the fleet's patrol plane squadrons as rear admiral, and the fleet's carriers as vice admiral, interspersed with study at the Naval War College and duty as chief of the Navy's Bureau of Aeronautics.

Promoted full admiral in 1941 King commanded the Atlantic Fleet during the undeclared naval war with Germany and at the end of the year was appointed commander in chief U.S. Fleet (CominCh). Headquartered at the Navy Department in Washington, he received the additional appointment of Chief of Naval Operations (CNO) in March 1942, thereby centralizing the Navy's operations and logistics under his authority. A superior administrator, he directed virtually all facets of the wartime navy. As CominCh-CNO, King represented the navy on the U.S. Joint Chiefs of Staff (JCS) and on the Anglo-American Combined Chiefs of Staff (CCS). He worked closely with his Army counterpart in both bodies, General George C. Marshall. But he resisted attempts by the U.S. Army and the U.S. Army Air Forces to dominate strategic employment of naval forces and to cut back naval construction. King countered British efforts to dominate wartime strategy in the Atlantic and to have a larger role in the Pacific. But he earned the grudging respect of British leaders for his strategic acumen and support of their operations.

---

doctrine, tactics, and specialized landing craft needed to be honed in battle—a reality driven home in August 1942, when an Anglo-Canadian landing raid at **Dieppe** on the French coast suffered heavy losses.

The Atlantic partners agreed to land in North Africa in November 1942, but the Americans rejected Churchill's ultimate goal to drive up the Italian peninsula into Germany via the "soft underbelly" of Europe. Led by the forceful **Admiral Ernest J. King** (see essay), commander in chief of the U.S. Fleet, they insisted on a direct cross-Channel assault after Italy's surrender.

The North Africa landings coincided with Soviet counterattacks on the eastern front. In September 1942, Russian naval aircraft and coastal warships resisted Ger-

From his wide reading of history and study of strategy King fully appreciated the global dimensions of World War II. Alone among his American and British peers, he insisted that the war against Japan be prosecuted with equal vigor with the struggle against Hitler, in spite of the Allied agreement to defeat Germany first. He adhered to the traditional maritime strategy of concentration in both theaters, namely, that the Allied navies must win control of the sea in order to supply major continental Allied armies which would defeat those of Germany and Japan. In Europe this meant overcoming the U-boat in order to support the Soviet army and then invade occupied France. He agreed with the British to invade Italy but only on the condition that Britain give the United States a free hand to fight Japan in the Pacific. He dominated Pacific strategy, against the opposition of General Douglas MacArthur.

The single-minded determination of "Ernie" King—as he was nicknamed—caused friction all around. President Franklin D. Roosevelt in 1942 appointed a former CNO, Admiral William D. Leahy, to chair the JCS and thus exert a modicum of control over King. But when King reached the mandatory retirement age of 64 in late 1942 Roosevelt ignored the rule. King resented civilian control of the Navy's expansion by the brilliant James V. Forrestal, under secretary until April 1944 and thereafter Secretary of the Navy. But the 2 men eventually converged in their mutual desire to fashion a balanced fleet with which to dominate the oceans of the postwar world.

King was promoted to the 5-star rank of fleet admiral in December 1944. He retired 1 year later. The American press corps, pleased with King's off-the-record candor throughout the war, honored the tough fighter with the story that he was reputed to shave with a blowtorch!

man naval and amphibious attacks in the Gulf of Finland and helped to lift the siege of Leningrad. They were later joined by Russian subs attacking German shipping in the Baltic, forcing the Germans to adopt convoys and lay a mine barrage off Kronstadt. In the Black Sea the Germans drove Russian naval forces eastward until November when the Red Army counterattacked and in February 1943 captured the entire German army at Stalingrad. Hitler had to divert forces from the Mediterranean to strengthen his eastern front, a boon to the Allied offensive in the middle sea. Meanwhile, the Allies made a secret deal with the Vichy French forces defending North Africa to change sides after only a token resistance against the landings.

The Mediterranean (1942–44). Axis and Allied naval and air forces defended their respective bases and convoys to and from North Africa against each other. On 22 March 1942 Admiral **Philip Vian** and a cruiser-destroyer force repulsed a gun force under Admiral Iachino off Syrte, Libya, but lost the 4 cargo ships under escort to dive bombers. Over 10–15 August a British fleet of 4 carriers, 2 battleships, 7 cruisers, and 27 destroyers fought its way from Gibraltar to Malta with a convoy of 13 cargo ships and tanker *Ohio* laden with aviation gas. German dive and torpedo bombers, U-boats, and torpedo boats sank the carrier *Eagle,* 2 cruisers, a destroyer, and 9 merchantmen, but *Ohio* got through.

The British successfully assaulted and captured Vichy French Madagascar in May 1942 to defend their Indian Ocean shipping. Rommel's Africa Corps spent the summer advancing toward Suez. Then, on 3 November, the British 8th Army counterattacked at El Alamein, driving Rommel westward out of Egypt. Five days later, the **North African landings** occurred. With Cunningham in over-all command and utilizing the expert amphibious skills of Admiral **Bertram Ramsay,** Anglo-American assault forces invaded Vichy French Morocco and Algeria. Both invasion armadas—that of the United States directly from Nor-folk, Virginia—passed undetected and unopposed by central Atlantic U-boats because Doenitz had concentrated them against a convoy off Morocco. Their late October attack sank 11 of 37 merchantmen, but the Allied fleets slipped by.

The 8 November 1942 landings occurred in 3 places simultaneously. They overwhelmed the token resistance by Vichy French forces, including several war-ships. Bombardment forces of battleships, cruisers, escort carriers, and destroy-ers supported the U.S. Army assaults at Moroccan Casablanca and Algerian Oran and Anglo-American troops at Algiers. One British destroyer and 2 cutters were the only Allied ship losses, while Force H cruised the western Mediterranean lest the Italian fleet interfere. Admiral François Darlan, Vichy French commander in North Africa, ordered all fighting to cease on 11 November, and his forces came over to the Allied side.

The Allied landings and Vichy defection enraged Hitler, who occupied the rest of France. When German troops entered Toulon, however, the local French ad-miral scuttled his 3 battleships, 7 cruisers, and 30 destroyers. The British imme-diately established a cruiser-destroyer striking force at Bone in eastern Algeria and Allied air forces moved into Algerian bases to attack Italian warships and merchantmen at sea and in port. The Germans rushed reinforcements to Tunisia, only to be trapped by a pincers movement of the Allied armies—U.S. general Dwight D. Eisenhower from Algeria, British general Bernard Montgomery from Egypt and Libya. Cunningham's fleet swept the Mediterranean of Axis shipping, sinking 100 Italian merchantmen in April 1943 alone. Rommel escaped by air, but the Africa Corps surrendered in May. Convoys now safely transitted the middle sea, expediting the supply of Russia through Iran via the Suez Canal.

With command of Mediterranean waters the Allied forces under Eisenhower prepared for the invasion of Italy. The U.S. Navy transported some 2,000 newly developed amphibious vessels to its bases in North Africa: tractored "dukw" (duck), LST (landing ship, tank), and specialized landing craft—LCI, LCT, and LCVP (for infantry, tanks, and vehicles and personnel). The first phase of the Italian campaign was the **landing on Sicily,** 10 July 1943. Covered by Force H, Cunningham lent highly effective shore bombardment to the assaults; land-based air support from North African fields was less satisfactory. The western task force under **Admiral H. Kent Hewitt** of the United States landed the American 7th Army, the eastern task force under Admiral Ramsey its British 8th Army. With Allied air forces battling the Luftwaffe, the 2 armies raced across Sicily until the Axis armies escaped across the Straits of Messina into Italy in August.

Mussolini's regime fell, and Italy changed sides. On 3 September the British 8th Army was sealifted across the Straits of Messina. On the 9th, Admiral Hewitt's bombardment forces supported the U.S. 5th Army's landing at **Salerno** near Naples. To defend Italy the Germans added radio-guided missiles which damaged several Allied ships. Force H escorted the surrendered Italian fleet to Malta for internment; the Luftwaffe sank an Italian battleship en route.

A German army counterattack stopped the Allied advance north of Naples, and on the night of 2–3 December 1943 German bombers sank 16 Allied supply ships at Bari on the southern Adriatic coast. The Allies decided to land in the German rear on the western coast of Italy. On 22 January 1944 cruisers and destroyers covered the 2-division Anglo-American assault at **Anzio.** But long-range air coverage from bases in North Africa proved so inadequate that the Allied troops were pinned down at their beachhead by the German army, and a guided missile sank a British cruiser. The Italian campaign bogged down in a virtual stalemate, but it had given the Allied navies invaluable amphibious experience.

Battle of the Atlantic (1943–45). In May 1943 Admiral King undertook a concerted offensive to defeat the U-boat by creating the Tenth Fleet under his personal command, in addition to his larger duties as U.S. Navy chief. His main striking forces were the hunter-killer groups of the Anglo-American navies, which pooled new technologies and tactics: sonobuoys, aircraft searchlights, and airborne microwave radars for sub detection; aerial rockets, homing torpedoes, and faster-sinking depth charges with which to kill U-boats; and "operations research," the application of quantitative analysis to antisubmarine tactics. U-boat losses mounted, and only once did a German sub sink a U.S. escort carrier. Also,

The German submarine *U-1229* is smothered by depth bombs from 3 TBM Avenger torpedo-bombers and machine-gun fire from 2 FM Wildcat fighters 300 miles southeast of Newfoundland, 20 August 1944. A TBM (*upper inset*) from escort carrier *Bogue* (*lower inset*) had damaged several battery cells with a bomb hit 2 hours earlier, causing deadly chlorine gas to leak. The U-boat had submerged, hoping to stay down using its schnorkel breathing tube (adjacent to the conning tower), but fear of the gas causing an explosion forced it to resurface. When these depth bombs exploded at keel depth, the crew abandoned ship as the sub sank. Taken prisoner by *Bogue*'s escorts were 41 crewmen and a spy bound for the coast of Maine. (U.S. Navy)

during the summer Allied bombers sank 16 U-boats in the Bay of Biscay, and vast numbers of new Allied merchant ships began to surpass the tonnage being lost.

Doenitz spent the summer of 1943 equipping his boats with a new acoustical homing torpedo and pressing development of the *schnorkel,* an underwater breathing device that enabled his subs to remain submerged instead of resurfacing periodically to recharge their batteries. But it would not become operational for another year. He deployed "milch cow" U-boats to resupply his subs at sea and renewed his attacks on the convoys in September when 19 U-boats sank only 9 of 88 merchantmen and escorts in 2 convoys covered by aircraft; 2 subs were lost. Allied ships and planes sank another 23 U-boats in October, and Allied scientists produced a decoy weapon which fouled German homing torpedoes.

A desperate Doenitz simultaneously unleashed his heavy gunships into the North Atlantic. In September *Tirpitz, Gneisenau,* and 10 destroyers raided the Arctic outpost of Spitzbergen, after which British midget subs stole into the Norwegian fjord anchorage of the *Tirpitz* to cripple her. On Christmas day *Scharnhorst* and 5 destroyers sortied against a Murmansk convoy only to be driven back next morning by escorting cruisers and destroyers. In the **Battle of North Cape,** Home Fleet commander Admiral Sir Bruce Fraser came up with battleship *Duke of York,* a cruiser, and 5 destroyers to slow down *Scharnhorst* with several hits, enabling the cruisers and destroyers to sink her with torpedoes. In April 1944 carrier planes disabled *Tirpitz* at her anchorage, and the RAF sank her in November. The remaining surface ships withdrew to the Baltic.

Doenitz shifted his U-boats to the Western Approaches at the beginning of 1944, only to have them so ravaged by hunter-killer groups that in March he discontinued the attacks on convoys, in effect conceding defeat. From July 1943 to May 1944 Germany lost 167 U-boats, faster than they could be replaced. Individual boats remained active throughout the Atlantic but found safer pickings in the distant Indian Ocean. Allied hunter-killer groups became so effective that in June one of them, built around escort carrier *Guadalcanal,* engaged and captured *U-505,* then towed it to Bermuda.

Normandy. By late spring 1944 the U-boat and Luftwaffe had been sufficiently weakened to enable the Allies to invade Hitler's Fortress Europe on the Normandy coast of France. Equally important, the counteroffensive of the Red Army tied down the main German army on the eastern front. The Soviet Black Sea Fleet and naval infantry liberated the Crimea and blockaded Axis Rumania and Bulgaria.

On 6 June 1944—D-Day—Eisenhower's Allied Expeditionary Force crossed the English Channel, preceded by 255 minesweepers clearing the way and by airborne troops dropped behind the beach. The British dominated the naval aspects of the operation, commanded by Admiral Ramsey, contributing most of the

2,468 landing craft and bombardment ships. Carriers were unnecessary, given the 12,800 Allied planes operating out of British airfields. Five British, American, and Canadian divisions successfully fought their way onto and behind the beach—175,000 men in all. During several days of German counterattacks by sea, Allied vessels sank 13 U-boats, 2 destroyers, and many coastal E-boats and motor torpedo craft. German mines, coastal guns, and aircraft claimed 4 Allied destroyers and assorted lesser craft. The British navy towed into place prefabricated harbor works, "Mulberrys," to create 2 artificial roadsteads, although 1 was soon destroyed by a violent storm.

After the bombardment ships helped capture the port of Cherbourg west of the Normandy beaches by 30 June, they redeployed to the Mediterranean for 1 more amphibious assault. The Allies broke out of the Normandy beachhead late in July, and on 15 August Admiral Hewitt landed the U.S. 7th Army, including a French corps, in southern France near Toulon. The Allied armies from Normandy and Toulon formed a pincers movement which liberated all France, forcing the U-boats to operate only from Baltic bases.

The Germans tenaciously defended Belgian Antwerp, whose port facilities the Allies needed to shorten supply lines as they invaded Germany. A British amphibious assault took Walcheren Island on 8 November, after which minesweepers began clearing the Scheldt for shipping. U-boats averaged only 50,000 tons of Allied shipping sunk monthly during the autumn of 1944 but doubled this amount over the winter. Allied bombers destroyed most of Germany's surviving cruisers in the Baltic during the spring of 1945, and British escort carriers, cruisers, and destroyers attacked the coast of Norway. Allied naval craft ferried troops across the Rhine River in March as the armies entered Germany from west and east. Just before Hitler committed suicide, he appointed Admiral Doenitz to succeed him. Doenitz signed the German surrender on 8 May.

Ultimate victory in Europe had hinged on the defeat of the U-boat in the Battle of the Atlantic. Axis submarines sank more than 2,800 merchant ships (almost 14.5 million tons), but Allied naval and air countermeasures destroyed 781 U-boats plus several Italian subs. By late 1942 the Allies were able to initiate naval offensives and amphibious operations that took Italy out of the war and restored control of the Mediterranean. The escorted convoys kept both Soviet Russia and Great Britain sufficiently supplied for the former to defeat the main German army in the east and the latter to mount the seaborne liberation of western Europe during the final year of the war. Britain's traditional maritime strategy of concentration against a continental foe had again succeeded but only because of the superior industrial, naval, and air power of its closest partner, the United States.

16

World War II in the Pacific

(1941–1945)

THE OUTBREAK OF WORLD WAR II in Europe in 1939 encouraged Japan to intensify its 2-year-old struggle to conquer China before attacking Russia for control of East Asia. In 1940 President Roosevelt moved the U.S. Fleet from California to Pearl Harbor to deter further Japanese aggression, initiated export embargoes of war materials to Japan, and increased economic and military aid to China. In February 1941 the U.S. Fleet was divided into the Atlantic and Pacific Fleets, with most battleships and aircraft carriers based at Pearl Harbor.

Japan began to fortify and build airfields on its mandated island groups in the Central Pacific—the Marianas, Carolines, and Marshalls. Fleet commander Admiral **Isoroku Yamamoto** conceived the idea of sinking the U.S. Pacific Fleet at its Pearl Harbor anchorage. In the summer of 1941 Japan occupied French Indochina, whereupon the United States halted the export of fuel to Japan. The Japanese therefore elected to conquer the oil-rich Dutch East Indies and to postpone the army's desired attack on Russia. General Hideki Tojo became prime minister in October and ruled that the navy would transport invasion forces into Southeast Asia—the Dutch East Indies, British Malaya, and the U.S. Philippines—after which Japan would win the war in China and invade Russia. All this was to take place after Yamamoto's carrier planes destroyed the U.S. Fleet in a sneak attack on Pearl Harbor, preventing it from interfering with the southern offensive.

Pearl Harbor. Admiral **Chuichi Nagumo** commanded the First Air Fleet—Japan's 6 largest carriers and their 423 fighters, horizontal and dive bombers, and torpedo-bombers. His air tactician, Commander **Minoru Genda,** devised a technique for aerial torpedoes to run in the shallow depths of the Pearl Harbor anchorage where the U.S. battleships and carriers were moored. The force crossed the North Pacific away from shipping lanes, maintaining radio silence. The U.S. commander, Admiral Husband E. Kimmel, kept his PBY Catalina patrol bombers on constant patrols to guard against a surprise attack. Because of the pressing demand for PBYs in the Atlantic, however, Kimmel only had enough of them to cover the most likely direction of an air attack—from Kwajalein in the Marshalls to the southwest. Nagumo's fleet therefore arrived undetected 275 miles northwest of Pearl before dawn on Sunday, 7 December 1941.

Launched from the carriers *Shokaku, Zuikaku, Akagi, Kaga, Hiryu,* and *Soryu,* the planes achieved complete surprise. Throughout the morning bombs and aerial torpedoes destroyed battleships *Arizona* and *Oklahoma,* holed *California* and *Tennessee* until they settled in the mud, damaged the other 4 battleships, and sank 2 destroyers. They obliterated over 200 parked planes at U.S. Army Air Forces, Navy, and Marine Corps air bases in Hawaii. The superior Zero fighters shot down most of the few U.S. planes that took off. American casualties exceeded 3,500. U.S. ships, planes, and antiaircraft guns claimed 29 Japanese planes, plus 5 midget submarines which tried to enter the harbor. No U.S. carriers were present: 2 were delivering landplanes to Wake and Midway islands. The Japanese did not bomb the valuable oil storage tanks, repair facilities, submarine pens, and command centers, but they neutralized the U.S. Pacific Fleet. Then Japan officially declared war.

Japanese amphibious forces easily landed in Malaya, Borneo, and the Philippines, covered by gun ships and land-based planes from Formosa (Taiwan), and Saigon, French Indochina. British battleship *Prince of Wales,* battle cruiser *Repulse,* and 4 destroyers sortied from Singapore to contest the Malayan landings. They lacked air cover, however, and Japanese navy torpedo-bombers sank both capital ships on 10 December. Next day a Japanese invasion force was driven away from Wake in the north-central Pacific by U.S. Marine shore batteries and aircraft which sank 2 destroyers and damaged a light cruiser. Two of Nagumo's carriers supported a second attempt, which overran the island on the 22nd.

Japan planned to create a defensive perimeter extending from Burma in the Indian Ocean, through Indonesia and New Guinea in the South Pacific, to the Gilbert and Marshall Islands in the Central Pacific. Operating from the interior position, Yamamoto's Combined Fleet and island-based naval air forces would defend these new oceanic possessions while simultaneously supporting the army on the Asian mainland. The Allies could only fight a futile defense of their Southeast Asian possessions, while the U.S. Navy initiated unrestricted submarine warfare against Japanese shipping. The new U.S. Navy chief, Admiral **Ernest J. King,** assumed direction of Allied strategy in the Pacific, administered by the able new Pacific Fleet commander, Admiral **Chester W. Nimitz.** Their few ships and troops protected the sea lanes between the United States and Australia in the South Pacific.

Southeast Asia (1942). The capture of Singapore and Manila were crucial to Japan's conquest of Southeast Asia. After landing in Malaya the 25th Army advanced on Singapore, instituting a landward siege that forced its surrender on 15 February 1942. Simultaneously, after Japanese planes destroyed U.S. air forces in the Philippines the first day of the war, the 14th Army landed on Luzon and advanced on Manila, which fell on 2 January. General Douglas MacArthur, the U.S. commander, retreated to the Bataan peninsula and Corregidor Island in the harbor and held out for 4 months. Navy PT (patrol torpedo) boats spirited him out of the Philippines to take command of U.S. forces in Australia just before Bataan surrendered in April and Corregidor in May.

During January the Allies formed the ABDA (American-British-Dutch-Australian) command to oppose the Japanese advance. Its naval forces were placed under Dutch admiral **Karel Doorman.** During landings by Japan's 16th Army on the northern coast of Borneo, 4 destroyers of the U.S. Asiatic Fleet managed to sink 4 out of 12 transports in the Makassar Strait on the 24th. On 4 February Doorman's cruisers and destroyers attacked landing craft in the strait but were driven back by Japanese planes. On the 19th 4 of Nagumo's carriers attacked Darwin on Australia's northern coast, sinking an American destroyer and 11 cargo ships.

Doorman contested the invasion of Java in the **Battle of the Java Sea** on 27 February. His 5 Allied cruisers and 9 destroyers tried to intercept a transport convoy but were engaged by its 4-cruiser, 14-destroyer covering force under Admiral Takeo Takagi. In the day-long fight Japanese torpedoes sank Dutch cruisers *Java* and *de Ruyter,* in which Doorman perished, and 2 Dutch destroyers, while a mine sank a British destroyer. As the surviving ships escaped through the Sunda Strait the night of the 28th they attacked a 56-transport invasion armada, sinking 4. But the huge covering force intercepted and sank U.S. cruiser *Houston* and Australian cruiser *Perth.* Before the following dawn, 1 March, 4 cruisers and planes from light carrier *Ryujo* sank British cruiser *Exeter* and 2 destroyers. The Dutch surrendered the East Indies on the 9th.

The British assigned Admiral **James Somerville** to command the Eastern Fleet, reinforced to 3 carriers (but with only 90 inferior aircraft) and 5 battleships to defend India and Ceylon's naval bases at Colombo and Trincomalee. But as Nagumo's victorious 5-carrier, 300-plane force approached Ceylon in April Somerville wisely kept his fleet out of carrier range south of India. On the 5th Nagumo's planes pummeled the port facilities and shipping at Colombo then intercepted and sank heavy cruisers *Cornwall* and *Devonshire* trying to reach Somerville. On 9 April Nagumo's bombers devastated Trincomalee and sank carrier *Hermes* and a destroyer as they fled. For the first time in the war, however,

Days after the 1 November 1943 landing of U.S. Marines on Bougainville in the northern Solomon Islands, LSTs (landing ship, tank) unload tractors, bulldozers, and trucks laden with supplies to strengthen the beachhead. On the right is an amphibious LVT (landing vehicle, tracked or "amphtrac") which "hit the beach" in the initial assault. The United States built more than 18,000 LVTs during World War II. Although the marines and army forces battled Japanese defenders in Bougainville's jungle for the rest of the war, they successfully protected the captured airfield essential for attacks on Rabaul and other Japanese island strongholds. (U.S. Navy)

Japan's carriers suffered losses: 70 planes shot down over Ceylon by land-based RAF Hurricane fighters flown by veterans of the Battle of Britain.

Britain withdrew its Eastern Fleet to safer ports in East Africa and Madagascar. Japanese cruisers and submarines plundered Allied shipping in the Indian Ocean, the protection of which was all the Royal Navy could address while struggling to defend its Mediterranean lifelines. The China-Burma-India (CBI) theater became a land war, and Britain depended on the U.S. Navy to defeat the Imperial Japanese Navy in the Pacific.

South Pacific. Under Admiral King's prodding, Admiral Nimitz mounted carrier raids against Japanese island bases in the South and Central Pacific, using task forces of 1 or 2 carriers each. This was a classic "fleet in being" stratagem: offensive hit-and-run tactics to keep the Japanese off balance while the United States remained on the strategic defensive, building up its fleet strength to the point when it could assume the offensive. Taking the "calculated risk" of possible carrier losses, King believed the Japanese would be so alarmed by such aggressiveness that they would redeploy major naval forces from other missions. He was proved correct when Nagumo's carrier force was recalled from Southeast Asian waters to counter Nimitz's carriers in the Pacific.

Usually commanded by Admiral **William F. Halsey Jr.,** these forces raided the Gilberts and Marshalls and Wake and Marcus islands during February and March 1942. No U.S. carriers were damaged except for *Saratoga,* torpedoed by a submarine. The Japanese, anxious to cut Allied sea communications between the United States and Australia, in March occupied Bougainville in the northern Solomons and Lae and Salamaua in northern New Guinea, where 2 U.S. carriers attacked their shipping. Then, in a bold move, Halsey in carrier *Enterprise* launched 16 B-25 Mitchell medium land bombers from *Hornet* which surprised the Japanese by bombing Tokyo on 18 April. Most of these planes, commanded by AAF Colonel J. H. "Jimmy" Doolittle, then crash landed in China.

The Halsey-Doolittle raid shocked Japanese leaders into mounting 2 offensives to extend their defense perimeter and put an end to Allied naval activity. They recalled Nagumo's carriers from the Indian Ocean to support landings in both operations. The first would capture Port Moresby in southern New Guinea from which planes and warships could cut the U.S.-Australian lifeline. The second would capture Midway, westernmost of the Hawaiian Islands, from which landplanes could neutralize Pearl Harbor. This operation was also designed to lure out and destroy the U.S. carriers. Both plans promised success, except that U.S. codebreakers discovered their basic outlines. This enabled Nimitz to send Admiral **Frank Jack Fletcher** to the Coral Sea with *Lexington* and *Yorktown* plus cruisers and destroyers to intercept the Japanese force bound for Port Moresby.

Battle of Midway

Alerted by cryptographers of the approach of the Japanese Combined Fleet under Admiral Isoroku Yamamoto to Midway Island, U.S. Pacific Fleet commander Admiral Chester W. Nimitz ordered his carrier task forces to sortie from Pearl Harbor at the end of May 1942. Rear Adm. Raymond A. Spruance departed with *Enterprise, Hornet,* 6 cruisers, and 9 destroyers on the 28th, followed 2 days later by Rear Adm. Frank Jack Fletcher with *Yorktown,* 2 cruisers, and 6 destroyers. By the time they rendezvoused north of Hawaii on 2 June they had been missed by the 18 Japanese submarines just arriving in Hawaiian waters hoping to intercept them.

Of the 230 U.S. carrier planes the F4F Wildcat fighter was inferior to the Japanese Zero except when flown by combat-experienced pilots. The SBD Dauntless dive bomber had proved its worth at the Coral Sea, although the sluggish TBD Devastator torpedo-bomber was extremely vulnerable to enemy fighters, thus requiring protection by its own escorting fighters. Nimitz used PBY Catalina flying boats to search for the Japanese fleet. They were based at Midway, along with AAF B-17 Flying Fortress bombers, some Wildcats and older planes, and a few new TBF Avenger torpedo-bombers.

On 3 June the B-17s sighted and briefly attacked—without effect—the 12 Midway-bound troop transports but then withdrew in the face of the covering force of 2 battleships, 1 light carrier, 10 cruisers, and 21 destroyers. The same day, planes from 2 light carriers attacked the U.S. base at Dutch Harbor in the Aleutians preparatory to the occupation of Attu and Kiska islands by amphibious forces which included 5 cruisers and 14 destroyers. Yamamoto hoped and believed that the U.S. carriers were moving north to protect the Aleutians, but Nimitz, already alerted to Yamamoto's lure, ignored it. Nimitz for his part deployed 25 U.S. submarines to assist his 3 carriers.

To begin the bombardment of Midway, Yamamoto sent ahead the First Air Fleet of carriers under Vice Adm. Chuichi Nagumo. Yamamoto remained 200 miles behind with his battle line of 7 battleships, 3 cruisers, 13 destroyers, and 1 light carrier. Nagumo pressed eastward behind a weather front with carriers *Kaga, Akagi, Soryu,* and *Hiryu,* 2 battleships, 3 cruisers, and 12 destroyers. He had 270 planes—Zero fighters, Val dive bombers, and Kate torpedo-bombers (codenamed by the Allies). Commander Minoru Genda had devised the Japanese carrier tactics: the 4 carriers would operate concentrated in a defensive box formation for easily coordinated air operations while attacking shore targets, as during the previous attacks on Pearl Harbor, Ceylon, and the Dutch East Indies. Whenever his scout planes located the U.S. carriers Genda intended for Nagumo's carriers to split into separate 2-carrier groups in order to maneuver independently during the naval battle—something they had never done before.

Just before dawn on 4 June a PBY sighted Nagumo's carriers 200 miles west-southwest of the U.S. carriers, the exact position of which Nagumo was still ignorant. He therefore launched 100 planes to attack Midway. The Zeros shot down 17 of 27 planes sent up to intercept them, but antiaircraft guns brought down a third of the attackers. Then, about 7:00 A.M., a collection of assorted Midway-based planes attacked Nagumo's force, only to be virtually annihilated. Spruance launched a search-strike of 116 planes from *Enterprise* and *Hornet,* followed by Fletcher's smaller flight from *Yorktown* half an hour later.

A Japanese scout plane then reported sighting a U.S. carrier, whereupon Nagumo began the tedious process of rearming his on-board planes with antiship bombs and torpedoes and of landing and reloading the planes from the Midway strike. These feverish activities consumed 2 hours, preventing Nagumo from dispersing his carriers according to Genda's doctrine. This left them extremely vulnerable, especially with bombs, torpedoes, and aviation gas exposed on deck.

At about 9:25 A.M. the U.S. carrier planes began their attacks. The several squadrons had been separated by clouds during their search, unable to communicate due to mandatory radio silence. Out of touch with their fighters, the unprotected TBDs bored in. Zeros and antiaircraft guns snuffed out all but 6 of the 41 TBDs, none of which scored a hit. Thus preoccupied, the Japanese failed to notice SBDs from *Enterprise* and *Yorktown* had arrived overhead and were commencing their 70-degree dive-bombing runs. In 3 minutes, 10:22 to 10:25, bombs exploded on *Akagi, Kaga,* and *Soryu,* turning them into conflagrations. When Zeros sped skyward Wildcats shot down 6, losing 1 of their own. At 10:45 *Hiryu* launched a strike of 18 Val dive bombers toward *Yorktown.* Eleven were shot down, but the others scored 3 direct hits. The *Hiryu* and *Yorktown* got off strikes in the afternoon. Kates torpedoed the latter, but *Yorktown*'s SBDs started fires on *Hiryu.*

All 4 Japanese carriers soon sank, *Soryu* also due to torpedo hits by submarine *Nautilus,* forcing Yamamoto to cancel the Midway landings. Two of the 4 heavy cruisers of the bombardment force collided trying to elude sub *Tambor* after midnight, 5 June, suffering damage that slowed them down. At midday on the 6th *Enterprise* and *Hornet* SBDs hit them, sinking *Mikuma* and severely damaging *Mogami.* Simultaneously, however, sub *I-168* torpedoed *Yorktown,* then under tow, and destroyer *Hammann,* which sank instantly. The *Yorktown* went down next day. Although hundreds of planes had been lost on both sides, many of their pilots and gunners were rescued after having "ditched" at sea or jumped overboard. The U.S. victory was measured by its having sunk Japan's 4 heavy carriers—as against only 1 of its own—which established the aircraft carrier as the dominant weapon in the Pacific war.

The **Battle of the Coral Sea** began on 3 May when light carrier *Shoho* supported landings on Tulagi in the southern Solomons, challenged only by *Yorktown* planes which sank several small vessels. The *Shoho* then moved into the Coral Sea to join the main Port Moresby–bound force under Admiral Takagi, but she was attacked and sunk by *Lexington* bombers on the 7th. Japanese planes sank a destroyer and an oiler. Next day, bombers and torpedo planes from *Zuikaku* and *Shokaku* fatally crippled *Lexington,* forcing her to be scuttled, and damaged *Yorktown.* But the American SBD Dauntless dive bombers severely damaged *Shokaku,* and F4F Wildcat fighters shot down half of *Zuikaku*'s 72-plane air group. Lacking adequate air cover, Takagi turned back to Rabaul, abandoning the Port Moresby invasion.

In spite of this reverse, Admiral Yamamoto pressed ahead with the Midway operation. Although deprived of the damaged *Shokaku* and of *Zuikaku,* in need of new pilots, he still had Nagumo's 4 other carriers to fight apparently only 2 surviving U.S. carriers. To lure them out of Pearl, he would land troops in the Aleutians, covered by 2 light carriers. He also deployed 18 submarines on a line north of Hawaii to attack the U.S. carriers as they sortied. Nagumo's 4 heavy carriers would bomb Midway preparatory to the landings and attack U.S. carriers. To finish off crippled ships Yamamoto would bring up the battle line, dominated by his flagship, new 72,000-ton superbattleship *Yamato,* the largest ship in the world.

Nimitz, aware of Yamamoto's strategy, recalled Fletcher and *Yorktown* to Hawaii where it was hastily repaired before joining Halsey's *Enterprise* and *Hornet.* Halsey himself, bedridden by fatigue, was succeeded by Admiral **Raymond A. Spruance,** to whom he loaned his staff of veteran officers. In the epic **Battle of Midway** the U.S. fleet defeated the Japanese, thereby ending their Pacific offensives (see essay).

Submarine Warfare (1942–44). Although both navies used their submarines in support of the fleets, they diverged fundamentally in their approaches to merchant shipping. Japan's admirals regarded commerce warfare as unglamorous and defensive, and they rarely diverted their subs to attack Allied cargo ships. They similarly avoided developing antisub measures to protect the 10.5 million tons of freighters, troop transports, and oil tankers which supplied their ground forces in China, Southeast Asia, and the Pacific islands. They did not undertake development of escort carriers, antisub destroyers and aircraft, and regular convoy routes until 1943, and even these measures were halfhearted and basically ineffective.

By contrast, the U.S. Navy divided up its 50 available submarines between the Southwest, Central, and the North Pacific in the spring of 1942 to begin a systematic *guerre de course* campaign. Using search radars, subs from Midway and Dutch Harbor in the Aleutians instituted the Empire Patrol in Japan's home waters. The Mandates Patrol blockaded the sea route between the main Japanese Pacific bases of **Truk** in the Caroline Islands and **Rabaul** in the Bismarck Archipelago. Subs from Australian Fremantle instituted the South China Sea Patrol between Singapore and Formosa; others from Brisbane covered New Guinea and the Solomons. A torpedo shortage forced them to lay mines instead, and a problem with defective torpedoes lasted until 1943.

Throughout 1942 U.S. subs sank 147 merchantmen, transports, and tankers, the lion's share of more than 1 million tons sunk. They also sank several warships and 22 Japanese subs they chanced upon. By year's end the 80 available U.S. subs were sinking vessels faster than Japan could replace them and at a cost of only 8 boats. Japan's initial antisub ships and planes sank 4 U.S. subs early in 1943, but the Americans adjusted their tactics and went on to destroy 23 of Japan's precious oil tankers that year.

Under the command of Admiral **Charles A. Lockwood** the growing Pacific submarine force mounted a concerted offensive against Japanese shipping in mid-1943. U.S. subs penetrated the Sea of Japan, and others formed the first 3-boat wolf packs, profiting from the German example. The Japanese abandoned their antisub effort, needing the ships and planes for fleet operations. Meanwhile, their 5 new escort carriers began to deploy, only to be eventually sunk by different subs. By the end of 1943 Japan had lost 1,803,000 tons of merchant shipping, two-thirds of it to submarines. The Japanese lost 22 more subs, the Americans another 15. But the U.S. onslaught increased. In March 1944 alone subs sank 67 freighters and 22 tankers; one of the most successful, *Flasher*, eventually sank 21 vessels in all (over 100,000 tons). By midsummer Japanese oil imports from the East Indies to Japan had been cut in half. As the United States captured islands ever further westward, subs operated from some of them to break the back of Japan's merchant shipping by the end of 1944.

Guadalcanal (1942–43). Japan abandoned its plans to invade Russia in mid-1942 to concentrate on shoring up its Pacific defenses. Determined to isolate Australia by air attacks on shipping from the United States, the Japanese began building an airfield on Guadalcanal in the southern Solomons. Alarmed, the Americans decided to capture the airfield. For the operation Nimitz appointed Admiral Robert L. Ghormley to command of the South Pacific area.

On 7 August 1942 the **Guadalcanal landings** surprised the Japanese, enabling the First Marine Division to establish its beachhead perimeter and occupy the airfield with ease. A smaller force had to overcome heavy resistance, however, to capture nearby Tulagi. The amphibious ships, commanded by Admiral **Richmond**

Kelly Turner, received fire support from 8 Allied cruisers plus destroyers and air support from Fletcher's *Enterprise, Saratoga,* and *Wasp.* Because of Rabaul-based air raids Fletcher withdrew from the confined waters of Guadalcanal next day, leaving the amphibious forces without air cover. That night, 8–9 August, Admiral Gunichi Mikawa led 7 cruisers and a destroyer down from Rabaul for a surprise attack on the bombardment ships. Firing starshells to illuminate them in the **Battle of Savo Island,** the Japanese sank 4 heavy cruisers—*Astoria, Quincy,* and *Vincennes* and Australia's *Canberra.* Mikawa made good his escape, except for heavy cruiser *Kako,* sunk by U.S. sub *S-44.*

For the next 5 months the Guadalcanal campaign raged over possession of the air strip, named Henderson Field by the U.S. Marines. The marines, later joined by U.S. Army units, continuously battled Japanese troops that held the rest of the island. The latter were periodically reinforced by the nighttime "Tokyo Express"—troop-laden destroyers from Rabaul covered by air raids. U.S. Navy, Marine Corps, and New Zealand planes operated out of Henderson Field by day against Japanese planes and shipping. A war of attrition between opposing fighter planes gradually turned in the Allies' favor. This was largely due to the U.S. policy of rotating home exhausted veteran squadrons to train new pilots while fresh squadrons replaced them. The shortsighted Japanese kept their best pilots in battle until they were finally killed.

Both sides periodically committed heavy fleet units to protect convoys of reinforcements to Guadalcanal and to destroy those of the enemy, leading to several naval battles. Nagumo's carriers covered a Truk-based convoy but were intercepted by Fletcher's carriers in the **Battle of the Eastern Solomons,** 22–25 August. *Enterprise* and *Saratoga* fighters shot down 90 planes from *Zuikaku, Shokaku,* and light carrier *Ryujo,* while their SBDs and TBF Avenger torpedo-bombers sank the latter at a cost of 20 aircraft. Land-based bombers from Henderson Field and the New Hebrides Islands turned back the convoy. On the 31st a Japanese sub torpedoed *Saratoga,* forcing her out of action, and on 15 September *I-19* sank carrier *Wasp.* The night of 11–12 October another Japanese convoy did get through during the **Battle of Cape Esperance,** a cruiser-destroyer action in which a Japanese cruiser was sunk.

Yamamoto committed his main naval forces to dislodge the Allies from Guadalcanal, and Nimitz replaced Ghormley with the aggressive Halsey. Nagumo's 4-carrier force led the attack but was engaged by 2 carriers under Admiral **Thomas C. Kinkaid** in the **Battle of the Santa Cruz Islands,** 26–27 October. The Japanese sank *Hornet,* heavily damaged *Enterprise,* and shot down 70 planes. The Americans put *Shokaku* out of action for a year and destroyed 100 planes, one-fourth of them by antiaircraft fire from the new battleship *South Dakota.*

Two weeks later Admiral Nobutaki Kondo's surface force bombarded Henderson Field while covering a landing. Both sides concentrated ships, planes, and subs in what became the **Naval Battle of Guadalcanal.** In the night action of 12–13 November the U.S. lost cruisers *Atlanta* and *Juneau* and 4 destroyers, Japan battleship *Hiei* and 2 destroyers. On the 14th *Enterprise* planes sank cruiser *Kinugasa,* and Henderson Field planes sank 7 troop-laden transports in the convoy. Kondo pressed on with the 4 surviving transports but was met during the night by Admiral **Willis A. Lee**'s gun force. The Japanese sank 3 destroyers, but battleship *Washington* destroyed battleship *Kirishima.* The Americans also sank the 4 transports and a destroyer.

This battle convinced Japan to abandon Guadalcanal and shift to the strategic defensive. The Americans were not aware of this, as the fighting continued unabated. The night of 30 November–1 December 1942, 8 Japanese destroyers and torpedo planes attacked 5 U.S. cruisers at the **Battle of Tassafaronga,** sinking *Northampton.* The following 29 January a torpedo-bomber sank cruiser *Chicago* off Rennell Island. The Allies otherwise controlled the air and sea around Guadalcanal, and in February 1943 the last Japanese troops evacuated the island.

Admiral Halsey immediately employed land-based planes, cruisers, destroyers, PT boats, and subs against a new Japanese airfield and anchorage at Munda on New Georgia in the central Solomons. Simultaneously, General MacArthur used Australian and U.S. troops to push overland from Port Moresby into northern New Guinea. His AAF commander, General George C. Kenney, retooled B-17, B-25, and A-20 bombers for low-altitude skip-bombing and strafing of enemy ships. A Japanese convoy of 8 destroyers and 8 transports attempted to move 6,900 troops from China via Rabaul to New Guinea but was intercepted by Allied planes off the northeastern coast. In the **Battle of the Bismarck Sea,** 2–5 March 1943, AAF P-38 and P-40 fighters shot down 24 Zero fighters, while U.S. bombers and Australian Beaufighters sank 7 transports and 4 destroyers. PT boats sank the last transport and numerous landing craft; more than 3,000 Japanese troops failed to reach shore.

In April 1943 Yamamoto moved all his carrier planes from their carriers at Truk to Rabaul for 2 massive 300-plane attacks on Halsey's and MacArthur's air forces and shipping at Guadalcanal and eastern new Guinea. But the green pilots were decimated by the Allied veterans. Meanwhile, Nimitz's codebreakers learned that Yamamoto himself would be flying on an inspection trip over the northern Solomons the morning of 18 April. Sixteen P-38s from Henderson Field intercepted and shot down his plane near Bougainville, killing him.

U.S. Strategy (1943). Spearheading the full-scale counteroffensive against Japan were new 30-knot fast carriers of the 27,000-ton *Essex* class (90 planes each) and light 11,000-ton *Independence* class (33 planes). Chief defense of the new fleet lay in two new fighters—the F6F Hellcat and F4U Corsair, coordinated by shipboard fighter director officers using radar. Carriers, battleships, cruisers, and destroyers were equipped with numerous antiaircraft guns; their 5-inch shells were fitted with proximity fuses that detonated close enough to an attacking plane to destroy it.

The U.S. strategy of concentration, largely devised by Admiral King, embodied the traditional components of hit and hold. The Chinese army, supported and supplied by Allied forces in the CBI theater, provided the main hitting force against the Japanese army on the continent of Asia. The holding element was to be the air-sea blockade of Japan by the Americans driving westward to destroy Japan's navy and merchant marine and capturing islands for forward naval and air bases.

With superior naval, air, and ground forces attacking from 3 different directions, the United States exploited the advantage of the **exterior position.** Japan defended its empire from the **interior position,** theoretically an advantage because its navy and naval air forces based at Truk and Rabaul could be shifted between the "unsinkable carriers"—its many island airfields—to counter the main U.S. attack. But because Japan's industrial output could not match America's, it lacked the ability to meet simultaneous attacks from all 3 directions.

Nimitz administered 3 subtheaters of the simultaneous offensives—the Southwest, South, and Central Pacific. In the Southwest Pacific, General MacArthur had supreme command for the conquest of New Guinea and the Philippines. He was independent of Nimitz, who however provided him with the Seventh Fleet of amphibious forces. In the South Pacific, Admiral Halsey commanded what became the Third Fleet to capture the Solomons and Rabaul, depending for air coverage mostly on landplanes from Guadalcanal. In the Central Pacific, Nimitz created the Fifth Fleet under Admiral Spruance. Using the new carriers and amphibious ships it targeted the mandated islands, especially Truk and the Marianas.

Two additional Allied areas played a role. The North Pacific, though plagued by foul weather, tied down more Japanese forces. In March 1943 a traditional cruiser-destroyer gunnery duel near the Komandorski Islands helped turn back a Japanese troop convoy bound for the Aleutians. In May Admiral Kinkaid assaulted and captured **Attu** with an army division, doing the same at Kiska in August, only to find it abandoned. U.S. Aleutian-based planes thereafter continually bombed the Kurile Islands north of Japan. The new Southeast Asia Command was assigned to Britain's Admiral Lord Louis Mountbatten after the defeat of Italy in 1943. Somerville's Eastern Fleet returned to its Ceylon bases to attack German U-boats in the Indian Ocean and Japanese forces in Burma and the East Indies during 1944.

U.S. Counteroffensive (1943–44). The attack began 30 June 1943 in the South and Southwest Pacific. MacArthur captured coastal positions in eastern New Guinea, and Halsey landed at Rendova then New Georgia in the central Solomons. His covering force repulsed a Japanese surface attack at Kula Gulf the night of 5–6 July and sank a cruiser off Kolombangara 12–13 July. Halsey bypassed Kolombangara to assault Vella Lavella on 15 August, and MacArthur landed at Lae and Salamaua in northeastern New Guinea on 3 September. With each capture, Navy "SeaBees" (Construction Battalions) and Army engineers built airfields from which Allied planes attacked Rabaul.

Nimitz and his admirals meanwhile organized Spruance's Central Pacific fleet at Pearl Harbor for the major drive westward. Admiral Turner's amphibious force included older battleships, new escort carriers, and assorted cruisers and destroyers for fire support. General **Holland M. Smith** of the U.S. Marines administered the assault forces. Eleven fast carriers developed their operating doctrine under the guidance of Nimitz's air commander, Admiral **John H. Towers.** Five fast battleships were commanded by Admiral Lee. But the old battle line was replaced by 4 circular task groups, each comprised of 3 carriers in the center, surrounded by a defensive circle of battleships and cruisers and an outer screen of destroyers. These task groups would cover and support the landing forces but break away to fight the Japanese fleet if it challenged the landings. Mobile service squadrons of tankers and supply ships replenished the warships at sea and at newly captured forward bases, giving the fleet unprecedented mobility.

After raiding several islands the fast carriers split up to support simultaneous landings in the South and Central Pacific in November. The *Saratoga* and *Princeton* covered Halsey's landings at **Bougainville** in the northern Solomons on the 1st. The next night his cruisers and destroyers drove off a similar Japanese force in **Empress Augusta Bay,** sinking a cruiser and destroyer. The Japanese rushed ships and planes from Truk to Rabaul, but Halsey's 2 carriers attacked Rabaul on the 5th, damaging 6 cruisers. The other 3 carrier groups headed toward the Gilberts, but 1 broke away to inflict more damage on Rabaul's shipping on the 11th. More than 100 Japanese planes attacked these carriers and the Bougainville shipping, only to be shot down or driven away by carrier and land-based fighters. With U.S. airfields on Bougainville, nearby Rabaul became too dangerous for warships, now withdrawn to Truk.

Marines and army troops assaulted **Tarawa** and **Makin** in the Gilberts on 20 November while fast carriers attacked enemy island airfields. In spite of fierce resistance and heavy losses the landings succeeded, but submarine *I-175* sank escort carrier *Liscome Bay* on the 24th. This loss, and damage from Kwajalein-based Betty torpedo-bombers, were attributed to the fact that the carriers had been restricted in their movements by remaining too close to the target islands. Henceforth, they would be allowed to operate independently as Task Force 58 under the aggressive Admiral **Marc A. Mitscher.** Similarly, the Tarawa assault provided lessons for improving amphibious tactics.

The 3 U.S. drives next moved simultaneously against Rabaul and Truk. In late December 1943 and early January 1944 MacArthur landed at Arawe and Cape Gloucester, New Britain, and moved further up the New Guinea coast. Halsey, whose destroyers sank 3 Japanese destroyers off **Cape St. George,** New Ireland, in late November, occupied Green and Emirau islands in early 1944, completing the encirclement of Rabaul. Spruance's Fifth Fleet landed marines and army troops at **Kwajalein** in the Marshalls on 31 January 1944, easily overcoming enemy resistance. Task Force 58 was released to attack the Japanese fleet at Truk, although it escaped westward before Mitscher's planes and gun ships struck on 17–18 February. They nevertheless destroyed 250 Japanese planes in the air and on the ground, more than 200,000 tons of merchant shipping, 2 cruisers, and 2 destroyers at a cost of 25 planes. Simultaneously on the 17th army troops overran **Eniwetok** in the western Marshalls. Two of Mitscher's 4 carrier groups then pressed on to the Marianas where on the 22nd they destroyed 74 Zeros and several merchantmen, leaving the rest to Lockwood's submarines.

The incredible striking power of the Fast Carrier Task Force so effectively neutralized Japanese air strength at Rabaul and Truk that Admiral King approved the recommendation of Nimitz and his admirals to bypass both island bastions. Abandoned by their warships, they would be neutralized by bombers from captured islands and eastern New Guinea. Task Force 58 ranged westward to destroy more planes and shipping in the Palau Islands in March 1944 then supported MacArthur's landings at **Hollandia** on 22 April. When the Japanese flew more planes into Truk, Mitscher's Hellcats destroyed 90 of them on the 29th and 30th. Japan tried to resupply its bypassed island garrisons using submarines, but many were tracked down by patrolling warships. In May destroyer escort *England* sank 6 subs between Bougainville and Truk.

To defend western New Guinea and the Marianas Japan shifted land-based planes to the Marianas and based its new Mobile Fleet of 9 carriers and 450 planes at Tawi Tawi west of the Philippines. When MacArthur landed at Wakde and Biak in western New Guinea in May the Japanese sent 200 planes down from the Marianas only to have them decimated by Kenney's AAF fighters. On 10 June the Japanese fleet dispatched 2 battleships as part of a convoy escort to

Biak. Next day, however, 200 Hellcats from Task Force 58 attacked the Marianas and destroyed an equal number of airborne and parked planes and with them an inbound 14-ship convoy. This marked the beginning of the **Marianas** campaign. While 1,000 planes from Mitscher's 15 carriers attacked the principal islands of Saipan, Tinian, and Guam, the Japanese fleet left Tawi Tawi to defend the Marianas and recalled the Biak-bound surface force to rendezvous with the fleet for the battle.

Spruance sent 2 of Mitscher's 4 carrier task groups north to attack airdromes at Chichi Jima and Iwo Jima on 15 June while Turner's amphibious ships landed 1 army and 2 marine divisions at **Saipan.** They were supported by a bombardment force of 7 older battleships, 8 escort carriers, 11 cruisers, and 60 destroyers. That night U.S. subs reported the Japanese fleet moving into the Philippine Sea toward Saipan. Spruance withdrew his transports 200 miles to the east out of harm's way and formed his bombardment ships into a battle line just west of Saipan. All 4 groups of Task Force 58 reconcentrated further west on the 18th— 7 heavy and 8 light carriers, 7 fast battleships, 21 cruisers, and 67 destroyers. Mitscher wanted to head west to attack the approaching enemy fleet, but Spruance elected to keep the fast carriers close to Saipan to prevent a possible Japanese "end run" around Saipan to attack the landing forces.

At dawn 19 June Admiral **Jisaburo Ozawa** launched his first air strikes 500 miles west of Saipan—beyond the range of Mitscher's carrier planes—to shuttle in and out of Tinian and Guam, attacking Task Force 58 en route. Flown by inferior pilots, these planes were intercepted by Mitscher's veteran Hellcat pilots to begin the **Battle of the Philippine Sea.** Meanwhile, U.S. subs attacked the Mobile Fleet of 5 heavy and 4 light carriers, 5 battleships, 13 cruisers, and 28 destroyers. Subs *Albacore* and *Cavalla* sank heavy carriers *Taiho* and *Shokaku,* respectively, and Mitscher's planes and antiaircraft guns shot down some 400 Japanese aircraft in the so-called **Marianas Turkey Shoot.** Task Force 58 pursued the fleeing Mobile Fleet next day and in a late afternoon strike sank heavy carrier *Hiyo* and 2 tankers and eliminated Ozawa's last 35 planes. The Americans lost 76 pilots and aircrewmen and no ships in the 2-day battle.

The fast carriers attacked the Jimas again then supported the troops on Saipan and the Fifth Fleet assaults on Guam on 21 July and Tinian on the 24th. The Seventh Fleet simultaneously landed MacArthur's troops further along the New Guinea coast. From captured airfields there AAF planes attacked the Halmaheras and adjacent sea lanes and supported MacArthur's assault on **Morotai** in September. Nimitz had airfields constructed in the Marianas for AAF planes, notably B-29 strategic bombers which in November began flying all the way to Japan.

Newly constructed naval bases at Guam and Saipan enabled Nimitz's amphibious forces to invade the Palau Islands in September, although fanatical Japanese resistance inflicted heavy losses at **Peleliu.**

The Philippines (1944–45). Conquest of the Marianas and New Guinea enabled Nimitz and MacArthur to coordinate their forces in a campaign to close off Japanese shipping between Southeast Asia and Japan's home islands. King wanted Nimitz to capture Formosa, but MacArthur convinced President Roosevelt to let him fulfill a promise to the people of the Philippines to liberate them instead. Furthermore, a massive Japanese army offensive overran most of southern China in 1944, making a landing in Formosa or China hazardous. With the Chinese army exposed as unreliable, the United States courted the Soviet Union to enter the Pacific war and defeat Japan's army on the Asian continent.

The Philippines campaign was expected to last several months. Kinkaid's Seventh Fleet would land MacArthur's army, supported by Nimitz's carriers, the nucleus of the Fifth Fleet; it was redesignated Third Fleet under Halsey while Spruance planned the next operation. Interservice differences, however, prevented any overall commander from directing the campaign: Halsey reported directly to Nimitz, Kinkaid to MacArthur, a potentially dangerous arrangement for a complex amphibious operation.

Loss of the Philippines meant ultimate defeat for Japan, its oil convoys from the East Indies cut off, the homeland vulnerable to invasion. From Tokyo Combined Fleet commander Admiral Soemu Toyoda planned to throw all his available naval and air power into the defense of the Philippines. He staged air forces into Formosa and planned an elaborate scheme for his remaining gun ships to destroy the invasion armada. Two battleship-cruiser forces—one from Japan, the other from Singapore—would converge on the Seventh Fleet assault ships while Japan's last carriers steamed south from Japan to lure Halsey's carriers away from the landing forces. This was in effect a suicide mission for Toyoda's entire fleet, given America's overwhelming naval power. He underscored this reality by creating the *Kamikaze Corps*—suicide planes flown by inexperienced pilots to crash into the American warships.

Halsey's initial air strikes on Mindanao in mid-September 1944 revealed Japanese air forces to be so weak that Allied leaders accepted his recommendation to bypass Mindanao in favor of early landings on Leyte in mid-October. The 16 fast carriers with their 1,000 planes ranged the Philippines, destroying nearly 900 aircraft and 67 ships. When they struck Formosa on 12 October Toyoda committed all his available planes to its defense, only to have over 600 of them destroyed in the air and on the ground in a 3-day struggle. U.S. losses were 90 planes. Toyoda then implemented his plan to attack the landing forces at Leyte.

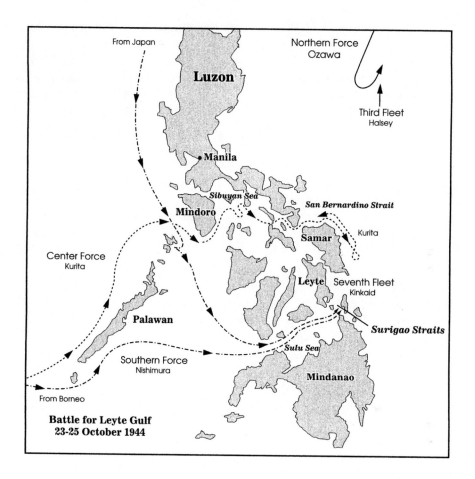

**Battle for Leyte Gulf
23-25 October 1944**

For a week Kinkaid's support ships attacked Leyte: 6 older battleships (some raised from the mud of Pearl Harbor), 18 escort carriers (with 400 planes), cruisers, destroyers, destroyer escorts, and PT boats. On 20 October 300 transports and assault craft began landing 200,000 men of the 6th Army. Halsey's carriers simultaneously attacked airfields in Luzon. The Japanese "Center Force" under Admiral **Takeo Kurita** left Singapore bound for Leyte Gulf but lost 2 cruisers to U.S. submarines *Darter* and *Dace* near Palawan Island on the 23rd. Kurita entered the **Sibuyan Sea** of the central Philippines where Halsey's planes attacked him next day, sinking superbattleship *Musashi* and crippling a cruiser. A land-based Japanese bomber succeeded in hitting light carrier *Princeton*, forcing it to be scuttled.

The **Battle for Leyte Gulf** had begun. By nightfall of 24 October Kurita's Center Force had turned around. But the "Southern Force" of 2 battleships, 4 cruisers, and destroyers from Japan had entered the Sulu Sea in the southern Philippines, surviving a carrier air attack. In addition, Halsey had detected the "Northern Force" of Ozawa's 4 carriers, 2 half-battleships (with flight decks), with cruisers and destroyers heading south from Japan. Halsey ran north during the night to intercept it at dawn, unaware that its planes had all flown ashore and that Ozawa had now turned around and was running north to draw Halsey further away from Leyte. At the same time, Kurita's Center Force resumed its eastward course to pass through San Bernardino Strait between Luzon and Samar, turning south to Leyte Gulf.

The divided U.S. command system now failed, because neither Halsey nor Kinkaid realized that the other was not guarding San Bernardino Strait. To destroy the Southern Force Kinkaid deployed his support ships in a battle line across **Surigao Strait** near Leyte. During the night they sank battleships *Fuso* and *Yamashiro* and 3 destroyers in the last major surface action in history. Next day 2 damaged cruisers were finished off by U.S. planes. At dawn of the 25th Halsey attacked the Northern Force east of Luzon's **Cape Engaño,** sinking heavy carrier *Zuikaku* and light carriers *Chitose, Chiyoda,* and *Zuiho.*

At the same time, sunup on the 25th, however, Kurita's Center Force suddenly appeared, without warning, off southern **Samar** near the Leyte roadstead. Spearheaded by *Yamato,* it sank escort carrier *Gambier Bay,* 2 destroyers, and a destroyer escort. But Kurita elected to break off the action, thinking Halsey's carriers were approaching. Just then the first land-based kamikazes attacked and sank escort carrier *St. Lo.* Kurita ran for the open sea but lost 3 heavy cruisers to furious U.S. counterattacks. Halsey turned south but failed to prevent Kurita's escape through San Bernardino Strait during the night, although over the next 2 days carrier planes sank 2 cruisers.

The Battle for Leyte Gulf saved MacArthur's beachhead and virtually annihilated the Japanese fleet: 300,000 tons of naval shipping lost (to 35,000 U.S.), 10,000 men killed (to 1,500), and 150 aircraft destroyed (to 100). Halsey's carriers continued to cover the 6th Army on Leyte for weeks as Japan rushed in reinforcements, supported by kamikazes which damaged several U.S. carriers. But carrier planes sank many troop transports, 13 escorting destroyers, and 3 cruisers. U.S. subs decimated Japan-bound convoys and sank battleship *Kongo,* carrier *Unryu,* and 68,000-ton *Shinano,* the world's largest carrier. They also accounted for most of the 2 million tons of Japanese merchant shipping sunk between July and December.

To secure the Philippines and close off Japanese shipping through the "Luzon bottleneck," MacArthur landed at **Mindoro** south of Luzon on 15 December and at **Lingayen Gulf** on Luzon's west coast 9 January. Halsey covered these operations while airfields were constructed on Leyte, although he took the fleet into a typhoon that sank 3 destroyers on 18 December. And kamikazes sank escort carrier *Ommaney Bay* at Lingayen Gulf. During January 1945 Third Fleet ranged the South China Sea sinking Japanese merchant shipping from Saigon to Formosa, while 4 carriers of the British Eastern Fleet attacked oil refineries in Sumatra. MacArthur liberated Manila which became a forward naval base along with Leyte-Samar, enabling the Seventh Fleet to land the 8th Army throughout the southern Philippines over ensuing months.

Air-Sea Blockade (1945). With the East Indies sealed off, the Allies began to close the vise on Japan. To defeat the Japanese army on the continent, Roosevelt and Churchill elicited a promise from Stalin that Russia would enter the war in the Pacific 3 months after the German surrender. The U.S. Army insisted on a massive Normandy-style invasion of the Japanese homeland late in 1945, but King and the navy believed their air-sea blockade would force Japan to surrender before an invasion was necessary.

The fast carriers joined AAF bombers from captured island bases in attacking Japanese merchant and naval shipping and airfields between Formosa and Japan and in bombing strategic targets in Japan itself. B-29s based in the Marianas had been bombing Japan since November 1944 but needed an intermediate airfield for emergency landings of damaged planes and as a base for fighters to escort them. Iwo Jima would be captured by Nimitz's amphibious forces for this purpose. Similarly, to shorten the range to Japan of U.S. land-based planes, Okinawa in the Ryukyu Islands had to be assaulted. In March 1945 B-29s commenced dropping the first of 12,000 aerial mines in the coastal waters of Japan, Manchuria, and Korea. By July these mines had destroyed 1.2 million tons of shipping and completely closed all harbors.

Spruance resumed command of the redesignated Fifth Fleet, with Mitscher as tactical commander of Task Force 58, for the Iwo Jima and Okinawa operations. To isolate Iwo, Mitscher's 16 carriers and 1,000 planes attacked airfields in the Tokyo area on 16–17 February. Japan's few veteran fighter pilots shot down 60 Hellcats but at a cost of some 300 Zeros and newer model fighters. The carriers moved to Iwo Jima, where Turner's gun ships and 11 escort carriers had been bombarding the island. On the 19th, 30,000 marines assaulted **Iwo Jima** and its tenacious defenders. Bombers and kamikazes attacked the U.S. Fleet 2 days later, sinking escort carrier *Bismarck Sea* and severely damaging *Saratoga*. The marines needed 2 weeks to capture Iwo's 3 airfields, and fighting still raged on 17 March when 16 B-29s made emergency landings—the first of 2,291. Also, AAF fighters began escorting the B-29s from Iwo to Japan. Nearly 7,000 marines died securing the island, whose 23,000 defenders were virtually annihilated.

For **Okinawa** the Fifth Fleet was joined by the new British Pacific Fleet under Admiral Sir Bruce Fraser, principally 6 fast carriers operating as one of Mitscher's 5 task groups. This brought Task Force 58's strength to 14 heavy and 6 light carriers, 1,600 aircraft, 10 fast battleships, 2 battle cruisers, 21 cruisers, and 80 destroyers. Mobile service squadrons not only supplied fuel oil and aviation gas but also ammunition and dry stores, enabling the fleet to remain at sea and not return to distant bases for many weeks. On 18 March Task Force 58 struck airfields on Kyushu, southernmost of Japan's home islands, and for 2 weeks attempted to isolate Okinawa from Japanese interference while braving heavy kamikaze attacks.

On 1 April Turner's 430 transports and assault craft landed 183,000 soldiers and marines of the 10th Army on Okinawa. Fire support was provided by 10 older battleships, 13 cruisers, numerous destroyers and rocket-firing craft, and 18 escort carriers with 540 planes. The 87,000 defenders offered little resistance, waiting until an attack of over 500 kamikazes against the carriers and amphibious shipping on 6 April. Mitscher's planes shot down 355 of them and next day sank superbattleship *Yamato*, a cruiser, and 4 destroyers on a suicide mission toward Okinawa. On the 8th the Japanese army on Okinawa counterattacked, matching the ferocity of the kamikazes.

Between April and June some 1,700 kamikazes pummeled the Allied warships off Okinawa daily and nightly, sinking 36 destroyers and landing craft and damaging 164 others, including several carriers. Navy, marine, and AAF planes operated from the island's captured airfields in supporting the troops and battling the suiciders. In the end the Japanese lost about 125,000 killed, the Allies over 12,000. But the island was immediately developed into an advanced naval and air base for the final attack on Japan. During spring and summer the British Eastern Fleet conducted landings along the coast of Burma and cleared Southeast Asian waters of enemy shipping. American and Australian troops landed in the East Indies.

Halsey relieved Spruance in command of the redesignated Third Fleet and led the carriers in attacks on the Japanese homeland during July. Kamikaze resistance was light because the Japanese were husbanding their forces for the expected invasion. Carrier planes destroyed hundreds of parked aircraft and sank a carrier and 3 battleships at the Kure naval base but at a cost of 133 planes to antiaircraft fire. In June a 9-sub U.S. wolf pack penetrated the Sea of Japan to sink 27 merchantmen, followed by other subs in July and August, effectively cutting off Japan from the continent. Japanese submarines were no less daring; on 30 July *I-58* sank unescorted heavy cruiser *Indianapolis* in the Philippine Sea.

Culmination of the Allied strategy of concentration occurred in early August. The hitting element was provided by the Soviet Union which declared war on the 9th. The Red Army swept into Manchuria, supported by 93 vessels of its Pacific Fleet and the Amur River Patrol. It crushed the Japanese army within a week, pushed into North Korea, and landed in the Kurile Islands. A new hitting element was the atomic bomb. B-29s dropped one on Hiroshima on the 6th, another on Nagasaki on the 9th. With Japan completely blockaded by aerial mines and submarines the holding element had been achieved, enabling Halsey to direct his carrier planes against strategic targets in Japan through the 15th. On that day Japan agreed to surrender. An invasion was never required. On 2 September the formal surrender was signed on board battleship *Missouri* in Tokyo Bay.

The greatest sea war in history marked the triumph of U.S. maritime strategy over a basically continental Japan, which however had used its formidable navy to stubbornly resist the American advance for nearly 4 years. In Mahanian tradition the U.S. Pacific Fleet won command of the sea by destroying the Imperial Japanese Navy in many naval battles determined largely by the aircraft carrier as the new capital ship. U.S. amphibious forces seized island bases critical for the air-sea blockade. Submarine *guerre de course* destroyed over half of the 2,345 merchantmen (8.5 million tons) sunk, at a cost of 52 subs. Subs also contributed importantly to the 687 Japanese warships sunk. Critical to U.S. victory, however, was the fact that Japan's main military force, its army, was tied down in China and ultimately defeated by the Soviet army. Strategic bombers destroyed Japan's home industries, underscored by the 2 atomic bombs at the finish. A combination of all these elements determined the American victory.

17

The American Pax

(1946–)

A BIPOLAR BALANCE OF 2 superpowers, the United States and the Soviet Union, replaced the World War II alliance. In spite of the United Nations, designed to prevent future wars, democratic America and communist Russia engaged in the Cold War (1946–90). It was defined by nuclear (atomic) weapons, which were never used, and by conventional armies and navies fighting limited wars. Simultaneously, independence movements of colonial peoples led to the disintegration of the British, French, and Dutch overseas empires, and the Chinese civil war ended in a Communist Chinese victory. The United States had the only navy capable of policing the world's oceans during and after the Cold War. As a result, the era has been one of general peace dominated by American hegemony—the **Pax Americana.**

Early Cold War (1946–50). Russia, a traditional continental power, and America, a basically maritime state, both emerged from World War II with informal empires that had to be defended and policed. Lacking coherent strategies, the 2 superpowers responded to real and perceived threats with ad hoc policies during the first 4 years of the Cold War. The Red Army fortified Russia's central European frontier—what Winston Churchill labeled the Iron Curtain—and the Soviet navy used captured U-boat technology to fashion a large submarine force. When Britain and the other western European nations faced possible economic collapse and vulnerability to the Soviet Union in 1947, the United States adopted the "containment" policy: thwarting Russian expansion by massive economic aid to Europe—the Truman Doctrine and Marshall Plan. American warships "showed the flag" in the Mediterranean and Black Seas while the main aircraft carrier strength of the U.S. Navy—scaled down by postwar demobilization—shifted from the Pacific to the Atlantic.

The presidential administration of Harry Truman depended on U.S. monopoly of the atomic bomb to intimidate the Russians. That this weapon threatened to eliminate navies altogether was graphically demonstrated in 1946 when 2 atomic bombs sank or gutted 2 retired fast carriers and assorted former American, Japanese, and German warships during tests in the Pacific. Because only land-based strategic bombers could carry "the bomb" the United States in 1947 reorganized its military structure to include the independent U.S. Air Force. Under a centralized Secretary of Defense, former Secretary of the Navy **James V. Forrestal,** the 3 unified services vied for constricted military budgets as the nation reduced defense spending.

The navy feared it would lose its carriers, patrol planes, and marine squadrons to the air force or at least suffer severe cutbacks. It therefore waged a bitter interservice struggle to have atomic bombs assigned to carrier planes. When the Truman administration canceled construction of a large carrier as an economy measure in 1949, the "revolt of the admirals" brought the navy's case before the public. In candid and heated congressional hearings the navy achieved success, and early in 1950 atomic bombs—now reduced in size—were assigned to existing carriers. Throughout these years both the navy and air force began to replace most of their piston-engine planes with jet-propelled aircraft.

Meanwhile, however, the atomic bomb failed to match the diplomatic leverage provided by conventional ground, naval, and air forces in numerous Cold War crises. In response to Russian pressure on Turkey and aid to Greek communists in that country's civil war, the United States created the permanent Sixth (Task) Fleet in the Mediterranean in 1948. The same year, the Soviet army blockaded Western access to occupied Berlin. The U.S. Air Force and 2 U.S. Navy patrol squadrons undertook a massive airlift of supplies to Berlin, which convinced the Russians to end the blockade in 1949. The United States then formed a military alliance—the North Atlantic Treaty Organization (NATO)—with the western European nations and Canada for the purpose of deterring the Soviet Union. The supreme NATO commander was stipulated to be an American general, its naval leader the same admiral who commanded the U.S. Atlantic Fleet.

The creation of NATO, the takeover of China by communists, and Russia's development of its own atomic bomb, all in 1949, led the National Security Council—the highest U.S. political and military leaders—early in 1950 to formulate a strategic policy of checking communist expansion throughout the world. General Dwight Eisenhower, supreme NATO commander, depended upon the British navy in the North Sea and the U.S. Sixth Fleet in the Mediterranean to guard the seaward flanks of western Europe, while NATO armies faced the Red Army across the Iron Curtain. U.S. strategic bombers deterred Russia's atomic forces, and the navy gave increased attention to antisubmarine operations. In the western Pacific, General Douglas MacArthur, supreme U.S.

commander, devised a cordon strategy of forward island defenses to contain the Soviet Union and "Red" China—which formed a military alliance in February 1950. The carriers of the Seventh Fleet patrolled East Asian waters, backed up from air bases in Japan, Okinawa, Nationalist Chinese Taiwan (Formosa), and the Philippines (independent since 1946). Whether this littoral defense perimeter included mainland Korea remained problematic.

Korean War (1950–53). U.S. opposition to the restoration of European colonial systems contributed to native independence movements in South and Southeast Asia. France had returned to Indochina with "river assault divisions" in 1945 to battle guerrilla forces in Vietnam, but it granted independence to Laos and Cambodia in 1949. The Indonesians fought a 5-year war against the Dutch in the East Indies before achieving independence in 1950. Britain granted independence to India, Pakistan, Burma, Ceylon, and Malaya in 1947–48. The latter, which did not include Singapore or North Borneo, was so beset with communist guerrilla activity that Britain would not leave until it was suppressed. From 1948 to 1954 British, Malay, and Commonwealth forces sealed off the Malay peninsula at the Kra Isthmus and defeated the guerrillas using Royal Navy gunfire support along the coasts. Korea, also a peninsula, had been jointly occupied by Soviet and American forces in 1945, north and south of the 38th parallel, respectively. These forces were gradually withdrawn by early 1950, at which time Russia's puppet communist regime in North Korea decided to conquer South Korea. The Russians, doubting the United States would intervene, acquiesced.

When the North Korean army crossed the 38th parallel on 25 June 1950 the United States immediately responded with carrier air strikes and began rushing troops to MacArthur in Japan. The United States was supported by Britain and other countries under the general auspices of the United Nations. As the Cold War's first limited shooting war—or "police action" as Truman described it—the Korean conflict was fraught with miscalculations by both sides. The parameters and "rules" of engagement had to be worked out on an ad hoc basis while the fighting raged. The one constant strategic factor, however, was unchallenged American naval supremacy. The Seventh Fleet and allied United Nations warships ranged the coasts of the Korean peninsula and throughout the Sea of Japan and Yellow Sea. U.S. vessels also patrolled the Taiwan Strait to prevent the Nationalist Chinese in Taiwan from attempting to return to the mainland and widen the war. With command of the sea the United States was able to contain the war in the Korean peninsula.

Neither Russia nor the United States wanted the struggle to escalate into a

World War III. The United States therefore refused to use atomic weapons, and the Soviet Union held back additional military aid which might have enabled the North Koreans to drive the allies out of South Korea. By August 1950 the North Korean army had driven South Korean and U.S. troops back to a defensive perimeter around Pusan in the southeastern corner of the peninsula. MacArthur then devised a masterful counterstroke—a landing at **Inchon** on the west-central coast near Seoul—in order to outflank the communists. On 15 September the U.S. Seventh Fleet under Admiral C. Turner Joy landed 2 divisions— 1 marine, 1 army—at Inchon, supported by 4 fast carriers (1 of them British) and 2 escort carriers, 7 cruisers, and 34 destroyers. Simultaneously, the troops at Pusan broke out, creating a pincers movement with MacArthur's landing forces that drove the North Korean army back across the 38th parallel. On 25 October allied forces captured Wonsan harbor on North Korea's eastern coast for use as an advanced anchorage.

When MacArthur's army reached China's border at the Yalu River, however, the new Chinese Communist regime sent its army across it, fearful that a unified pro-U.S. Korea would provide an avenue by which the Nationalists might reenter China to regain control. The massive Red Chinese army drove part of MacArthur's army back across the 38th parallel in November and the remainder to the eastern coast at Hungnam, where it was evacuated by the Seventh Fleet on 24 December. These unanticipated events had major strategic repercussions: Russia lost control of North Korea to China, and the Truman administration rejected MacArthur's entreaties to mount another counteroffensive into North Korea. The general responded by criticizing his superiors and was summarily relieved of command. MacArthur's arguments for seeking a complete victory at the risk of widening the war had no validity in the new era of limited warfare.

The Korean War settled into a virtual stalemate as the belligerents sought ways to terminate it through negotiations. Allied forces again advanced as far as the 38th parallel by April 1951, after which the battle line solidified across the mountainous neck of the Korean peninsula. Carrier bombing planes from Task Force 77—notably propeller-driven AD Skyraiders—attacked communist targets from the battle line to the Yalu but were prohibited from violating Chinese air space beyond the Yalu—an enemy **sanctuary.** By the same token, communist planes did not attack the carriers or U.S. bases in South Korea or Japan. Although the North Koreans held the coast adjacent to Wonsan Harbor, Seventh Fleet battleships and destroyers utilized the anchorage from which to bombard coastal railroads and to sweep mines. The fighting remained confined to North Korea from mid-1951 to mid-1953, at which time an armistice ended it and basically restored the status quo antebellum at the demilitarized battle line.

Nuclear Arms Race (1952–62). The new American president, Eisenhower, had pressured North Korea to come to terms by deploying nuclear weapons on board carriers off Korea in 1953. Their actual utility remained doubtful because of the danger of triggering another world war. The next year, France appealed to the United States to use its carriers to drop atomic bombs on the Vietnamese army besieging the French army at Dienbienphu. When the United States refused, Dienbienphu fell, and France granted independence to Vietnam. The country was divided at the 17th parallel, however, into communist North Vietnam and pro-U.S. South Vietnam.

In spite of the fact that only conventional weapons had been employed in the Korean War, the United States used the conflict as a pretext for general rearmament focusing on nuclear weapons to counter the Soviet Union worldwide. In addition to the atomic bomb the thermonuclear hydrogen bomb was perfected by the United States in 1952 and the USSR in 1954. To deter the Soviet Union from initiating a world war the Eisenhower administration adopted the threat of "massive retaliation" with superior numbers of nuclear warheads by land, air, and sea.

Crucial to this strategy were delivery systems. The air force developed long-distance jet-propelled strategic bombers (B-47, B-52) and intercontinental ballistic missiles (ICBM) from hardened silos in the continental United States. The navy constructed 60,000-ton attack carriers of the *Forrestal* class and the A3D Skywarrior carrier jet bomber capable of reaching targets inside Russia. Under the direction of Admiral **Hyman G. Rickover,** the navy harnessed nuclear power to drive its future submarines, beginning with the 3,500-ton new *Nautilus* in 1954. Nuclear-powered subs enjoyed virtually unlimited range, even while submerged, for attacking enemy surface ships and submarines. The first nuclear-powered carrier—the 76,000-ton new *Enterprise*—followed in 1961. From 1955 to 1961, the chief of naval operations, Admiral **Arleigh A. Burke,** fended off air force attempts to take control of the navy's new underwater-launched ICBM. This was the Polaris missile system, devised under the direction of Admiral William F. Raborn Jr. The first Polaris missiles were deployed on a 6,900-ton nuclear sub in 1960; the 16 missiles per "Polaris" sub had an initial range of 1,400 miles.

The Soviet Union held the initial lead in ICBMs but only from hardened silos, and it fashioned an air force of strategic bombers. To protect its coasts and threaten enemy shipping Russia retained a basically coastal, inshore navy with a large fleet of diesel-powered submarines. Its immediate concern, however, was consolidating its defenses against NATO in central Europe. When NATO rearmed West Germany and admitted it to membership in 1955, Russia created the Warsaw Pact of all the eastern European nations it controlled, including East

Germany, which it rearmed. When Hungary revolted in 1956, the Red Army crushed it. Russia also courted newly independent nations around the world in response to similar American initiatives, but it steadily lost favor with Communist China until China terminated their alliance in 1960.

The independence of the new Arab nations of North Africa and the oil-rich Middle East required active U.S. and British naval patrols to maintain political stability. The region was racked by turmoil, due especially to the creation of the Jewish nation of Israel in 1948 and continuing pressure against it by its Muslim neighbors. Soviet Russia exploited these tensions by providing aid to several Muslim states, notably Egypt. Egypt nationalized the Suez Canal in 1956, threatening international trade and Israel's access to the Red Sea. Britain, France, and Israel intervened militarily but without consulting the United States. In October amphibious and helicopter-borne troops from British carriers invaded Suez and Port Said, supported by 3 British and 2 French carriers, a French battleship, and several cruisers and destroyers. The **Suez crisis** brought immediate U.S. and UN pressure, which resulted in a cease-fire and the allied withdrawal.

Henceforth, no Western nation would be allowed to act militarily without U.S. approval—final recognition of U.S. global hegemony, especially by Britain, now dependent on American nuclear technology. The United States instituted the Eisenhower Doctrine by which it intervened on behalf of Middle East governments which requested assistance when threatened by communist takeovers. The Sixth Fleet escorted Israeli shipping in the Red Sea and landed marines in Lebanon in 1957 to prevent a pro-Soviet regime from taking power. Iraq ended its alliance with the West and attempted to annex Kuwait in the Persian Gulf in 1961 but was stopped by Royal Marine commandos and 2 British carriers. Throughout these years the European nations granted independence to their African colonies. The major naval activity occurred when France unsuccessfully fought to retain its presence in North African Tunisia and Algeria in 1961–62.

The United States established regional alliances throughout the world with which it created a ring of air and naval bases around the Soviet Union. But it grew particularly apprehensive over Russian-backed revolutionary movements in Latin America. Fidel Castro's institution of a communist regime in Cuba prompted the administration of President John F. Kennedy to underwrite an invasion of Cuba by anti-Castro emigrés in April 1961. They made an amphibious landing at the Bay of Pigs on Cuba's southern coast but were crushed when their supporting aircraft failed to appear. The next year Castro obtained Russian interrange ballistic missiles to prevent a possible U.S. invasion. Kennedy regarded the presence of nuclear warheads so close to American soil as a potential trigger for a thermonuclear World War III and in October 1962 openly challenged the Soviet Union.

Cuban Missile Blockade

During the summer and autumn of 1962 high-altitude American U-2 intelligence aircraft and Navy F8U Crusader photographic planes detected the presence of Soviet Russian military weapons in Cuba—MiG-21 fighter planes, *Komar*-class guided missile patrol boats, surface-to-air missiles (SAM), and SS-4 land-based Sandal medium range ballistic missiles (MRBM). The latter, each of which carried a nuclear warhead, were capable of hitting targets as far away as Washington, D.C., St. Louis, and the Panama Canal. In addition, American planes sighted components for even longer range SS-5 Skean missiles on board a Soviet cargo ship bound for Cuba.

President John F. Kennedy regarded all these missiles as a clear threat not only to the continental United States and Latin America but to the thermonuclear balance of power. The U.S. Army, Navy, Air Force, and Marine Corps chiefs who comprised the Joint Chiefs of Staff recommended bombing these missile sites and/or mounting an invasion of Cuba to capture them. Kennedy, however, elected a naval blockade instead, calling it a "quarantine" because "blockade" in international law meant an act of war. By it he hoped to avoid bloodshed and to convince Soviet Premier Nikita S. Khrushchev to remove the missiles before the United States was forced to attack them—and possibly trigger World War III.

Kennedy obtained the support of NATO and the Latin American Organization of American States (OAS) and turned to the chief of naval operations, Admiral George W. Anderson Jr., to execute the blockade. In mid-October 1962, to deter a possible nuclear attack on the United States from mainland Russia, 6 Polaris submarines deployed from their base at Holy Loch, Scotland, to underwater launch points, and land-based air force missiles and bombers of the Strategic Air Command were put on alert. The U.S. Second Fleet's Task Force 135, built around nuclear-powered carrier *Enterprise* and oil-driven *Independence,* patrolled off the southeastern coast of the United States, backed up by shore-based U.S. Air Force and Marine Corps fighters.

On 20 October Kennedy ordered the navy to stop and search any Cuba-bound Russian or Soviet bloc vessel suspected of transporting missiles. If any such vessel refused to allow an inspection party to come aboard the navy was instructed to use force. Next day Admiral Anderson established Task Force 136 as the Quarantine Force under Vice Adm. Albert G. Ward, Second Fleet commander. Its 2 cruisers, 22 destroyers, 2 missile frigates, and antisubmarine carrier *Essex* took up blockade station across Atlantic waters some 500 miles north and east of eastern Cuba. They were eventually joined by warships of Britain, Canada, Venezuela, Argentina, and the Dominican Republic.

Kennedy declared the quarantine to begin midmorning of 24 October. At that time U.S. warships began moving toward the nearest of the 18 Russian and 8 Soviet bloc freighters then in the Atlantic heading toward Cuba. By midafternoon most of these ships had begun to turn back toward Russia, evidence that Khrushchev had yielded to the blockade. Nevertheless, to demonstrate U.S. resolve, early next morning destroyer *Joseph P. Kennedy Jr.* (named for the President's late brother, a naval aviator killed in World War II) stopped and searched a Soviet-contracted freighter. It was selected because it obviously carried no weapons, a less-volatile inspection than one of a missile-laden Russian ship. Carrier planes simultaneously tracked Soviet submarines withdrawing from the area. Early on the 27th several destroyers fired warning shots at a Russian oil tanker crossing the quarantine line, whereupon it stopped then turned about for home. But on the same day a land-based SAM missile shot down a U-2 over eastern Cuba, killing the pilot. Tensions mounted, and an antisub destroyer dropped hand grenades over a Soviet sub, convincing it to surface and identify itself; the destroyer escorted it into the open Atlantic.

On the morning of 28 October Khrushchev indicated his intention to withdraw the missiles from Cuba, but the blockade remained in force and was tightened even closer around Cuba on the 30th. More subs were forced to the surface, and additional U.S. and OAS warships reinforced the quarantine. On 1 November the crisis seemed to have passed, and 4 days later Soviet freighters began departing from Cuban ports carrying missiles which they clearly displayed on deck. On 20 November the United States terminated the blockade. Kennedy by his actions had added a new dimension to international law in the nuclear age—the use of limited coercive force to interdict foreign weapons which threatened American security and the delicate equilibrium of global peace. This traditional use of historical naval strategy had effectively neutralized high-tech material weapons of the nuclear age.

By instituting the **Cuban missile blockade** (see essay) and negotiations, he forced the Russians to withdraw their weapons from Cuba.

The Cuban crisis did not end the Russo-American nuclear arms race, but it did reveal the folly of nuclear weapons as viable tools in Cold War military confrontations. The risk of nuclear war had become so great that both superpowers initiated discussions for arms control agreements. On the other hand, from the Cuban blockade the Russians had learned the efficacy of conventional naval forces. Henceforth they accelerated construction of surface warships. For the United States, the Suez and Lebanon crises of 1956–57 had drawn attention to the need for a "flexible response" to regional crises. So too had Seventh Fleet support of Nationalist Chinese forces on several offshore islands threatened by Red China in 1955 and 1958. The result was renewed American attention to conventional ground, naval, and air forces. As in both world wars, historical strategy again prevailed over material strategy.

The United States failed to realize, however, that the Soviet Union was not orchestrating a monolithic global communist revolution. Instead, the many "wars of national liberation" throughout the world were genuine people's struggles to throw off superpower domination. These movements often involved playing off the United States and Russia against each other when convenient, thereby heightening Cold War tensions. This was especially the case in Southeast Asia.

Vietnam War (1964–73). By 1960 the United States was providing military advisers to South Vietnam and Laos against native communist guerrillas, and the Dutch navy battled Indonesia for retention of Dutch West New Guinea. The Dutch finally withdrew late in 1962, whereupon Indonesia moved against Malaya. The next year Malaya was reorganized into Malaysia, including Singapore and North Borneo, and it welcomed British naval assistance against Indonesia. Two carriers, many escorts, minesweepers, submarines, commandos, and Malaysian and Commonwealth troops isolated and battled Indonesian ground forces in North Borneo from 1963 to 1965. The British carefully observed Indonesian territory and air space as sanctuaries and avoided bombing jungle targets for fear of hitting innocent civilians, thereby winning their support. In 1965 a coup overthrew the pro-communist Indonesian regime and terminated the war.

The U.S. Seventh Fleet and military and naval advisers shored up the autocratic regime of South Vietnam as part of America's anti-Soviet containment policy—to prevent a "domino effect" of Southeast Asian nations falling to communism. Unlike Borneo, however, South Vietnam was not an island. Its western border and the "Ho Chi Minh Trail" through neutral Laos and Cam-

U.S. battleship *New Jersey* fires one of her 9 16-inch main batteries at communist army positions up to 23 miles away at Tuy Hoa on the central coast of South Vietnam, late March 1969. Commissioned in 1943, the 45,000-ton *Iowa*-class "battlewagon" served as flagship of the Third/Fifth Fleet in the Pacific war (1944, 1945) and of the Seventh Fleet in the Korean War (1951, 1953), where her guns bombarded North Korean coastal targets. In 1983, displacing 57,600 tons, she was equipped with Tomahawk "land attack" cruise missiles. Her sister ships *Missouri* and *Wisconsin* fired Tomahawks at Iraqi positions during the Persian Gulf War (1991). Although *New Jersey*'s 50 years of active service were interrupted by periods in decommissioned reserve ("mothballs"), her 50-year service life was typical of major warships over the preceding 500 years. (Naval Historical Center)

bodia could not be sealed off from North Vietnamese troops and supplies assisting Vietcong guerrillas in the South. The coastline was another matter, and in February 1964 President Lyndon B. Johnson's administration ordered U.S. destroyers to patrol the Gulf of Tonkin while South Vietnamese PT boats raided the North Vietnam coast. On 2 and 4 August, North Vietnamese PT boats in the Gulf mistakenly attacked U.S. destroyers, which repulsed them. On the 4th and 5th 2 U.S. carriers launched retaliatory strikes which sank 2 PT boats in the Gulf and 25 more at their bases. Similar incidents ensued, leading Johnson to commit U.S. ground forces to South Vietnam in February 1965 and to initiate constant carrier strikes north of the 17th parallel, thereby escalating the war.

As in the Korean War, rules of engagement developed which confined the fighting to South Vietnam, with North Vietnam, Laos, and Cambodia becoming **sanctuaries** from ground attacks. The only really successful U.S. interdiction of communist supplies occurred along the South Vietnamese coast and Mekong River system. The 4 carriers of Task Force 77 flew close air support missions for ground forces; a battleship, cruisers, and destroyers provided shore bombardment; and helicopter carriers airlifted troops ashore. The Mobile Riverine Force employed specialized Navy and Coast Guard assault patrol boats, monitors, hovercraft, and cutters alongside the South Vietnamese Navy Junk Force. They eventually cut off communist water traffic south from the 17th parallel all the way to the coast of Cambodia and throughout the Mekong delta to protect the capital, Saigon. But the roles and missions of U.S. Army, Navy, Air Force, and Marine Corps forces developed on an ad hoc and confusing basis as the United States tried to adjust to the demands of counterinsurgency warfare.

Pursuing a strategy of "graduated response" to enemy activities the United States escalated the war by gradually increasing naval and air attacks on North Vietnam. From 1966 to 1968 Seventh Fleet warships extended their aerial, surface, and mining operations against North Vietnamese shipping and inland targets from the 17th parallel to Hanoi, the capital. Carrier planes ranged as far west as Laos and battled Russian-made MiG fighters. The major carrier fighter, the F-4 Phantom II, doubled as a bomber alongside the A-1 (formerly AD) Skyraider, A-4 Skyhawk, A-6 Intruder, and A-7 Corsair II (all jets except the A-1). U.S. aircraft dominated the skies but at a cost of 421 planes by the end of 1968, many shot down by Soviet-made SAMs (surface-to-air missiles). Sensitive to possible hostile Russian and/or Chinese reactions, the United States refrained from an outright naval blockade of North Vietnam and, until 1967, from bombing North Vietnamese targets close to the Chinese border.

Damaging as the carrier and air force strikes were, North Vietnam's Tet offensive into the South early in 1968 heightened American public criticism of the war and convinced Johnson to de-escalate it and seek a negotiated settlement. In April he halted all bombing north of the 19th parallel and in October all bombing of North Vietnam. The United States also began to turn over ground and river operations to the South Vietnamese. In October Admiral E. R. Zumwalt Jr. initiated a campaign by U.S. and Vietnamese riverine forces which cleared the Mekong River and delta and was extended temporarily into Cambodia in 1970. The successful operation was completed 1 year later, when the South Vietnam Navy assumed full responsibility for policing its inland waters.

Six Seventh Fleet carriers and the air force continued their attacks, however. In the spring of 1972 air strikes and shore bombardments were resumed virtually everywhere in North Vietnam by President Richard M. Nixon in response to a fresh enemy offensive. In December these attacks were extended to Hanoi and its major port of Haiphong, which they mined, resulting in a formal cease-fire the next month. The United States then withdrew from South Vietnam, but in 1975 the country was overrun by the North which unified it under the native communist regime.

Naval Arms Race (1963–89). The failure of the United States to win the Vietnam War did not alter the general balance of the 2 superpowers, for Vietnam was of no vital strategic importance to either the United States or the Soviet Union. The latter's priorities remained defensive: countering U.S. nuclear weapons and the U.S. Navy; continuing distrust of neighboring China; and internal order, reflected in the brutal suppression of Czechoslovakia's bid for independence in 1968.

Under the leadership of Admiral **Sergei G. Gorshkov,** naval commander in chief from 1955 to 1986, the Soviet navy undertook a massive expansion to imitate the growing American fleet. It developed nuclear-powered attack and ballistic missile submarines and created a surface fleet of carriers with vertically launched (VSTOL) planes and helicopters, cruisers (some nuclear-powered), destroyers, and patrol boats. Like the U.S. Navy, the Russian navy employed an array of missiles against various targets: antiship, antiair, surface to air, surface to surface ("cruise"), air to air, air to surface, and underwater launched. Both navies incorporated modern electronic and computer technology in their ships and aircraft, but the quality of Russian weapons systems rarely surpassed the Americans.

Despite Cold War competition at sea, on land, in the air, in space, and in Third World regions, both superpowers shared with other nations common concerns over controlling nuclear weapons and refining international law. The hallmark of several arms control agreements was SALT I—the first Strategic Arms Limitation Treaty—in 1972. Its main feature was parity in land-based and submarine-launched nuclear warheads and the number of ballistic missile subs—42 for Soviet Russia, 41 for the United States, with adjustments for future construction. The treaty, designed to last for 5 years, was superseded by SALT II in 1979. Although the latter agreement was never ratified, the terms of SALT I remained in force by mutual consent, so valuable had it proved in reducing nuclear tensions.

Four Law of the Sea conferences between 1958 and 1982 involved most of the world's nations trying to define their respective rights in territorial waters. Although the major powers often joined together in countering the small nations, most agreed in 1982 that each nation had jurisdiction of its coastal waters from 3 out to 12 miles. Each nation also enjoyed exclusive economic zones out to 200 miles except in international straits where all ships had transit rights. The agreement eventually became binding in 1994 even though the United States did not sign because of disputes over exploitation of the seabed for minerals and the need for U.S. warships to police politically troubled waters.

Patrolling the world's oceans fell increasingly on the United States as British naval power declined. By 1960 Britain's economy could no longer afford the 8 attack carriers and 54 conventional submarines necessary to sustain the country's global naval commitments. In 1964 British naval forces intervened to help stabilize several new East African nations and then concluded Malaysia's struggle with Indonesia: In 1966, however, Britain decreed that it would no longer conduct naval operations without allies. It ceased construction of attack carriers and declared it would withdraw all its naval forces from regions east of Suez by 1971. As a consequence, the United States had to fill the political vacuum in the Indian Ocean and Persian Gulf, although the Royal Navy delayed several final departures—from South African Simonstown (1975), Singapore (1976), and Hong Kong (1997). By 1970 it was down to 3 carriers, 4 Polaris missile subs, and 35 attack subs, plus escorts—all concentrated for operations in European waters. The same was true of the French navy, roughly the same size.

The global strategy of the U.S. pax centered on 2 objectives in the wake of the 1962 Cuban missile crisis: (1) deterring the Soviet Union from nuclear war and from an attack on the "Central Front" of western Europe, and (2) maintaining stability throughout the oceans of the world. Whenever possible, the United States worked through the auspices of the United Nations, NATO, or regional alliances—all of which it dominated—or it acted unilaterally, if need be. During the 1960s the navy increased the range of its submarine-launched Polaris missiles from 1,700 to 2,900 miles and added a nuclear-powered cruiser and frigate as escorts for nuclear carrier *Enterprise*. More *Forrestal*-class oil-driven carriers raised the inventory of fast attack carriers to 15. Polaris subs and carrier bombers ringed Soviet Russia, which now employed 400 land-based navy Backfire bombers with a range of 3,000 miles. To augment its attack subs the U.S. Navy designated several World War II era *Essex*-class carriers as antisubmarine carriers to operate in hunter-killer groups. "Vertical envelopment" of amphibious beachheads was provided by helicopters operating off specialized helicopter carriers.

In addition to fighting the Vietnam War the American navy responded to other crises throughout the 1960s. The creation of the Soviet Mediterranean Fleet in 1963 greatly complicated Sixth Fleet operations in that politically turbulent region, especially during the Arab-Israeli Six Day War in June 1967. Fifteen Israeli destroyers plus PT boats captured an Egyptian naval base and closed the Suez Canal as other Israeli forces humbled 5 Arab nations. A Soviet naval squadron put into Alexandria as the tense cease-fire took effect. Four months later Egyptian PT boats sank an Israeli destroyer off Port Said with Russian-made Styx cruise missiles. NATO aircraft henceforth closely watched Russian naval movements in the Mediterranean. In Asia, China organized coastal fleets in response to U.S. involvement in Vietnam, and Russia supplied warships to India for its inconclusive war against Pakistan in 1965. The U.S. Navy continued to police Korean waters but suffered the capture of spy ship *Pueblo* in Wonsan harbor by 5 North Korean patrol boats in 1968.

The naval arms race of the superpowers accelerated during the 1970s. Soviet Russia deployed its *Yankee*-class ballistic missile submarines carrying Sawfly missiles with a 3,500-mile range. The Polaris missile was replaced on U.S. "boomers" with the Poseidon and its multiple independently targeted reentry vehicle (MIRV)—up to 14 separate H-bomb warheads per missile. The United States introduced the first of several new 92,000-ton *Nimitz*-class nuclear-powered carriers with the usual nuclear-strike capability. Russia developed its first conventional 38,000-ton *Kiev*-class carrier for operating VSTOL aircraft to protect its surface fleets. The widely scattered Soviet fleets were coordinated in global "Okean" naval exercises during the decade but without the benefit of permanent overseas bases like those of the United States. Because the number of Soviet missile, attack, and coastal submarines reached 375 the U.S. Navy gave up trying to track them all with hunter-killer groups. It decommissioned its antisubmarine carriers and depended instead on the jet-propelled 2,500-mile S-3 Viking on board attack carriers and the shore-based turboprop 2,300-mile P-3 Orion patrol plane.

The most active regions of naval combat activity during the 1970s remained Southeast Asia, the Indian Ocean, and the Middle East. Bangladesh, supported by India, proclaimed its independence from Pakistan. In the India-Pakistan war of December 1971, Indian carrier-based planes and torpedo boats successfully bombed and blockaded the Pakistani coast, sinking a destroyer though losing a frigate to a submarine attack. A Soviet naval squadron made an appearance, prompting the United States in 1974 to develop a naval and air base on the island of Diego Garcia and to establish a joint base with the Australians at Fremantle. In 1975 a Cambodian gunboat seized American merchantman *Mayaguez* in the Gulf of Thailand. The United States responded with a Marine Corps landing on Tang Island to retake the ship as carrier planes from *Coral Sea* sank 3 Cambodian gunboats and bombed airfields. Israel sealifted commandos to 2 Red Sea islands in 1972 to protect Israeli oil tankers, and in the Arab-Israeli Yom Kippur War of October 1973 Israeli patrol boats used Gabriel cruise missiles to sink several Syrian missile boats.

Britain's withdrawal from the Persian Gulf left a political vacuum that pro-U.S. Iran tried to fill by purchasing missile-equipped warships. The United States in 1971–72 based 3 warships at Bahrain in the Gulf and supplied Saudi Arabia with corvettes and landing craft. Iraq turned to Soviet Russia for naval assistance, whereupon the United States sent a carrier into the Gulf in 1974. Concurrent Russian naval visits to Yemen and East African ports threatened the Red Sea, and in 1979 the Soviet Union backed a political coup in Afghanistan which touched off a civil war. That same year anti-Western elements seized control of Iran and took U.S. diplomats hostage. The United States dispatched 3 carriers to the Indian Ocean, developed naval bases in Saudi Arabia, received support from alarmed East African and Persian Gulf states, and in 1980 declared its intention to deny domination of the oil-rich Gulf by any one nation. Late that year Iraq attacked Iran, whose warships sank 11 Iraqi vessels in 1 action. Although the conflict dragged on until 1988, the United States had otherwise succeeded in restoring a precarious stability to the Gulf region.

Isolated from the larger power struggles was Argentina's sudden invasion and occupation of the British-owned Falkland Islands in the South Atlantic in April 1982. Despite the downsizing of its navy Britain immediately counterattacked in the **Falklands War.** It dispatched an expeditionary force, covered by 2 carriers, to the islands, only to be challenged by the Argentine fleet. On 2 May the nuclear sub *Conqueror* torpedoed and sank cruiser *General Belgrano,* causing the Argentine navy to return to port. Over the ensuing weeks, however, land-based Argentine planes sank 2 British destroyers, 2 frigates, 1 assault ship, and a supply vessel with bombs and Exocet cruise missiles. But British fighters, missiles, and antiaircraft guns shot down 75 planes, enabling the landing forces to go ashore on 21 May and secure the Falklands by mid-June.

The U.S. Sixth Fleet actively patrolled the Mediterranean as a counterforce to increasing Arab terrorism throughout the world. In 1981 Soviet-built Libyan fighters attacked 2 F-14 Tomcat fighters from U.S. carriers on maneuvers, but the F-14s shot down 2 of them. In 1986 the Libyans fired missiles at planes from 3 carriers, whereupon the carriers launched strikes against Libya with A-6, A-7,

U.S. ballistic missile submarine *Ohio* on patrol in the Pacific in 1982. First in her class of "boomers," the nuclear-powered sub carried 24 Trident strategic missiles mounted in tubes aft of the "sail" (conning tower). Launched while the sub remained submerged, each Trident held several independently guided H-bomb warheads capable of striking targets more than 4,500 miles away. The United States and Soviet Union used their boomers to deter each other from initiating a mutually destructive thermonuclear exchange during the Cold War. (U.S. Naval Institute)

F-14, and F/A-18 Hornet aircraft—joined by U.S. Air Force planes based in Britain. The American aircraft destroyed Libya's air defense system and sank 2 missile boats. In the Persian Gulf a U.S. frigate was damaged by an Iranian mine in 1988, whereupon a U.S. cruiser shot down an Iranian fighter with a missile, and several ships sank 2 Iranian frigates and some patrol boats. Following another clash between U.S. and Iranian warships in July a U.S. cruiser mistakenly shot down an Iranian commercial airliner, killing everyone on board.

Cold War naval rivalry reached its peak during the 1980s. The United States introduced 18,700-ton *Ohio*-class ballistic missile subs, each mounting 24 4,500-mile Trident missiles. The Soviet Union produced 25,000-ton *Typhoon*-class boats, each carrying 20 4,000-mile SS-N-20 MIRV-directed missiles. The U.S. Navy supplemented its vastly superior 15 attack carriers and new model aircraft with a renaissance in surface warfare. This was made possible by digital electronics, improved ship design, and a plethora of new missiles, some with multiple capabilities including land attack. Sea Sparrow, Standard, Harpoon, Tomahawk, and Aegis missiles were developed concurrently with new classes of cruisers, destroyers, frigates, and destroyer escorts. New torpedoes and mines were added to dozens of new 6,900-ton *Los Angeles*-class nuclear attack submarines. Under the presidency of Ronald Reagan, the 4 World War II-era *Iowa*-class battleships were recommissioned and fitted with missile systems as part of an immense naval revitalization program aimed at overpowering the Soviet navy.

The American naval expansion program quickly outpaced a Russia increasingly plagued by internal economic and social problems, including the prohibitive expense of pacifying restive Warsaw Pact nations and settling what had become a disastrous intervention in Afghanistan. Neither could the Russians afford to match Reagan's projected "Star Wars" space missile system or the U.S. Navy's proposed "Maritime Strategy." Though never officially adopted as national policy, this strategy aimed at countering any Soviet advance into western Europe with massive carrier air attacks on Russian naval bases in northern waters, including U.S. operations from Norway. Neither could mere visits of Russian warships to foreign ports stand up against Reagan's Rapid Deployment Joint Task Force of new amphibious assault vessels, hovercraft, troop helicopters, mine hunters and mine countermeasures ships, hydrofoil patrol boats, teams of special operations SEAL swimmers, and advanced Harrier vertical takeoff aircraft.

The U.S. containment policy of deterring Soviet arms and policing the world's oceans resulted in American victory in the Cold War. Although the sheer expense of the Maritime Strategy caused it to be abandoned in 1987, the Soviet Union had already begun to retrench. In 1989–90 it granted independence to the Warsaw Pact nations, agreed to the reunification of Germany, recalled its warships

to home ports, and signed arms control treaties with the United States in 1988
and 1991 reducing the number of nuclear warheads and allowing for open in-
spections. The end result was the disintegration of the Soviet Union in 1990–91.

Soviet influence abroad had waned inversely to the active projection of U.S.
naval power, including the American occupation of Grenada in the West Indies
in 1983 which overthrew a communist regime. Indeed, between 1946 and 1991,
naval forces had participated in 83 percent of the 270 U.S. military interventions
throughout the world, in half of them as exclusively naval operations. All had
been conducted in coastal waters against no naval opposition. The U.S. success
was due not only to military and industrial might; it represented the final moral
triumph of American democracy over Soviet communism.

Post–Cold War Navies. The Pax Americana continued without interruption during the 1990s. The U.S. Navy maintained its nuclear deterrent against
newly democratic Russia and communist China but was heavily downsized for
lack of a real threat. The Strategic Arms Reduction Treaties (START) of 1991
and 1993 fixed the number of U.S. Trident missile submarines at 18, by century's
end Russia's 44 allotted boomers (with fewer warheads) had declined to 26.
The United States maintained a force of 12 carriers and 2,100 aircraft and introduced the first 9,200-ton *Seawolf*-class sub to augment its 55 other nuclear attack boats in countering Russia's similar but shrinking numbers. Indeed, the
Russian navy declined so rapidly that by the end of the century it had fewer operational subs of all types than the United States and lacked the funds for personnel and equipment to effectively operate its deteriorating fleet units. By
contrast, the 300-ship American navy maintained its customary efficiency in
spite of downsizing, with ongoing construction replacement programs and ever
improving technology.

The U.S. Navy dominated the seas as the most flexible component of the ongoing American global hegemony, although all nations with coastlines maintained small inshore navies. The navies of NATO, the most formidable, were also
downsized: Britain—3 carriers, 3 missile and 10 attack subs; France—1 and 4, respectively. China had 5 nuclear attack subs. Spain, Thailand, and Brazil each had
1 carrier, but all the world's carriers, except for America's 12 and France's 1, were
of the smaller antisub variety, equipped mostly with VSTOL aircraft. The only
regional navy of any size was Japan's with over 60 destroyers and frigates and
15 diesel-powered submarines. All navies generally followed the leadership of the
U.S. Navy in policing their home waters.

The United States during the 1990s enforced its traditional interpretation of
international law by keeping the oceans and coastal areas of the world free for
trade against pirates, smugglers (primarily of drugs), terrorists, and regional ag-

gressors. The United States worked through the United Nations and NATO and unilaterally to maintain global stability. As during the years of the Cold War, its navy provided optimum mobility and flexibility.

Tensions in the Middle East reached a critical stage in 1990 when Iraq invaded and overran tiny Kuwait in the Persian Gulf and threatened to assert control over the world's major oil resources. The United States led the international response. In the **Gulf War** of early 1991 the United States employed 6 carriers as well as battleships, cruisers, and destroyers firing Tomahawk missiles and ships' guns against Iraqi forces. They sank the entire Iraqi coast defense navy and neutralized enemy mines, which succeeded only in damaging 2 U.S. warships. During the buildup of allied ground forces 2 U.S. Marine Corps brigades threatened to mount an amphibious assault on Kuwait, thus tying down 6 Iraqi divisions there. Two entire marine divisions attacked Kuwait during the main allied ground invasion to the west of Kuwait on 24 February, outflanking it. The Kuwait defenders broke and fled in 1 day. Iraq sued for peace on the 28th. Over ensuing years the U.S. Navy and other armed forces enforced UN sanctions against a troublesome Iraq.

Beginning in 1992 U.S. warships and aircraft joined NATO forces in patrolling the Adriatic Sea and stabilizing wartorn Serbia and Bosnia in the ethnic wars of the Balkan region. In 1996 U.S. carriers patrolled the Taiwan Strait to thwart Chinese pressure against Taiwan. In the late 1990s American naval vessels policed the waters of turbulent West African states and evacuated foreigners. In 1998 3 U.S. carriers entered the Persian Gulf to force Iraq to conform to UN sanctions against chemical weapons production. And so it goes. . . .

At the advent of the 21st century A.D. naval power continued to play the same important roles in human affairs that it had since the beginning of the 21st century B.C. As long as people have travelled upon the sea, which comprises over 70 percent of the earth's surface, navies have been—and will continue to be— necessary components of global relationships.

Appendix 1

Functions of Navies in History

I. Maritime great powers: politically liberal, economically capitalistic, culturally open, navy seniority.

Naval missions:

1. *Offensive* strategic posture.
2. Strongest battle fleet in the world to control the sea.
3. Defended against invasion.
4. Protected merchant shipping and attacked that of the enemy (*guerre de course*).
5. Blockaded enemy coasts.
6. Engaged in combined/amphibious operations.
7. Engaged in strategic bombardment (20th century).

II. Continental great powers: politically authoritarian, economically centralized, culturally closed, army seniority.

Naval missions:

1. *Defensive* strategic posture.
2. Formidable fleet but not employed to dominate the sea.
3. Defended against invasion.
4. Attacked enemy merchant shipping (*guerre de course*).
5. Engaged in coastal and combined operations.
6. Maintained strategic bombardment capability (20th century).

III. Small states: dominated by relationships to great powers.

Naval missions:

1. Defended against invasion.
2. Policed local waters.
3. Attacked small enemy warships.
4. Attacked enemy commerce (*guerre de course*).

Appendix 2

Modern Naval Ranks (20th Century, U.S. Navy)

A. "Flag" officers (commanders of any naval force of 2 or more vessels; each flies own "flag" over the command "flagship")

Commissioned Rank	USN Insignia (on Collar, Sleeve) One broad sleeve stripe, plus	Army, Marine Corps, Air Force Equivalents
Fleet admiral	5 stars; 4 stripes	Field/air marshal, general of the army
Admiral (full)	4 stars; 3 stripes	General (full)
Vice admiral	3 stars; 2 stripes	Lieutenant general
Rear admiral (upper half)	2 stars; 1 stripe	Major general
Rear admiral (lower half)	1 or 2 stars; 1 stripe	Brigadier general
Commodore	1 star	Brigadier general

B. Ship's commissioned officers (each capable of commanding some kind of naval vessel—the smaller the ship, the lower the actual rank of its "captain"; whatever his/her actual rank, the commanding officer of any vessel is "the captain" or, informally, the skipper)

Commissioned Rank	USN Insignia (on Collar, Sleeve)	Army, Marine Corps, Air Force Equivalents
Captain	Eagle; 4 stripes	Colonel
Commander	Silver oak leaf; 3 stripes	Lieutenant colonel
Lieutenant commander	Gold oak leaf; 2½ stripes	Major
Lieutenant	2 silver bars; 2 stripes	Captain
Lieutenant (junior grade)	1 silver bar; 1½ stripes	First lieutenant
Ensign	1 gold bar; 1 stripe	Second lieutenant

C. Noncommissioned officers/enlisted personnel

Noncommissioned Rank	USN Insignia (on Sleeve)	Army, Marine Corps, Air Force Equivalents
Midshipman/naval cadet	Half-stripe	Cadet
Warrant officer	Broken stripe	Warrant officer
Petty officer, chief and 3 classes	Eagle and chevrons	Sergeant, first and lesser grades
Seaman, 3 classes	Half-chevrons	Corporal and private

Appendix 3

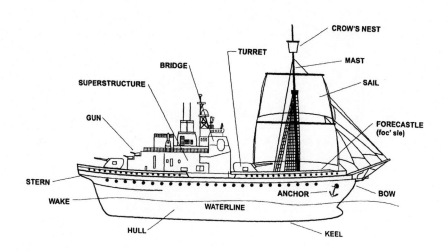

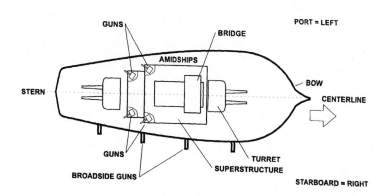

Appendix 4

Warship Profiles U.S. Navy

Further Reading

Listed herein are selected important English-language books and a few articles written since 1950 (most recent date of printing is given). Students doing research should examine the **bibliographies in recently published books** for listings of earlier and more specialized works. Not included are reference books; primary sources (documents, diaries, autobiographies); or works about naval technology or individual battles, ships, or weapons. This listing is arranged in eight categories:

1. General Naval History
2. Specific Navies
3. Ancient and Medieval Periods
4. Age of Sail (1500–1815)
5. Nineteenth Century (1815–1914)
6. Twentieth Century
7. Biographies
8. Anthologies

1. General Naval History

Corbett, Julian S. *Some Principles of Maritime Strategy* (1988).

George, James L. *History of Warships: From Ancient Times to the Twenty-first Century* (1998).

Hughes, Wayne P., Jr. *Fleet Tactics: Theory and Practice* (1986).

Pemsel, Helmut. *A History of War at Sea* (1989).

Potter, E. B. *Sea Power: A Naval History* (1981).

Reynolds, Clark G. *Command of the Sea: The History and Strategy of Maritime Empires.* 2 vols. (1983).

———. *History and the Sea: Essays on Maritime Strategies* (1989) (United States, Japan, Russia, Mahan, King).

———. "The U.S. Fleet-in-Being Strategy of 1942." *Journal of Military History* 58 (January 1994): 103–18 (background from 1690).

Roskill, Stephen. *The Strategy of Sea Power* (1962).

Scheina, Robert L. *Latin America: A Naval History* (1987).

2. Specific Navies

a. Austria

Sondhaus, Lawrence. *The Naval Policy of Austria-Hungary, 1867–1918: Navalism, Industrial Development, and the Politics of Dualism* (1994).

b. Britain

Clowes, William Laird. *The Royal Navy: A History from the Earliest Times to the Present.* 7 vols. (1897–1903; 1996–97) (ends at 1903).
Hill, J. R., ed. *The Oxford Illustrated History of the Royal Navy* (1995).
Kennedy, Paul. *The Rise and Fall of British Naval Mastery* (1994) (covers 1500 to 1970s).

c. China

Swanson, Bruce. *Eighth Voyage of the Dragon: A History of China's Quest for Seapower* (1982).

d. France

Jenkins, E. H. *A History of the French Navy* (1973).

e. Japan

Evans, David C., and Mark R. Peattie. *Kaigun: Strategy, Tactics, and Technology in the Imperial Japanese Navy, 1887–1941* (1997).

f. Netherlands

Boxer, C. R. *The Dutch Seaborne Empire, 1600–1800* (1988).
Bruijn, Jaap R. *The Dutch Navy of the Seventeenth and Eighteenth Centuries* (1993).

g. Portugal

Boxer, C. R. *The Portuguese Seaborne Empire* (1969).

h. Russia

Mitchell, Donald W. *A History of Russian and Soviet Sea Power* (1974).

i. Spain

Parry, J. H. *The Spanish Seaborne Empire* (1990).

j. United States

Albion, Robert Greenhalgh. *Makers of Naval Policy, 1798–1947* (1980).
Beach, Edward L. *The United States Navy: 200 Years* (1986).

Love, Robert W., Jr. *History of the U.S. Navy.* 2 vols. (1992) (divides at 1941).
Millett, Allan R. *Semper Fidelis: The History of the United States Marine Corps* (1991).

k. Venice

Lane, Frederick C. *Venice: A Maritime Republic* (1973).

3. Ancient and Medieval Periods

Casson, Lionel. *The Ancient Mariners: Seafarers and Seafighters of the Mediterranean in Ancient Times* (1991).
———. *Ships and Seamanship in the Ancient World* (1995).
Fahmy, Aly Mohamed. *Muslim Sea-Power in the Eastern Mediterranean from the Seventh to the Tenth Century* (1966).
Jordan, Borimir. *The Athenian Navy in the Classical Period* (1975).
Lewis, Archibald R., and Timothy J. Runyan. *European Naval and Maritime History, 300–1500* (1990).
Morrison, John, ed. *The Age of the Galley* (1994).
Reynolds, Clark G. "The Maritime Character of Minoan Civilization." *American Neptune* 56 (Fall 1996): 315–51 (includes Bronze Age navies).
Sandars, N. K. *The Sea Peoples* (1985).
Starr, Chester G. *The Influence of Sea Power on Ancient History* (1989).
———. *The Roman Imperial Navy, 31 BC to AD 324* (1966).

4. Age of Sail (1500–1815)

Baynham, Henry. *From the Lower Deck: The Royal Navy, 1780–1840* (1969).
Bromley, J. S. *Corsairs and Navies, 1660–1760* (1987).
Brummett, Palmira. *Ottoman Seapower and Levantine Diplomacy in the Age of Discovery* (1994).
Creswell, John. *British Admirals of the Eighteenth Century: Tactics in Battle* (1972).
Dull, Jonathan. *The French Navy and American Independence: A Study of Arms and Diplomacy, 1774–1787* (1976).
Fowler, William M., Jr. *Jack Tars and the Commodores: The American Navy, 1783–1815* (1984).
Goodman, David. *Spanish Naval Power, 1589–1665: Reconstruction and Defeat* (1997).
Guilmartin, John F. *Gunpowder and Galleys: Changing Technology and Mediterranean Warfare at Sea* (1974).
Lavery, Brian. *The Ship of the Line, I: The Development of the Battlefleet, 1650–1850* (1983).
Mahan, Alfred Thayer. *The Influence of Sea Power upon History, 1660–1783* (1970).

——. *The Influence of Sea Power upon the French Revolution and Empire, 1793–1812.* 2 vols. (1968).

Martin, Colin, and Geoffrey Parker. *The Spanish Armada* (1992).

Miller, Nathan. *Sea of Glory: A Naval History of the American Revolution* (1992).

O'Brien, Patrick. *Men-of-War: Life in Nelson's Navy* (1995).

Palmer, Michael A. "'The Soul's Right Hand': Command and Control in the Age of Fighting Sail, 1652–1827." *Journal of Military History* 61 (October 1997): 679–705.

——. *Stoddert's War: Naval Operations During the Quasi-War with France, 1798–1801* (1987).

Phillips, Edward J. *The Founding of Russia's Navy: Peter the Great and the Azov Fleet, 1688–1714* (1995).

Powell, J. R. *The Navy in the English Civil War* (1962).

Pritchard, James. *Louis XV's Navy, 1748–1762* (1987).

Stark, Suzanne J. "Women at Sea in the Royal Navy in the Age of Sail." *American Neptune* 57 (Spring 1997): 101–20.

Symcox, Geoffrey. *The Crisis of French Sea Power, 1688–1697: From Guerre d'escadre to Guerre de course* (1974).

Tracy, Nicholas. *Nelson's Battles: The Art of Victory in the Age of Sail* (1996).

Tunstall, Brian. *Naval Warfare in the Age of Sail: Evolution of Fighting Tactics, 1650–1815* (1991).

5. Nineteenth Century (1815–1914)

Bauer, K. Jack. *Surfboats and Horse Marines: U.S. Naval Operations in the Mexican War, 1846–48* (1969).

Brown, David K. *Warrior to Dreadnought . . . 1860–1905* (1997).

Browning, Robert F., Jr. *From Cape Charles to Cape Fear: The North Atlantic Blockading Squadron During the Civil War* (1993).

Daly, J. K. *Russian Seapower and the Eastern Question, 1827–1841* (1991).

Gough, Barry M. *The Royal Navy and the Northwest Coast of North America, 1810–1914* (1971).

Hamilton, C. I. *Anglo-French Naval Rivalry 1840–1870* (1993).

Herwig, Holger H. *"Luxury Fleet": The Imperial German Navy, 1888–1918* (1987).

Howell, Raymond C. *The Royal Navy and the Slave Trade* (1987).

Lambert, Andrew D. *The Last Sailing Battlefleet: Maintaining Naval Mastery 1815–1850* (1991).

Luraghi, Raimondo. *A History of the Confederate Navy* (1996).

Marder, Arthur J. *The Anatomy of British Seapower: A History of Naval Policy in the Pre-Dreadnought Era, 1880–1905* (1976).

Musicant, Ivan. *Divided Waters: The Civil War at Sea* (1995).

Preston, Antony, and John Major. *Send a Gunboat! A Study of the Gunboat and Its Role in British Policy, 1854–1904* (1967).

Reckner, James R. *Teddy Roosevelt's Great White Fleet* (1988).

Ropp, Theodore. *The Development of a Modern Navy: French Naval Policy, 1871–1904* (1987).

Schurman, Donald M. *The Education of a Navy: The Development of British Naval Strategic Thought, 1867–1914* (1965).

Semmel, Bernard. *Liberalism and Naval Strategy: Ideology, Interest, and Sea Power during the Pax Britannica* (1986).

Shulman, Mark Russell. *Navalism and the Emergence of American Sea Power, 1882–1893* (1995).

Sondhaus, Lawrence. *Preparing for Weltpolitik: German Sea Power before the Tirpitz Era* (1997).

Still, William N., Jr. *American Sea Power in the Old World . . . 1865–1917* (1980).

Symonds, Craig L. *Navalists and Antinavalists: The Naval Policy Debate in the United States, 1785–1827* (1980).

Wise, Stephen R. *Lifeline of the Confederacy: Blockade Running During the Civil War* (1988).

6. Twentieth Century

Alexander, Joseph H. *Storm Landings: Epic Amphibious Battles in the Central Pacific* (1997).

Alexander, Joseph H., and Merrill L. Bartlett. *Sea Soldiers in the Cold War: Amphibious Warfare, 1945–1991* (1994).

Auphan, Paul, and Jacques Mordal. *The French Navy in World War II* (1959).

Baer, George W. *One Hundred Years of Sea Power: The U.S. Navy, 1890–1990* (1994).

Barlow, Jeffrey. *Revolt of the Admirals: The Fight for Naval Aviation, 1945–1950* (1994).

Barnett, Correlli. *Engage the Enemy More Closely: The Royal Navy in the Second World War* (1991).

Blair, Clay. *Silent Victory: The United States Submarine War Against Japan* (1975).

Braisted, William R. *The United States Navy in the Pacific, 1897–1909* (1969); *1909–1922* (1971).

Cable, James. *Gunboat Diplomacy* (1994) (covers 1919–91).

Cagle, Malcolm W., and Frank A. Manson. *Sea War in Korea* (1957).

Coletta, Paolo E. *The United States Navy and Defense Unification, 1947–1953* (1981).

Cutler, Thomas J. *Brown Water, Black Berets: Coastal and Riverine Warfare in Vietnam* (1988).

Dingman, Roger. *Power in the Pacific: The Origins of the Naval Arms Limitation, 1914–1922* (1976).

Dull, Paul S. *A Battle History of the Imperial Japanese Navy (1941–1945)* (1978).

Fanning, Richard W. *Peace and Disarmament: Naval Rivalry and Arms Control, 1922–1933* (1995).

Field, James A., Jr. *History of United States Naval Operations: Korea* (1962).

Friedman, Norman. *Carrier Air Power* (1981).

Gordon, Andrew. *The Rules of the Game: Jutland and British Naval Command* (1997).

Halpern, Paul. *A Naval History of World War I* (1993).

Hood, Ronald Chalmers, III. *Royal Republicans: The French Naval Dynasties Between the World Wars* (1985).

Inoguchi, Rikihei, and Tadashi Nakajima. *The Divine Wind: Japan's Kamikaze Force in World War II* (1994).

Kaplan, Philip, and Jack Currie. *Wolfpack: U-Boats at War, 1939–1945* (1997).

Layman, R. D. *Naval Aviation in the First World War* (1996).

Lundstrom, John B. *The First South Pacific Campaign: Pacific Fleet Strategy, December 1941–June 1942* (1976).

Marder, Arthur J. *From the Dreadnought to Scapa Flow: The Royal Navy in the Fisher Era, 1904–1919.* 5 vols. (1961–70).

Massie, Robert K. *Dreadnought: Britain, Germany and the Coming of the Great War* (1991).

Miller, Edward S. *War Plan Orange: The U.S. Strategy to Defeat Japan, 1897–1945* (1991).

Morison, Samuel Eliot. *History of United States Naval Operations in World War II.* 15 vols. (1947–62).

Muir, Malcolm, Jr. *Black Shoes and Blue Water: Surface Warfare in the United States Navy, 1945–1975* (1996).

Palmer, Michael A. *On Course to Desert Storm: The U.S. Navy and the Persian Gulf* (1992) (Gulf War).

——. *Origins of the Maritime Strategy: The Development of American Naval Strategy, 1945–1955* (1990).

Prados, John. *Combined Fleet Decoded . . . World War II* (1995).

Reynolds, Clark G. *The Fast Carriers: The Forging of an Air Navy* (1992).

——. *War in the Pacific* (1990).

Roskill, Stephen. *Naval Policy Between the Wars.* 2 vols. (1968, 1976) (Anglo-American).

——. *The War at Sea.* 3 vols. (1954–62) (British).

Rohwer, Jürgen. *War at Sea, 1939–1945* (1996).

Sadkovich, James J. *The Italian Navy in World War II* (1994).

Schreadley, Richard L. *From the Rivers to the Sea: The U.S. Navy in Vietnam* (1992).

Stephen, Martin, and Eric Grove. *Sea-Battles in Close-up: World War 2.* 2 vols. (1988, 1993).

Sumida, Jon Tetsuro. *In Defense of Naval Supremacy: Finance, Technology and British Naval Policy, 1889–1914* (1989).

———. "Sir John Fisher and the *Dreadnought:* The Sources of Naval Mythology." *Journal of Military Affairs* 59 (October 1995): 619–60.

Syrett, David. *The Defeat of the German U-Boats: The Battle of the Atlantic* (1994).

Thomas, Charles S. *The German Navy in the Nazi Era* (1990).

Utz, Curtis A. *Cordon of Steel: The U.S. Navy and the Cuban Missile Crisis* (1993).

van der Vat, Dan. *Stealth at Sea: The History of the Submarine* (1994).

Wildenberg, Thomas. *Gray Steel and Black Oil: Fast Tankers and Replenishment at Sea, 1912–1992* (1996).

Yerxa, Donald A. *Admirals and Empire: The United States Navy and the Caribbean, 1898–1945* (1991).

7. Biographies

Akawa, Hiroyuki. *The Reluctant Admiral: Yamamoto and the Imperial Navy* (1979).

Baumber, Michael. *General-at-Sea: Robert Blake and the Seventeenth-Century Revolution in Naval Warfare* (1990).

Bradford, Ernle. *The Sultan's Admiral: The Life of Barbarossa* (1968).

Buell, Thomas B. *Master of Seapower: A Biography of Fleet Admiral Ernest J. King* (1995).

———. *The Quiet Warrior: A Biography of Admiral Raymond A. Spruance* (1987).

Duncan, Francis. *Rickover and the Nuclear Navy* (1989).

Dyer, George Carroll. *The Amphibians Came to Conquer: The Story of Admiral Richmond Kelly Turner.* 2 vols. (1972).

Hearn, Chester G. *Admiral David Dixon Porter: The Civil War Years* (1996).

Mackay, Ruddock F. *Admiral Hawke* (1985).

———. *Fisher of Kilverstone* (1973).

Morison, Samuel Eliot. *John Paul Jones* (1990).

Ollard, Richard. *Pepys: A Biography* (1974).

Oman, Carola. *Nelson* (1996).

Potter, E. B. *Admiral Arleigh Burke* (1990).

———. *Bull Halsey: A Biography* (1985).

———. *Nimitz* (1976).

Reynolds, Clark G. *Admiral John H. Towers: The Struggle for Naval Air Supremacy* (1991).

Roskill, Stephen. *Admiral of the Fleet Earl Beatty: The Last Naval Hero, An Intimate Biography* (1980).

Seager, Robert, II. *Alfred Thayer Mahan: The Man and His Letters* (1977).

Spinney, David. *Rodney* (1969).

Taylor, Theodore. *The Magnificent Mitscher* (1991).

8. Anthologies

Bradford, James C., ed. *Quarterdeck and Bridge: Two Centuries of American Naval Leaders* (1997) (essays on Hopkins, J. P. Jones, Decatur, O. H. Perry, Stockton, M. C. Perry, Farragut, Semmes, D. D. Porter, Luce, Mahan, Dewey, Sims, Moffett, King, Nimitz, Halsey, Burke, Rickover, Zumwalt).

Howarth, Stephen, ed. *Men of War: Great Naval Leaders of World War II* (1992) (essays on Pound, Raeder, King, Yamamoto, Nimitz, Spruance, Doenitz, Cunningham, Halsey, Mitscher, Nagumo, Ozawa, Conolly, Hewitt, Kinkaid, Ramsey, Turner, Kretschmer, Prien, Lockwood, Walker, Horton, Stark, Somerville, Fraser, Vian, Burke, Godfrey, Rochefort, Moreell, Holland M. Smith).

Sweetman, Jack, ed. *The Great Admirals: Command at Sea, 1587–1945* (1997) (essays on Drake, Tromp, Blake, de Ruyter, Juel, Hawke, Suffren, Nelson, Miaoulis, Farragut, Tegetthof, Dewey, Togo, Jellicoe, Scheer, Cunningham, Yamamoto, Spruance, Halsey).

Acknowledgments

This book is the result of a career studying navies in history. It also reflects the impact of many individuals on my thinking; to them I extend my profound gratitude. My undergraduate adviser at the University of California at Santa Barbara (B.A., 1961), A. Russell Buchanan, allowed me to pursue my initial interest in naval history. Theodore Ropp, my inspiring graduate mentor at Duke University (Ph.D., 1964), typified the global perspective of his colleagues and their attention to the phenomenon of organized conflict. Philip K. Lundeberg enriched my knowledge of U.S. naval history while I was his summer intern at the Smithsonian Institution (1962).

As civilian professor at the U.S. Naval Academy (1964–68), I was required to learn to sail in order to teach the age of fighting sail. I also profited from the collective knowledge of several colleagues—E. B. Potter for the broad sweep, William H. Russell for the ancient period, and Robert W. Daly for Russian naval history. There, and at the University of Maine (1968–76), my intellectual skills were further sharpened by Robert Seager II. My knowledge of commercial shipping improved during my tenure heading the humanities department at the U.S. Merchant Marine Academy (1976–78). The veterans of the second carrier *Yorktown* taught me about life and work at sea when I was curator of that and other ships at Charleston's Patriots Point Naval and Maritime Museum (1978–87). Its engineer, James R. Blandford, gave me a hands-on education about the innards of modern men-of-war.

To my students over the years, including at the University/College of Charleston, South Carolina (since 1988), I recognize their enthusiasm and insights, which stimulate any teacher. I also acknowledge many patient editors of my works, notably Clayton R. Barrow Jr. of the U.S. Naval Institute. Finally, the one absolutely indispensable person in my personal and professional life has been Connie, my devoted wife, typist, and proofreader of all our manuscripts over the first 35 years of my career. In addition, I thank Dwight, Ward, and Colleen for their patience in enduring Dad's passion for research and writing when they were kids. And I must salute "Commander," our authoritarian schnauzer who for 14 years has pulled rank on me to be taken on his afternoon sniff-walk. May this short remembrance inform students that education and the study of history are lifelong endeavors.

Index

◆

Maps

The maps, except the last one, are over-the-horizon projections designed to liberate the student of naval history from the conventional Mercator north-at-the-top view of modern cartographers. With this perspective, one can understand how naval strategists and commanders throughout history regarded the relationships of important waterways to land masses and why this perspective influenced their operations.

1. The Ancient World—and Sicily
2. The Mediterranean—and Ancient Aegean
3. The Bottleneck of Europe—and the English Channel
4. The European Peninsula
5. The Periphery of Asia
6. American Sea Lanes—and West Indies
7. The Indian Ocean

Suggestion for the student: Make enlarged copies of these maps for your study of specific periods and events in history. Mark important port cities, terminal points (straits), trade routes, particular naval movements and campaigns, and the location of significant naval battles. Use these maps to illustrate research projects.

Suggestion for the instructor: Make copies of these maps for quizzes and examinations, asking the students to identify important locations or to illustrate their answers to essay questions about specific naval operations.

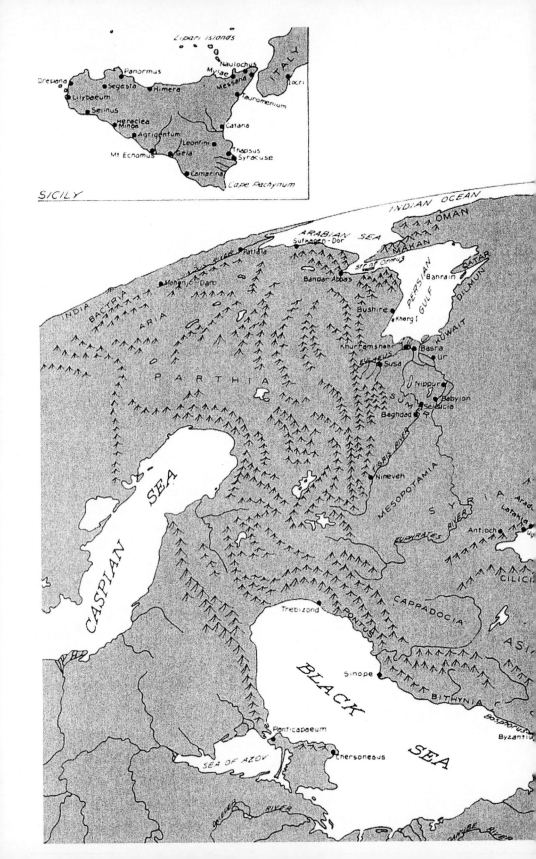

THE MEDITERRANEAN

ANCIENT AEGEAN

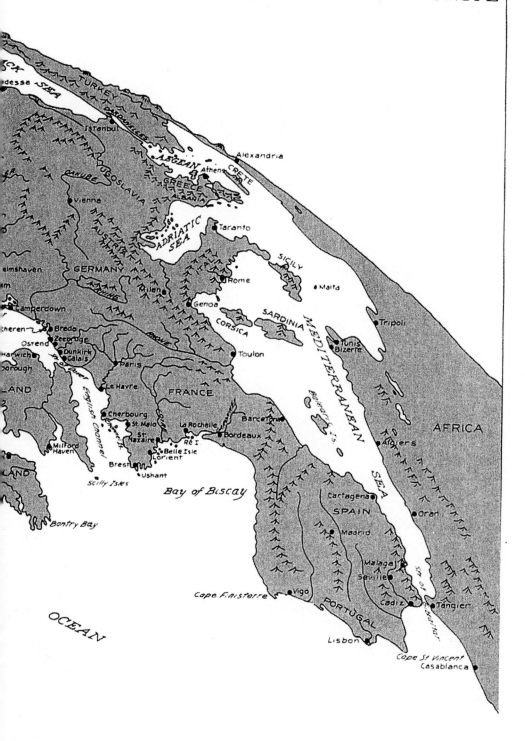

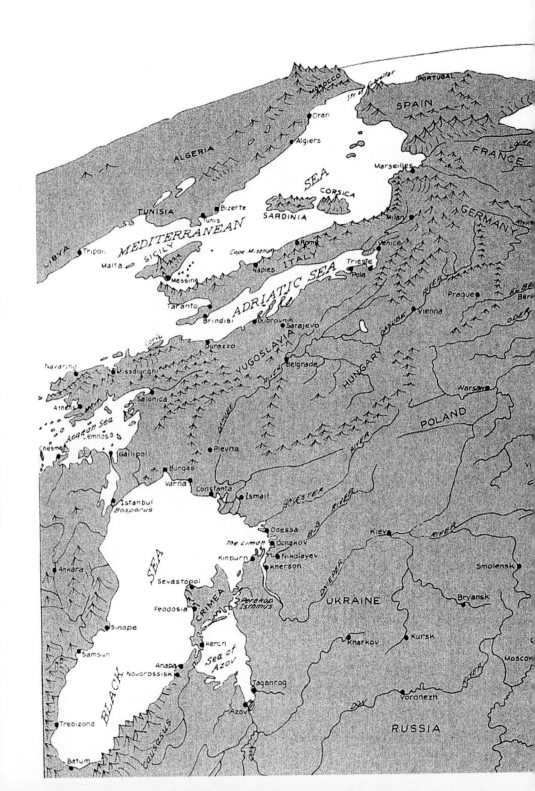

ATLANTIC

OCEAN

Quiberon Bay

NORMANDY

Paris

English Channel

IRELAND

Dublin

London ENGLAND

Hebrides

Rotterdam

Amsterdam

HOLLAND

Orkney Is

NORTH

SEA

Wilhelmshaven

Bremen

Heligoland

Hamburg

Hedeby

Shetland Is.

Faeroe Is.

Lübeck

Wismar

KIEL DENMARK

ICELAND

Warnemünde

Stralsunde

Rügen I.

GOTLAND

Copenhagen

Stavenger

Trelleborg

Elsinore

Kattegat

Bergen

Malmö Helsingborg

SKANE

Bornholm I.

Oland I.

Oslo

Karlskrona

Skagerrak

Gydnia

Baltiisk

Königsberg

SWEDEN

Trondheim

Memel

Libau

Gotland

Wisby

BALTIC

Stockholm

SEA

Oesel I.

Aland I.

LITHUANIA

Riga

Dago I.

RIVER

Abo

NORWAY

Bodö

LIVONIA

Hango Head

Gulf of Finland

Porkkala

Lofoten Is.

LATVIA

Revel

Helsinki

Gulf of Bothnia

ESTONIA

Narvik

Lake Peipus

Hogland

Svensksund

I.

Fredrikshavn

Narva

Viborg

Kronstadt

Leningrad

Novgorod

Neva

Lake Ladoga

FINLAND

RIVER

Onega

Petsamo

Murmansk

WHITE SEA

BARENTS SEA

RIVER

NORTH DVINA

Archangel

Kola Inlet

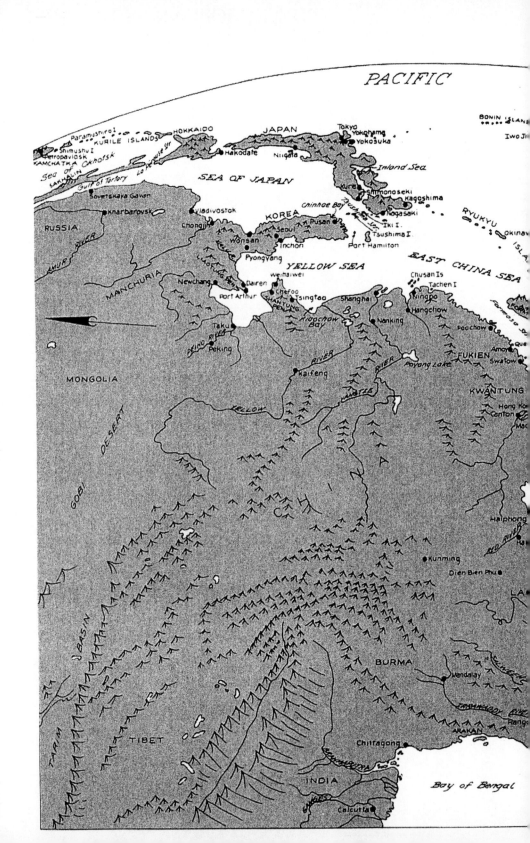

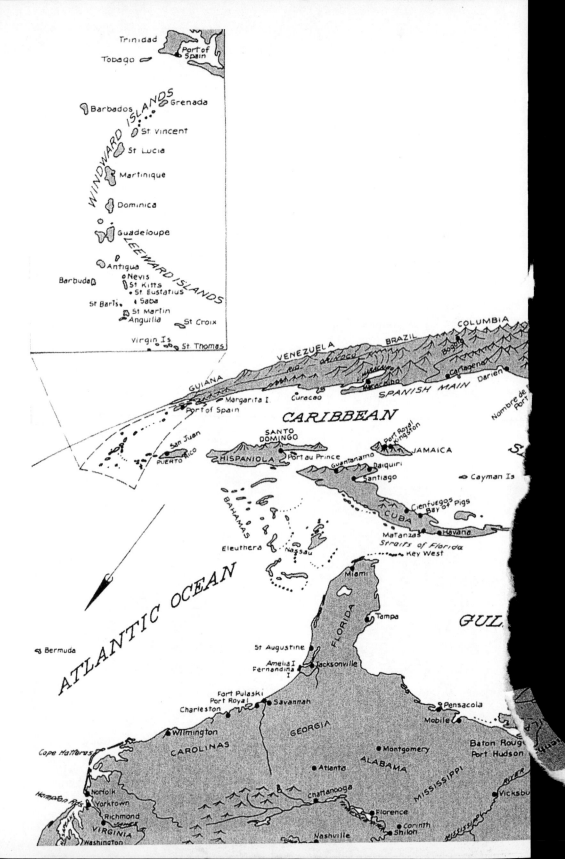

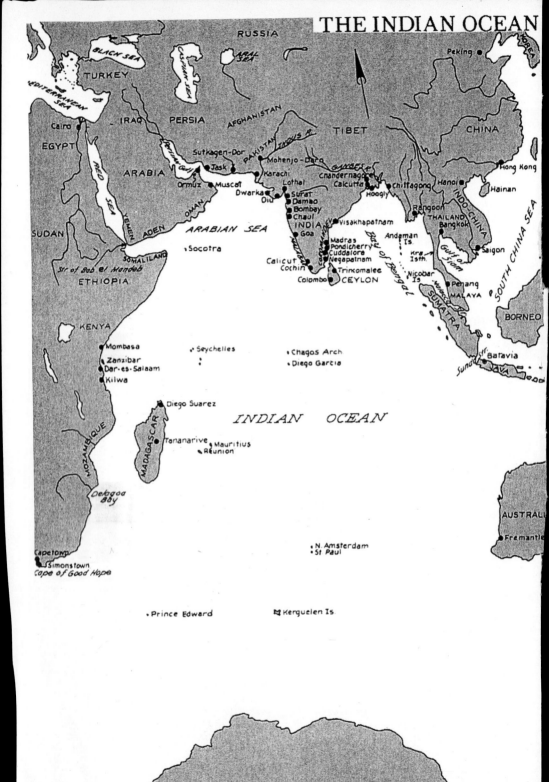

THE INDIAN OCEAN

◆

About the Author

Clark G. Reynolds is author of *Command of the Sea: The History and Strategy of Maritime Empires; The Fast Carriers: The Forging of an Air Navy;* the award-winning *Admiral John H. Towers: The Struggle for Naval Air Supremacy,* and several other works on naval history. He has taught naval history at the U.S. Naval Academy, U.S. Merchant Marine Academy, the University of Maine, and the University/College of Charleston, S.C., where he is currently professor of history. He has served on the Secretary of the Navy's Advisory Committee on naval history and received his Ph.D. at Duke University

The Naval Institute Press is the book-publishing arm of the U.S. Naval Institute, a private, nonprofit, membership society for sea service professionals and others who share an interest in naval and maritime affairs. Established in 1873 at the U.S. Naval Academy in Annapolis, Maryland, where its offices remain today, the Naval Institute has members worldwide.

Members of the Naval Institute support the education programs of the society and receive the influential monthly magazine *Proceedings* and discounts on fine nautical prints and on ship and aircraft photos. They also have access to the transcripts of the Institute's Oral History Program and get discounted admission to any of the Institute-sponsored seminars offered around the country.

The Naval Institute also publishes *Naval History* magazine. This colorful bimonthly is filled with entertaining and thought-provoking articles, first-person reminiscences, and dramatic art and photography. Members receive a discount on *Naval History* subscriptions.

The Naval Institute's book-publishing program, begun in 1898 with basic guides to naval practices, has broadened its scope in recent years to include books of more general interest. Now the Naval Institute Press publishes about 100 titles each year, ranging from how-to books on boating and navigation to battle histories, biographies, ship and aircraft guides, and novels. Institute members receive discounts of 20 to 50 percent on the Press's nearly 600 books in print.

Full-time students are eligible for special half-price membership rates. Life memberships are also available.

For a free catalog describing Naval Institute Press books currently available, and for further information about subscribing to *Naval History* magazine or about joining the U.S. Naval Institute, please write to:

Membership Department
U.S. Naval Institute
118 Maryland Avenue
Annapolis, MD 21402-5035
Telephone: (800) 233-8764
Fax: (410) 269-7940
Web address: www.usni.org

THE SEA SERVICE FORUM FOR 25 YEARS

U.S. NAVAL INSTITUTE